Algorithmic Trading
Questions and Answers

Venice Trex, Ph.D.

Contents

3

Preface

In the intricate dance of global financial markets, where vast sums change hands at the speed of light, algorithmic trading has emerged as the choreographer, directing the rhythm and flow of capital. As we stand at the nexus of finance and technology, the age-old art of trading is being redefined by algorithms, data science, and machine learning. This transformation raises questions that straddle both finance and technology, and this book aims to answer them.

"Algorithmic Trading: Questions and Answers" is more than just a compendium of mostly asked questions about algorithmic trading; it's a journey through the evolving landscape of modern trading. We delve deep into the mechanics, strategies, and technologies that are reshaping the world of finance. Whether you're a seasoned trader adapting to the digital age, a technologist venturing into the realm of finance, or a student eager to break into the industry, this book is designed to equip you with the knowledge you need.

Each chapter builds upon the previous, forming a comprehensive tapestry that covers not just the 'how' but also the 'why' of algorithmic trading. We've carefully curated questions that not only prepare you for interviews but also deepen your understanding of the field. Our answers, while rooted in expertise, are crafted to be engaging and accessible, often drawing upon real-world analogies and examples.

The world of algorithmic trading is vast and ever-changing. However, the principles, once understood, provide a robust foundation upon which one can build. As you turn the pages of this book, our hope is that you gain not just knowledge, but also an appreciation for the innovation and sophistication that algorithmic trading brings to the financial markets.

Thank you for embarking on this journey with us. Let's demystify the world of algorithmic trading together.

Chapter 1

Introduction to Algorithmic Trading

1.1 How did algorithmic trading evolve over the past two decades?

Algorithmic trading, like so many things in the world of finance and technology, has been on quite a journey over the past two decades. From its infancy to the complex, highly sophisticated systems we have today, the evolution of algorithmic trading is a fascinating tale of innovation, challenges and remarkable accomplishments.

Let's rewind back to the early 2000s. At this time, algorithmic trading had just stepped onto the financial stage. It was like introducing the first car - an invention that had the potential to change everything. However, much akin to that first automobile's crude form compared to today's sleek, high-tech vehicles, early algorithmic trading was basic and largely unrefined. The key objective was to break up large transactions into smaller, less noticeable chunks to limit market impact. This simple, yet efficient strategy, dubbed as "Volume Weighted Average Price" (VWAP) was widely adopted.

Just as with the development of the automobile, where horse-powered carts became supercars, in the mid-2000s, algorithmic trading started to evolve to optimize trading strategies. With mathematical and statistical models like Bollinger Bands, Moving Average Convergence Divergence (MACD), and Relative Strength Index (RSI), the paradigm shifted from simple slicing strategies to predicting future market movements to make profits, much like going from free-riding a straight road to steering through tricky curves.

Then, the 2010s came roaring in with High-Frequency Trading (HFT), akin to the advent of Formula One races in algorithmic trading. HFT firms started leveraging ultra-low latency connections (nano-seconds level) coupled with complex algorithms for arbitrage, market making, momentum ignition etc., to make profits. Much controversy also arrived around this time with debates about market fairness and systemic risk, similar to arguments on the dangers and ethics of high-speed racing.

Around 2015 onwards, algorithmic trading underwent further evolution with the introduction of Machine Learning (ML) and Artificial Intelligence (AI), akin to integrating advanced AI driver-assisting systems in cars. Trading algorithms started learning from historical data, adjusting strategy parameters automatically, and predicting market movements more accurately. The core goal went beyond price discovery to adaptively learning & changing strategy, akin to self-driving cars in the world of automobiles.

And here we are today, with algorithmic trading algorithms employing cutting-edge technology, and evolving at an unprecedented pace. From strategies based on order book dynamics, reinforcement learning, sentiment analysis on social media data, to event-driven trading; the horizon continues to expand. Remember, just as the automobile industry required norms and regulations to ensure safety while maintaining the spirit of innovation, the algorithmic trading environment also necessitates high-level regulatory considerations to ensure a level playing field and to limit the risks of unforeseen market disruptions.

To sum up, the evolutionary journey of algorithmic trading over the past two decades is a story of iterative progress and innovation, taking us from simple order slicing algorithms to the incorporation of AI and ML, expanding the horizons of predictability, adaptability, and profitability in financial trading. It's a thrilling ride, and we can only speculate about how much more advanced this landscape will become in the future.

1.2 Which events or technological advancements significantly influenced the rise of algorithmic trading?

Algorithmic trading has seen an exponential rise over the years, heavily influenced by both specific historical events and technological advancements. Here's a quick snapshot:

1. **Computers and the internet (1980s onwards):** The biggest game-changer was the advent of personal computers. This democratized access to programming, allowing many people to write algorithms and apply them to trading. The internet, of course, globalized and revolutionized the way information was shared and accessed. Imagine the difference between checking postal mails and instant emails!

2. **Electronic Trading (1990s onwards):** With the emergence of electronic trading platforms, such as those started by NASDAQ, the trading process became faster and more efficient. This is somewhat like going from snail mail to instant messaging. With continuous access to real-time price information, high-speed internet, and powerful computers, algorithmic strategies could be devised and executed at a scale and speed that hadn't been possible before.

3. **Financial Crises:** The stock market crash of 1987, often called

"Black Monday", resulted in an increased use of automated trading systems. After observing the chaos caused by human panic, market participants began to see the appeal in automated, emotionless trading. Many years later, during the global financial crisis of 2008, algorithmic trading demonstrated the ability to react more rapidly to market events, further increasing its popularity.

4. **Regulation National Market System (Reg NMS, 2005):** This set of SEC rules was designed to improve market fairness but inadvertently led to future growth in algorithmic trading by mandating a "trade-through" rule. This rule required trades to execute at the best available price, leading to an increase in the use of algorithms designed to hunt for the best prices.

5. **High frequency trading (Late 2000s onwards):** Technological advancements allowed traders to execute trades in microseconds. High Frequency Trading (HFT), a subset of algorithmic trading, became very popular, resulting in a significant percentage of trades on daily basis. It's akin to upgrading from a bicycle to a race car, and the pace of trading took off at a speed never seen before.

6. **Cloud Computing (2010s onwards):** Cloud computing technology has enabled traders to deploy complex algorithmic strategies without investing in expensive hardware and infrastructure. Now, they have the capacity to process enormous volumes of data in real time and execute trades in various markets simultaneously. It's akin to having the power of an entire oracle in your pocket, readily accessible whenever you wish.

7. **Machine learning and AI (Current):** The latest advancements in machine learning and artificial intelligence have allowed for the creation of algorithms that can "learn" from past data and improve their own performance. Implementing AI in trading is like having a seasoned Grandmaster Chess Player, who not only plays chess exceedingly well but also learns from each move, refining its strategy for the next games.

These advancements have altogether made it possible for trading algorithms to take decisions based on complex mathematical models, execute trades at lightning speeds, and constantly evolve their strategies based on new data. This is a long way from the manual, emotion-driven trading of yesteryears!

1.3 How did early algorithmic trading strategies differ from today's strategies?

Algorithmic trading has significantly evolved over the years, particularly as computing power and software development have improved. Looking back, you'll notice substantial differences between the earlier and the modern algorithmic trading strategies.

In the early stages of algorithmic trading, strategies were relatively simple. They were primarily rules-based, programmed to follow a set of instructions without the capability to learn or adapt from historical or real-time market data. One could liken these algorithms to a novice chess player who understands all the rules but doesn't have the ability to strategize or anticipate their opponent's moves.

For instance, a simple strategy could be a moving average crossover, where one would buy when the short-term moving average rises above the long-term moving average, and sell when the short-term moving average falls below the long-term moving average. This is represented by the equation:

$$Difference = MA_{shortterm} - MA_{longterm}$$

However, these methods were quite rigid and couldn't adaptively respond to market changes.

Today, with advancements in machine learning and artificial intelligence, the landscape of algorithmic trading has drastically evolved. Trading algorithms are more sophisticated and capable of undertaking complex strategies, like market making and statistical arbitrage, efficiently and on multiple assets simultaneously.

Consider today's algorithmic trading as a highly skilled chess player. Using their understanding of the game (i.e., the financial market), this player constantly learns from every move or strategy played (every trade made or data pattern), to refine their strategy and make forecasts about their opponent's (the market's) next moves.

One such example is pairs trading, where two co-integrated securities are identified. When they deviate from their usual equilibrium, the algorithm will short the outperforming security and go long on the underperforming one, anticipating that they will eventually revert to their mean.

Now, many modern day algorithms also utilize machine learning methods to learn from real-time and historical data and adapt the strategy accordingly. This is a considerable advantage as it enables the algorithms to update themselves based on current and continually changing market conditions.

All these advancements contribute to enhancing the predictive accuracy, speed, and therefore, profitability, in the algorithmic trading realm.

1.4 How have market structures changed with the advent of algorithmic trading?

The advent of algorithmic trading has led to significant changes in market structures, all of which are akin to transforming a traditional marketplace to a high-speed, digitally-enhanced environment. Let's look at some key areas.

1. **Market Liquidity:** Algorithmic trading has increased market

liquidity. It's as if one has left a spigot open, allowing a constant flow of water (stocks in our case) into a pond (the market). Algorithms can trade out of huge positions in a fraction of a second, offering a constant stream of buying and selling opportunities.

Algorithms also tend to exude 'latent liquidity', somewhat like an iceberg lurking beneath the water's surface. While only a fraction is visible on the order book (the tip of the iceberg), the majority lies beneath, ready to be deployed when conditions are right.

2. **Speed of Trading:** Because of the automated nature of algorithmic trading, the speed of trading has significantly increased. Where humans used to be runners in a marathon, algorithms are high-speed trains. We're talking making trades at a millisecond or even a microsecond level!

3. **Transparency vs Opacity:** The rise of algorithmic trading has intensified the ongoing debate between transparency and opacity in financial markets. On one hand, it can create transparency in terms of rapid dissemination of trade information (similar to how a fast-flowing river carries information quickly downstream). However, traders using algorithms often cloak their trades, making it tougher for others to identify their strategies - the murky waters below the surface of our river.

4. **Price Discovery and Efficiency:** With algorithmic trading, price discovery has become more efficient. Due to their ability to quickly process vast amounts of data, algorithms act like ultra-efficient detectives, continually searching for any price inefficiencies and correcting them. This leads to markets that more accurately reflect the real value of the assets being traded.

5. **Fragmentation of Markets:** The advent of algorithmic trading has also led to the fragmentation of markets. Think of it as a large pizza that used to be in one piece, but has now been sliced into several bits. Liquidity is split across these bits, which are the various traditional exchanges and alternative trading systems. Algorithms can work across these slices, seeking out the best prices and liquidity.

6. **Increase in Trading Volume:** Lastly, algorithmic trading has contributed to an increase in trading volume. As trillions of transactions can be executed algorithmically, markets see a surge in trading volume, like a supermarket seeing increased footfall when it introduces automated checkouts.

In conclusion, market structures have undergone significant transformations with the advent of algorithmic trading, impacting everything from liquidity to efficiency, trading speed to market fragmentation. These transformations have complex implications, creating new opportunities and risks in the financial markets. The challenge for market participants and regulators is to leverage these changes while managing the risks.

1.5   What role did electronic exchanges play in the rise of algorithmic trading?

The development of electronic exchanges was like a catalyst in the chemical reaction of algorithmic trading's growth, substantially accelerating the process.

To understand this process, let's draw upon an analogy. Consider one era in history - the invention of roads and the wheel. Before these inventions, moving goods from one place to another was a strenuous, slow, and inefficient process. The advent of the wheel and subsequent development of roads revolutionized transportation, making it faster and more effective.

In a similar fashion, electronic exchanges transformed the way trading was conducted. Before electronic exchanges, trades were executed manually, which was a slow and inefficient process. There were limitations in terms of the speed of execution, the volume of transactions, and the geographical boundaries. The involvement of humans also introduced a level of error and bias.

Electronic exchanges, like our roads in the analogy, have provided the infrastructure required for algorithmic trading to thrive. They introduced automation in trade execution, eliminating human error and bias. Variances in execution times were enormously reduced, providing a more uniform trading environment.

Just as the speed limit on a highway describes how fast you can get from point A to point B, the speed of electronic exchanges outlines how quickly trades can be executed. As you can imagine, in a competitive trading environment, even milliseconds count.

Moreover, electronic exchanges have extended the capacity of transactions per day, providing the "volume" needed for high-frequency trading strategies, where algorithms make thousands - or even millions - of trades per day.

Also, with electronic exchanges, geographical boundaries were no longer a restriction in trading. An algorithm sitting in New York can analyze the market data of Tokyo stock exchange and execute trades in a matter of seconds, opening up new horizons for international trading strategies.

Just as wheels are useless without the roads, algorithmic trading wouldn't have seen such a dramatic expansion without the advent of electronic exchanges. It's like having a high-speed sports car (algorithmic trading), but without a highway to drive it on (electronic exchange), it's pointless.

In conclusion, electronic exchanges played a crucial role in the rise of algorithmic trading by providing a faster, more efficient, and error-free infrastructure for the execution of trades.

1.6   Why has algorithmic trading gained such prominence in recent years?

Algorithmic trading has gained prominence in recent years due to a variety of reasons. To help illustrate these points, let's use the analogy of driving. Nowadays, we see more self-driving vehicles on roads. They are designed to drive more efficiently, reduce human error, and hopefully, make the journey more consistent and reliable. The same principles can be applied to algorithmic trading in the financial markets.

1. **Efficiency and Speed**: Unlike human traders, who need to spend time analyzing information and executing trades, algorithmic trading systems can process vast quantities of data and execute trades virtually instantaneously. This is akin to how a self-driving car reacts quickly to changing traffic conditions.

2. **Reduction of Human Error**: Just as self-driving cars eliminate human error, algorithmic trading reduces the risk associated with human emotion or mistakes. Trading algorithms follow instructions precisely, making them less prone to errors compared to a trader who might misinterpret information or enter an incorrect order.

3. **Consistency**: Algorithmic trading brings consistency, just as our self-driving car consistently follows the rules of the road. Trading algorithms will consistently follow the trading plan, regardless of market conditions.

4. **Backtesting Capability**: In the same way that self-driving cars are tested in various traffic conditions, trading algorithms can be backtested on historical market data to see how they would have performed in different market situations.

5. **Ability to navigate high-frequency trading (HFT)**: Algorithmic trading can operate at an incredibly high speed, processing large volumes of trades in fractions of a second. This is much like how self-driving cars can quickly and accurately respond to split-second changes on the road. In a market increasingly dominated by high-frequency trading, algorithmic trading systems have the ability to keep pace.

6. **Reduced Transaction Costs**: Just as self-driving cars aim to reduce the cost of travel (by eliminating the need for a human driver), trading algorithms can help reduce transaction costs. They're able to

find the most cost-efficient way to execute trades, taking into account factors like bid-ask spreads and market impact.

The rise of technology in finance, or "FinTech", is a significant factor in the increased use of algorithmic trading. Just as advancements in technology have made self-driving cars a reality, they've also made the development and implementation of trading algorithms more accessible and cost-effective.

1.7 How does algorithmic trading impact market liquidity and volatility?

Algorithmic trading has a significant impact on the market in terms of liquidity and volatility. Liquidity and volatility are two important characteristics of a vibrant and efficient market. Let's first define the terminology before we delve into how algorithmic trading impacts both cornerstones.

Liquidity refers to the ease with which an asset or security can be bought or sold in the market without affecting its price. Ideally, a healthy market should allow participants to swiftly enter and exit positions at stable and predictable prices. Liquidity is akin to a bustling farmers' market: a corn farmer can quickly sell his products at a fair price, and a hungry customer can immediately buy corn without causing the price to skyrocket or plummet.

Volatility, on the other hand, refers to the degree of variation of a trading price series over time. This fluctuation can be caused by factors like changes in supply and demand, geopolitical events, or financial news. Volatility is comparable to the changing seasons which may affect the prices and availability of crops in our previously discussed farmers' market.

Now, let's discuss how algorithmic trading affects these characteristics.

1. **Impact on Market Liquidity**

Algorithmic trading can both increase and decrease market liquidity. On one hand, it can enhance liquidity. Algorithmic traders constantly buy and sell securities, effectively acting as market makers. With high-frequency trading, they provide a continuous supply of buy and sell orders, which serves as the oil that keeps the engine of the market moving smoothly, just like the bustling farmers' market we mentioned.

On the other hand, algorithmic trading can decrease liquidity in certain situations. In periods of stress, when markets experience sharp declines, algorithmic traders may pause or withdraw their strategies, which can exacerbate liquidity shortages. This is akin to our corn farmer deciding not to sell during a rainy day, making the corn hard to find and possibly more expensive.

2. **Impact on Market Volatility**

Algorithmic trading may also impact market volatility in different ways. They can decrease short-term volatility by providing more liquidity and smoothing out price discrepancies through arbitrage and market-making activities, much like our corn farmer helps to stabilize corn prices through consistent supply.

However, algorithmic trading can increase volatility in certain situations as well. Some algorithms respond to market movements and may add to price swings in times of market stress. For example, during sharp market drops, trend-following algorithms may exacerbate price declines by selling more. This could be compared to a rumor about a bad corn season causing all the corn farmers to suddenly sell, resulting in a sudden increase in corn supply and a decrease in corn prices.

To sum up, while algorithmic trading can certainly contribute to the overall functioning of the markets, like many innovations, it's not without potential drawbacks. Regulators and market participants need to understand its impacts to ensure its benefits are captured while minimizing any adverse risks.

1.8   What are the key advantages of algorithmic trading over manual trading?

Algorithmic trading has several key advantages over manual trading:

1. **Speed and Accuracy:** An algorithm can process massive amounts of data and issue trade orders much faster than a human can. Imagine yourself in a car race where algorithmic trading is a modern Formula 1 car and manual trading is a classic sports car. Both can get you to the finish line, but the F1 car (algo trading) can do it much quicker and more efficiently.

2. **Elimination of Emotional and Human Errors:** We, humans, are prone to emotions such as fear and greed that can lead to poor trading decisions. With algorithmic trading, this pitfall is completely eliminated as algorithms are purely based on logic and data analysis, just like a robot performing a task, impervious to emotions.

3. **Backtesting Capabilities:** Backtesting involves applying trading rules to historical market data to determine the viability of the strategy. It's like testing a bridge model under various stress conditions before actually building it. With manual trading, backtesting is a labor-intensive, slow, and error-prone process. With algo trading, it's fast, reliable, and can be performed on multiple strategies at once.

4. **Lower Transaction Costs:** Since algorithms are able to evaluate more efficiently when, how and where to trade, they help reduce transaction costs. In our car race metaphor, that translates into being able to find the quickest, shortest and least congested route to the finish line.

5. **Constant Market Monitoring:** Algorithms can monitor and trade in multiple markets or assets simultaneously, around the clock, something that's practically impossible for humans. This is similar to having hundred of eyes watching across a variety of different landscapes all at the same time.

6. **Discipline and Consistency:** Algorithms execute trades to the letter, without deviation. They don't get tired, need breaks, or go on vacation. They're consistent in a way humans can't be - like a marathon runner with the stamina to run at a constant speed indefinitely.

In conclusion, algorithmic trading, with the power of speed, accuracy, lower costs, and discipline, offers significant potential advantages over manual trading. However, it's important to note its own risks and challenges like technical failures or anomalies that can lead to trade errors. Properly designed and thoroughly tested trading algorithms can significantly enhance trading practices, but as with all technology - their usage requires understanding, management, and vigilance.

1.9   How do institutional investors utilize algorithmic trading?

Institutional investors often utilize algorithmic trading to enhance their trading strategies, decrease operational costs and risks, and increase trading efficiency. Think of algorithmic trading like a skilled and experienced chef who can prepare a meal with precision and consistancy while keeping an eye on multiple factors such as time, temperature, and quantity.

In the same way, algorithmic trading utilizes sophisticated mathematical models and formulas to rapidly execute trades under certain pre-set conditions. Let's dive more into how institutional investors use it.

1. **Trade Execution Algorithms**: These types of algorithms, also known as 'Execution Algorithms', are commonly used by institutional investors to reduce market impact and execution costs. They divide a larger order into smaller pieces to minimize the stock's price movement caused by the trade. This is similar to slicing an apple into small pieces rather than eating it all at once to avoid catching attention in

a library.

2. **Index Fund Rebalancing**: Index funds have specific rules for when they rebalance their portfolios. Algorithmic trading is used to follow these guidelines and execute trades at the exact precise moment, ensuring minimum deviation from the index. This is much like setting an alarm to wake up at exactly 6 AM to go jogging, to keep up with a strict fitness routine.

3. **Arbitrage Strategies**: Algorithms can rapidly identify pricing inefficiencies between securities in different markets or in derivative forms, buying low from one place and selling high in another, bringing in profits. Imagine you see a missed pricing in a supermarket where a pack of six apples is more expensive than six individual ones - you simply choose the cheaper option.

4. **Statistical Algorithms**: Here, academic data and predictions of market movement are used to generate trades. It's a bit like forecasting the weather - using historical patterns and data to anticipate what's coming next.

5. **High-Frequency Trading (HFT)**: Algorithms can execute trades within microseconds to take advantage of market inefficiencies and price discrepancies. Think of this like a professional photographer with a high-speed camera capturing hundreds of photos within seconds at a sports event.

Overall, the use of algorithmic trading can lead to optimized execution, better market prediction, and increased profits for institutional investors. This is similar to how the use of specialized tools can help a craftsman deliver better products more efficiently.

1.10   Can algorithmic trading lead to market inefficiencies?

Absolutely, algorithmic trading can indeed lead to market inefficiencies in certain cases. This is quite akin to a group of cars (traders) following a single GPS strategy (algorithm) on a road (market). If all of them take the same turns at the same time (place similar trades simultaneously), it's going to create bottle-necked traffic (market inefficiency).

In a perfectly efficient market, security prices always fully reflect all available information. However, algorithmic trading, by its very nature, creates scenarios where this principle can be violated. Let's understand this with a few common examples:

1. **Flash Crashes**: Algorithmic trading can lead to situations known as "flash crashes" where the price of a security or an entire market rapidly plummets and then rebounds. This is due to high-frequency trading algorithms placing large sell orders, leading to a rapid drop in price. Other algorithms, seeing the drop in price, also 'panic' and start selling, exacerbating the drop. This could be likened to a sort of 'domino effect' - when one domino falls, it triggers all the rest to topple in quick succession.

Mathematically, it resembles something like this:

If S_t is the security price at time t and τ is the time the first algorithm starts selling, then for $t > \tau$, S_t may rapidly decrease because of the cumulative impact of all the algorithmic sell orders.

2. **Front Running**: Some predatory algorithms use a strategy known as "front running", where they detect the orders of large institutional investors before they are fully executed, and then place orders before these large trades, benefiting from the price movement these large orders cause. It's as if a sniffer dog (algorithm) catches a scent (trade order) and runs ahead to grab the prize (execute a trade for its own benefit).

Let's use formula for illustration:

If P_{buy} is the price that a large investor intends to buy at a certain time t_0, a 'sniffer dog' algorithm can detect that at slightly earlier $t_0 - \delta t$, and buy the item at $P_{buy} - \epsilon$ where $\epsilon > 0$. The algorithm then makes a profit by selling at P_{buy}.

3. **Quote Stuffing**: Another technique, known as quote stuffing, involves an algorithm quickly sending and then cancelling orders to create market uncertainty and gain a price advantage. Such practice can sometime leads to inefficiency.

These algorithm-induced inefficiencies have led to calls for more regulation and control of algorithmic trading strategies, to prevent scenarios that can destabilize the entire market. Despite these potential issues, it is also worth mentioning that algorithmic trading has equally contributed to market efficiency by providing higher liquidity, reducing transaction costs, and allowing quicker price discovery. But, as with any powerful tool, the crux really lies in how it's used.

1.11   What distinguishes high-frequency trading from other forms of algorithmic trading?

High-Frequency Trading (HFT) is a specialized subset of algorithmic trading. The distinguishing characteristics of HFT include a high turnover of orders, low latency, and a lead focus on speed.

To give you a more relatable analogy, consider a bustling city marketplace. Now, imagine a particularly fast trader who is able to complete transactions at an incredibly rapid pace, purchasing goods from one vendor and selling them to another before anyone else even has time to react. That's akin to an HFT algorithm in the financial markets.

Now, on a more technical note, HFT algorithms utilize advanced hardware infrastructure and direct connectivity to exchanges - think of it as having a shop right next to the source, allowing for faster transactions. These algorithms send out a vast number of orders and cancellations each second, potentially millions of them. They capitalize on infinitesimal price discrepancies that may only exist for milliseconds.

For instance, if a stock is being sold for $10.00 on one exchange and $10.01 on another, a high-frequency trading algorithm might buy the stock on the first exchange and sell it on the second, making a profit of $0.01 per share. The aim is to make numerous such trades in a day and gain an aggregated profit.

However, do note that the techniques employed and levels of involvement in the market of HFT are not consistent across all algorithmic trading. Algorithmic trading in a broader sense is about executing trade orders via pre-programmed trading instructions accounting for variables such as time, price, and volume.

Think of algorithmic trading like automated vehicles. All automated vehicles navigate roads and transport passengers leveraging artificial intelligence, but those designed for high-speed races have additional features, are fine-tuned for speed, and prioritize rapid decision-making - similar to HFT in the field of algorithmic trading.

1.12   How do the goals of quantitative trading differ from purely algorithmic strategies?

While closely related, quantitative trading and algorithmic trading have some differences in focus and methodology; their goals, too, are slightly distinct yet complimentary. Think of them as two cooks in the same kitchen: while they may use the same ingredients and equipment, their specific roles and specialties might differ.

Algorithmic Trading is like our fast-paced, precision-oriented chef whose goal is ensuring consistency, speed, and accuracy of executing orders. The main objective of algorithmic trading is to minimize the cost of trading and ensure that the trades are executed at the best possible prices, as fast and as efficiently as possible, without significantly impacting the market prices. This is largely about the logistics of trading, such as handling large orders, implementing stop losses, or slicing an order into smaller pieces to prevent substantial market impact. Algorithmic trading can also refer to more complex strategies, such as statistical arbitrage or market making.

On the other hand, Quantitative Trading is like our innovative chef, always tinkering with exotic spices, whose goal is to come up with creative, statistically-driven trading strategies. It addresses questions like what should be bought or sold, when it should be done, and how much should the trade volume be. It the use of advanced mathematical models, historical data, and rigorous research to identify and exploit trading opportunities, with sharp ratio or alpha generation as primary objectives.

Quantitative strategies might include, but are not limited to, trend following, mean reversion, sentiment analysis, and event-driven strategies. For example, a quant trader might design a strategy to buy stocks that have had three days of losses in a row, based on the historical statistic that they have a tendency to bounce back on the fourth day.

However, keep in mind that while different in goals, these concepts often go hand in hand in practice. A quantitative strategy can determine your trading decisions, but the actual trades are carried out using algorithms. Basically, you can think of quants as strategy designers, while algorithms are their efficient executioners. They work together to optimize your trading operations, each contributing their unique strengths and compensating for the other's weaknesses. And just as in a restaurant, success depends on the harmony and cooperation between these two roles.

1.13 What are the infrastructure requirements unique to high-frequency trading?

High-frequency trading (HFT) is a subset of algorithmic trading where transactions happen in microseconds. If we think of trading as a high-speed highway, then HFT is like driving a sports car which is capable of speeding at 300 mph. To operate at such speed and keep up with the competition, HFT firms require high-quality, advanced technical infrastructure. Here are the main requirements:

1. **Low-latency network infrastructure:** In the world of HFT, speed is king. Every millisecond counts and can make the difference between a profitable and a loss-making trade. Therefore, sophisticated low-latency network setup is crucial. This can include high-speed fiber-optic lines, microwave links or even satellite communications. It's as if you need an express lane on our highway to overtake the regular traffic.

2. **Co-location services:** HFT firms often lease space in data centers located as close as possible to the exchange's servers to minimize transmission time (latency). To keep up with our analogy, imagine moving your home next to the highway entrance to cut down on your travel time.

3. **High-performance computing hardware:** superior processors (CPUs), high-frequency servers, application-specific integrated circuits (ASICs), and graphics processing units (GPUs) are used to execute orders in microseconds. It's like having the most powerful engine in your sports car to ensure maximum speed.

4. **Advanced Order Routing Systems:** These systems determine the routing of orders over different exchanges to minimize the market impact and achieve the best execution. They act like an advanced navigation system in your car, determining the fastest route to your destination.

5. **Advanced algorithms:** HFT makes use of complex algorithms to analyze market conditions and execute trades. These algorithms need to identify profitable opportunities and execute trades faster than other participants. It's like an elite racing driver who can react faster than others on the highway.

6. **Redundancy systems:** Due to the volatile nature of HFT, redundancy systems are an integral part of HFT's infrastructure. These systems protect against potential system failures and data loss, similar to having a spare tire in your car for unexpected flat tires.

7. **Real-time Risk Management Systems:** Real-time monitoring and risk management systems are used to limit risk exposure at any given point of time. Consider it as a car's ABS and airbag systems which work in real-time to prevent any accidents.

8. **High-speed Data Feeds:** HFT firms rely on direct data feeds from exchanges. These feed handlers analyze, normalize and disseminate data to the respective algorithms. It's like having a scout car ahead of you that communicates the traffic conditions to you in real time.

9. **Sophisticated Backtesting platforms:** HFT strategies need to be tested rigorously before they can be deployed. It's like testing your car around a circuit track before it's ready for the public highway.

All these requirements essentially turn HFT into a technology arms race, where the best and fastest technology secures an edge over the competition. In other words, to compete in HFT, you need a meticulously designed sports car, excellent highway infrastructure, and a proficient driver with an advanced navigation system.

1.14   How do regulators view high-frequency trading compared to other algorithmic trading methods?

Regulators view high-frequency trading (HFT) in a somewhat different light compared to other algorithmic trading methods. To provide an analogy, if algorithmic trading is a motor race, then high-frequency trading is like Formula 1. Both involve cars (trading algorithms in this case), but while the typical motor race is focused on many metrics — tactful overtaking, pit stop strategies, etc., Formula 1 is most often about pure top-speed and precision.

Regulators are concerned with high-frequency trading primarily due to the following factors:

1. **Speed and Volume**: High-frequency trading, as the name implies, executes trades at an incredibly high speed, sometimes making thousands of trades per second. Like the Formula 1 cars tearing off at the beginning of the race and the tremendous noise they make, this speed and volume can be disruptive.

2. **Market Volatility**: High volume of trades can result in increased market volatility. It's kind of like introducing a very fast, agile creature (HFT) among others in a jungle. It might disrupt the normal flow of life (market activities) and cause sudden, unexpected movements (price swings).

3. **Unfair Advantage**: Firms that employ HFT use sophisticated technologies to execute trades faster than other market participants, which can potentially lead to an unfair advantage. Imagine if in our motor race, one driver had a map of the track before anyone else - it wouldn't be very fair, would it? This is a key issue in HFT, where access to faster data and execution can create a non-level trading field.

Given these factors, regulators like the Securities and Exchange Commission (SEC) in the U.S., or the Financial Conduct Authority (FCA) in the U.K., have enacted several measures to supervise HFT. These measures aim to prevent market abuse, ensure fairness, and maintain stability in the financial markets.

For example, the SEC introduced the Market Access Rule (Rule 15c3-5) that imposes risk management controls on brokers routing orders on behalf of HFT firms. This is equivalent to placing safety measures and speed restrictions on our Formula 1 cars to ensure a safe and fair race!

Overall, regulators recognize that HFT is a part of the evolving landscape of trading and finance. They aim to manage the distinctive risks posed by HFT while ensuring that its benefits can continue to add value to the financial markets.

1.15   Can you provide an example of a typical quantitative trading strategy?

One classic example of a quantitative trading strategy is a "Mean Reversion" strategy.

Mean Reversion is based on the theory stating that prices and returns eventually move back towards their mean or average. In simpler terms, if you imagine a rubber band expanding as prices move away from the mean, the eventual snap back of the rubber band is akin to prices reverting back to their mean -hence the term 'Mean Reversion'.

Let's break down this concept with an example:

Consider a simplified model where you have a single asset whose price fluctuates over time. For this example, let's imagine that our asset is a share of a popular tech stock - let's call it "TechCo".

1. We start by calculating the mean (average) price of TechCo stock over a chosen historical period. This part is purely computational:

we total up the closing prices for each day, then divide by the number of days. We might represent this as follows:

$$\bar{P} = \frac{1}{N} \sum_{i=1}^{N} P_i$$

where P_i is the closing price on day i, and N is the total number of days.

2. Now comes the "trading" part of the strategy. Each day, we check the current price of TechCo stock against its historical average, or mean, $\bar{P}$.

a) If the price of TechCo stock is significantly lower than the mean (let's say it's fallen more than two standard deviations below the mean), we would expect the price to increase in the future to move closer to the mean. So, we buy the stock.

b) If the price of TechCo stock is significantly higher than the mean (greater than two standard deviations above it), we expect it to decrease in the future. So, we sell the stock.

So, in essence, our strategy is buying low, selling high - but in a statistical sense rather than comparing to absolute price levels. We're saying that if the price moves 'too far' from the average, we expect it to 'revert' back, hence we can trade on it.

This example of Mean Reversion is one of many quantitative trading strategies used in algorithmic trading. Each strategy has its pros and cons and is used in different market conditions. As market conditions change over time, so do the effectiveness of each strategy. Therefore, it's crucial for algorithmic traders to continuously evaluate and adjust their strategies.

Chapter 2

Basics of Financial Markets

2.1 How do the trading mechanics differ between stocks, bonds, commodities, and forex?

Given that we're discussing the basics of financial markets, let's delve into the differences in trading mechanics between stocks, bonds, commodities, and forex. This is equivalent to looking at how different games in a casino work - while the underlying principle of gambling does not change, the rules, strategies, and outcomes can vary significantly from poker to roulette.

1. Stocks Trading:

Trading stocks is like buying a share of ownership in a company. When you buy a share, you essentially acquire a small part of the company and have a claim on its future earnings and assets. Stocks

are primarily traded on exchanges like the New York Stock Exchange
(NYSE) and Nasdaq.

Most stock trading is matching buyers and sellers in electronic markets, much like an auction house. You place your bid (buy order) or
offer (sell order), and when someone appears willing to take the other
side of your trade at your specified price, the trade is executed.

2. Bonds Trading:

Bonds trading is a bit like lending money to your friend with the
promise of getting it back, plus a little interest. When you purchase
a bond, you're actually providing a loan to the issuer (which might
be the government or a corporation). They, in turn, promise to repay
the debt with a fixed interest over a certain period.

Unlike stocks, most bonds aren't traded on public exchanges. They're
primarily traded over-the-counter (OTC), which means the transactions occur directly between the buyer and the seller, often brokered
by investment banks or brokers.

3. Commodities Trading:

Commodities trading often involves futures contracts and is like betting on where prices will go. Commodities include tangible goods like
gold, oil, natural gas, soybeans, etc. A futures contract is an agree-
ment to buy or sell a specific quantity of a commodity at a particular
price on a certain date.

Most commodity trading occurs on futures exchanges like the Chicago
Mercantile Exchange (CME). Unlike stocks and bonds, commodities
can be physically delivered, but most futures contracts are settled in
cash, giving a trader no actual coffee beans or crude oil barrels but
the monetary value instead.

4. Forex Trading:

Forex trading, on the other hand, is like exchanging money when
traveling to another country. It involves the simultaneous buying of

one currency and selling of another. The foreign exchange (forex) market is, by far, the world's largest and most liquid market, with trillions of dollars traded every day.

Forex is an over-the-counter (OTC) market, which means trading takes place directly between two parties without a central exchange or intermediary. It operates 24 hours a day, five days a week, with operations distributed across global financial centers.

As you can see, while the objective remains the same - buying low and selling high - the mechanics of how you do that differ from market to market.

2.2 Which of these markets is most susceptible to algorithmic trading and why?

Algorithmic trading is broadly used across various financial markets, which typically include the Equity Market, Forex Market, Commodity Market, Derivatives Market, Cryptocurrency Market, Bond Market, ETFs, and many more.

However, the Equity market (stocks) and the Forex market tend to be the most susceptible to algorithmic trading. This is due to several factors:

1. **Liquidity**: Both the Equity and Forex markets are very high in terms of liquidity. Liquidity refers to the ability to quickly buy or sell an asset without causing a significant change in its price. High liquidity is important in algorithmic trading because it allows algorithms to execute large-volume trades without significantly impacting market prices.

2. **Market Efficiency**: Forex and Equity markets are often considered 'efficient' markets. This means that information is rapidly digested by the market and reflected in the pricing of assets. Algorithmic trading thrives in markets that efficiently process information,

as trading algorithms rely on analysis of historical and real-time data to predict future price movements.

3. **Data Availability and Analysis**: Both Forex and Equity markets have a bounty of data available, and much of this can be accessed in real-time. Algorithmic trading fundamentally relies on data - the more data available, the more informed & precise the trading algorithms can be.

Imagine trading algorithms as a team of super-efficient, ultra-fast auction bidders; they analyze past sales, monitor the ongoing auction, and make rapid-fire bids based on that data. If they were in a tiny local auction house (low liquidity, less efficient market) they would struggle – their efforts would significantly impact prices and they'd soon run out of things to bid on. However, place them in a vast, bustling international auction market (like Forex or Equity), and they can bid and buy with ease, using a wealth of information (data) and not significantly impact auction prices with their actions.

In summary, while algorithmic trading is increasingly prevalent across all financial markets, it tends to be most impactful and effective in efficient, high-liquidity markets with vast amounts of data; this typically means the Forex and Equity markets.

2.3 How do dividend payouts impact stock trading algorithms?

Trading algorithms, or algos, are typically designed to consider a multitude of variables when making decisions, including potential dividend payouts. Dividends can impact the stock price and the overall trading strategy in a few ways.

1. **Dividend Capture**: A common strategy is the 'Dividend Capture' strategy, which revolves around buying a stock just prior to the ex-dividend date to collect the dividend then selling it off once the dividend has been received. However, this might not always result in

profit due to the "dividend drop".

Look at it this way, consider a $40 stock which pays a $1 dividend. On the ex-dividend date, the stock price will drop to $39, assuming no other price influencing scenarios. This is like a typical scenario of having a pie, and after sharing a portion (the dividend), the remaining pie is smaller (the stock price).

So the algorithm would need to determine whether the stock's price will rise enough after the dividend payout to offset this initial 'dividend drop', and still provide a profit.

2. **Dividend Discount Models**: Trading algorithms might also use 'Dividend Discount Models' (DDM), which evaluate a stock's price based on expected future dividends.

Imagine forecasting the weather; if we predict rain (an upcoming dividend), we take an umbrella (buy the stock). If tomorrow's weather forecast changes (dividend expectations change), we alter our plans accordingly (adjust the stock holding).

So if a company has strong expected future dividends, the DDM will produce a higher stock price, potentially triggering a 'buy' signal in a trading algorithm.

The Dividend Discount Model can be expressed like this:

$$P_0 = \frac{D_1}{(1 + k) + \frac{D_2}{(1+k)^2} + \frac{D_3}{(1+k)^3} + \cdots}$$

where:

P_0 = price of the stock today

D_1 = dividend expected at end of first year

D_2 = dividend expected at end of second year

k = required rate of return (or discount rate)

In conclusion, trading algorithms need to consider dividends and how they will impact trading strategies, just as a traveler would need to consider and plan for any upcoming weather changes.

2.4 How are commodities affected by macroeconomic factors, and how can algorithms account for this?

Commodities are basic goods that are interchangeable with other commodities of the same type, like crude oil, gold, coffee, and grains. They are major indicators of the economy's health and are significantly influenced by macroeconomic factors such as inflation, interest rates, currency strength, and geopolitical events. It's similar to how a cold wind influences your decision on what to wear: if you anticipate the cold, you'll dress appropriately, like wearing a coat.

1. **Inflation and Interest Rates:** When inflation increases, the value of money decreases, leading to higher commodity prices, just like how a severe cold would make you add an extra layer of clothing. Similarly, when interest rates are low, it's cheaper to borrow money, leading to increased spending and investment in commodities, causing prices to increase.

2. **Currency Strength:** Commodities are primarily priced in US dollars. So, if the dollar weakens, commodities become cheaper in other currencies, leading to increased demand and higher prices. Conversely, if the dollar strengthens, commodities become more expensive in other currencies, leading to decreased demand and lower prices. It's like how the cost of your coat may increase or decrease if you were to buy it from a foreign country due to exchange rates.

3. **Geopolitical Events:** These can disrupt supply chains, leading to changes in commodity prices. It would be like if a snowstorm blocked your roadway, making it harder for you to go out and buy a coat, thereby increasing its price due to lack of supply.

In algorithmic trading, sophisticated statistical techniques and machine learning algorithms can be used to predict how these macroeconomic factors will influence commodity prices. These techniques take large amounts of historical and real-time data, analyze patterns and trends, and generate predictions that can be implemented in trading algorithms. For instance:

- **Regression Analysis:** This can be used to model the relationship between commodity prices and macroeconomic factors. Think of it like estimating how many layers of clothing you need based on the temperature.

- **Time series Analysis:** This can be used to predict future commodity prices based on past data. Similar to how you would consider last year's winter temperatures to inform your winter shopping this year.

- **Machine Learning:** Techniques, like Decision Trees or Neural Networks, can identify complex nonlinear relationships between commodity prices and macroeconomic indicators, like how you might consider several factors besides just temperature (like wind speed, humidity, etc.) when deciding how to dress.

- **News Parsing:** Algorithms can parse economic news and geopolitical events in real-time to predict their impact on commodity markets. Imagine having an assistant who reads all weather forecasts and news related to winter clothing for you and gives you shopping recommendations.

Keep in mind, of course, the algorithms are not perfect — much like how the most meticulously planned outfit might still leave you feeling cold or too hot. They work on probabilities, not certainties, and are as good as the data they are trained on. However, they are a valuable tool for traders in the complex world of commodity trading.

2.5   What are the challenges of algorithmically trading forex compared to stocks?

Algorithmic or systematic trading in both forex and stock markets come with their unique challenges influenced by the inherent characteristics of these markets. Here are some distinct differences and challenges you might face while performing high-frequency trades in these markets:

1. **24-Hour Market:** Forex markets operate 24 hours a day during the weekdays, unlike stock markets which usually operate for 8 hours a day. This around-the-clock liquidity offers significant opportunities but also poses certain challenges such as maintaining a constant algorithmic monitoring system. Imagine running a store that never shuts, the utilities required, and the round the clock management necessary.

2. **Liquidity:** Forex market is the most liquid market in the world with a daily trading volume exceeding 5 trillion dollars, that's about the equivalent of the world's largest ocean, the Pacific Ocean. On the other hand, the liquidity in a stock market is more like a lake, robust but not as expanse as Forex. Hence, a forex trading algorithm needs to be more robust to accommodate the large volume fluctuations.

3. **Regulation:** In general, the forex market is less regulated than the stock market, where a central body like the SEC governs the stock market operations. An analogy here might be comparing a city with strict law enforcement (stock market) versus one with less stringent rules (forex market).

4. **Transaction Costs:** The costs associated with each transaction might be larger in the forex markets as most Forex trading algorithms are sensitive to bid-ask spread costs, especially for high-frequency strategies. It's similar to paying a higher toll tax (read: transaction cost) when you're driving on the forex highway compared to the stock market one.

5. **Macro vs Micro:** Stocks are greatly influenced by firm-level

data while forex markets are influenced by macro-level data. This difference in input data factors may require varying infrastructure needs.

6. **Market Impact:** Due to the high liquidity in the Forex market, large trades won't have a substantial impact on price movements. This is analogous to throwing a big rock into the Pacific Ocean (Forex) vs. a small lake (stock market). The rock has less effect on the ocean than on the lake.

It's important to note both markets involve real financial risks and positions should be adopted based on thorough research and understanding of these nuances.

2.6 Who are the major participants in the financial markets and what are their roles?

Financial markets are highly complex entities, composed of various participants, each playing a specific role. These players can be broadly classified into:

1. **Institutional Investors:** Think of them as the whales of the financial ocean. As the name indicates, these are institutions such as mutual funds, pension funds, and insurance companies. They typically have a large amount of capital to invest. Due to their trading volume, these players can significantly influence market trends. For instance, mutual funds and pension funds collect money from numerous individuals and invest it across various assets. Think of them like a chef who uses ingredients (funds) collected from different people to prepare a dish (the diversified investment portfolio).

2. **Banks:** Banks are the backbone of the financial system. They act as intermediaries between all market participants. They not only provide necessary liquidity to the market but also offer financial prod-

ucts like loans and deposits. Banks perform the role of market makers
in the Foreign Exchange market, setting bid-ask spreads for currency
pairs. It's like a local shop that buys goods from wholesalers (bid)
and sells them to customers (ask).

3. **Retail Investors:** These are individuals like you and me who
invest their personal capital in the financial markets. They generally
invest through intermediaries like brokers or mutual funds. Although
each retail investor typically has limited capital, collectively, retail
investors can significantly impact market dynamics.

4. **Brokers/Dealers:** Essentially, these are the market's facilita-
tors — the connectors. They match buyers with sellers and vice versa.
They receive a commission for their services, much like a real estate
broker who links sellers and buyers and earns a commission from the
deal.

5. **Hedge Funds:** My favorite analogy for hedge funds is they're
like the hawks of the financial markets. They seek to maximize returns by taking both long (buying) and short (selling) positions in
securities, often using sophisticated algorithms and high-frequency
trading technologies. They usually manage money for wealthy individuals and institutions.

6. **Regulatory Bodies:** Not to be forgotten are the guardians
of the markets, regulatory bodies like the Securities and Exchange
Commission (SEC) in the U.S. or the Financial Conduct Authority
(FCA) in the UK. Their role is to ensure that all participants follow
the rules of the game. They help maintain fair and transparent markets by preventing fraudulent activities and providing all necessary
information to the market participants.

So, similar to a bustling city's ecosystem, financial markets are composed of various participants, each playing its own unique, important
role in maintaining the system's balance and ensuring the smooth
operation of the intricate economic machinery.

2.7 How do market makers influence the liquidity of a particular asset?

Market makers play a crucial role in influencing the liquidity of a particular asset. They can be likened to the heart of the financial market that facilitates regular flow of buy and sell orders and ensures that transactions can be easily executed, just as the heart enables blood circulation in the body, keeping an organism alive and functional.

They improve market liquidity by leveraging the bid-ask spread. The bid price is the price at which a market maker is willing to buy an asset, while the ask price is the price at which they're willing to sell. This difference between the bid and ask price is called the "bid-ask spread" and it's basically how market makers earn their income.

To comprehend the impact of this, imagine a street market or a bazaar. The market makers are like shopkeepers who set up their stalls early in the morning. They make sure that there are goods to buy by keeping an inventory (either by producing the goods themselves or buying from other sources). When someone wants to buy an apple, there's always a shopkeeper who can provide it, and when someone wants to sell an apple, there's always a shopkeeper willing to buy it. In this way, the market makers in our analogy (the shopkeepers) ensure there's always liquidity (availability of apples to buy and sell).

In financial markets, the market makers commit to buying and selling securities at any time during the trading hours. They always "make a market" available by quoting both a buy and a sell price, thus ensuring that traders can transact at any time. So, in times of uncertainty or stress when most traders are trying to sell, market makers step in to buy, and vice versa.

However, it's noteworthy to mention that while market makers enhance liquidity, they assume substantial risk as they may end up holding a large amount of a certain security if there are more sellers than buyers (or more buyers than sellers). This could potentially result in a loss if the price of that asset moves against their position.

In summary, market makers play a significant role in shaping the liquidity of an asset and, by extension, the health of the broader market by always being ready to buy and sell, thereby ensuring smooth and consistent trading activity.

2.8 How might institutional investors use algorithmic trading differently from retail investors?

The difference between how institutional investors and retail investors utilize algorithmic trading is like the difference between a master chef using a kitchen to prepare an exquisite meal and a home cook using the same kitchen to prepare dinner. Both are using the same tools — the kitchen in this case — but their scale, proficiency, resources, and outcomes are vastly different.

In the context of financial markets, the kitchen is the trading platform and the cooking ingredients are the investment assets. Institutional investors, like large-scale master chefs, have access to more tools (financial instruments), more resources (more capital), and they have a higher proficiency (more sophisticated algorithms).

Institutional investors often use algorithmic trading in several ways:

1. **High-Frequency Trading (HFT)**: This is akin to preparing instant, but repetitive meals on a large scale, like a fast-food chain. Institutional investors use complex algorithms to transact thousands or millions of orders at extremely fast speeds, often in microseconds, exploiting minute price differences for a sizeable aggregate gain.

2. **Statistical Arbitrage**: Quite similar to a master chef, who uses his experienced palate to harmonize contrasting ingredients into a refined dish, this strategy involves complex models that hunt for

price discrepancies across similar assets in different markets to earn risk-free profits.

3. **Index Fund Rebalancing**: An institutional investor may manage an index fund that mirrors the S&P 500. At times, rebalancing is needed (like tweaking a recipe) to ensure the fund continues to accurately mirror the index. This is where algorithmic trading comes into play by automating these vast number of trades that might need to be done at once.

Now, let's visit the realm of retail investors. Retail investors generally don't have the same resources. They're similar to the home cook preparing dinner. The scale is smaller, the tools are fewer but efficient, and the ambition is to make a wholesome meal. They mainly use algorithmic trading for:

1. **Trading Automation & Discipline**: Just like using a slow cooking pot to have dinner ready precisely when needed, retail traders might use algorithmic trading to automate trades when specific market conditions occur, taking emotions out of the equation.

2. **Dollar-Cost Averaging**: Like a home cook portioning out weekly meals, retail traders might use algorithms to invest fixed amounts at regular intervals, regardless of the asset's price, to reduce the impact of volatility.

In summary, the main differences between institutional and retail investors in using algorithmic trading are about scale, complexity, sophistication of algorithms and differing strategic objectives.

2.9   How do algorithms account for actions by central banks?

Algorithms can indeed account for actions by central banks through news-based trading and economic indicators.

A central bank's actions often have a significant impact on the financial market, affecting interest rates, liquidity, and inflation, among other things. For instance, if the Federal Reserve (central bank of the United States) alters its monetary policy, the effect on the stock market will most likely be significant and quick.

Understanding this, algorithmic trading strategies can be designed to react to these economic news events. This is called "news-based trading" or "event-driven trading". In these strategies, algorithms are set to parse financial news, press releases, or sometimes even social media in seconds. They can understand the type of event (e.g., interest rate change), which bank is involved (e.g., Federal Reserve), and the direction of change (increase or decrease). Based on these inputs, they execute trades milliseconds after the news is out.

Think of it this way - it's like having a super-fast newscaster. As soon as the central bank's decision is released, this newscaster not only delivers the news, but also how this is likely to impact various financial instruments and executes trades with lightning speed.

Another way to account for actions by central banks is by using economic indicators. This is a more long-term and predictive approach. Economic indicators like GDP, unemployment rates, consumer price index, etc. help traders anticipate central bank actions. If an economy is overheating with high inflation, a central bank like the Federal Reserve may raise interest rates to cool things down. Algorithms can track these indicators and adjust the trading strategy accordingly.

It's similar to forecasting the weather. Just like meteorologists use indicators like temperature, humidity, and wind velocity to predict whether it will rain or shine tomorrow, traders can use economic indicators to predict what central banks might do next.

In both cases, it is not a simple task. Both news-based trading and prediction based on economic indicators require complex programming, significant backtesting and are subject to potential misinterpretations or unexpected reactions from the market. Because of that, while they offer potential benefits, they can also lead to sizable losses if not managed properly.

2.10 What is the role of arbitrageurs in the market?

Arbitrageurs play a pivotal role in financial markets. They help maintain financial stability and market efficiency. If you think of the financial markets as a large machine, arbitrageurs serve as the 'grease' that keeps the gears running smoothly.

Specifically, they take advantage of price discrepancies across different markets or securities. Let's say we have an apple market, where apples are selling for $1 each in New York (Market A) and $1.20 in San Francisco (Market B). If you're an arbitrageur, you'd want to buy the apples in New York and sell them in San Francisco, making a profit of 20 cents per apple with no real risk. This is essentially what arbitrageurs do in financial markets - looking for inefficient pricing across markets, quickly jumping in to correct these inefficiencies, and profiting from the pricing differentials.

Arbitrageurs help create market efficiency through their actions. Referring back to our apple example, their actions of buying apples in New York and selling them in San Francisco would eventually lead to a price equilibrium in both the markets. This is because as demand increases in New York (due to arbitrageurs buying), the price would rise, while a larger supply in San Francisco (caused by arbitrageurs selling) would cause a price drop there.

This mechanism, thanks to arbitrageurs, allows information to be seamlessly reflected in prices across all markets. In terms of the financial markets, this can refer to the prices of securities, currencies, commodities or derivative contracts.

In theoretical academics, the "Law of One Price" assumes a world without arbitrage opportunities, meaning identical goods should trade at the same price. But in the real world, perfect efficiency doesn't exist. Therefore, there's need for arbitrageurs who continuously work on minimizing these price discrepancies, thus contributing to a more efficient and fair market.

2.11   Describe the difference and use-cases for market orders, limit orders, and stop orders.

Think about trading orders like placing an order at a restaurant:

1. **Market Orders**: This is like walking into a restaurant and telling the waiter, "I want a pasta, and I want it now, whatever the cost". Market orders represent a desire to buy or sell a security immediately at the best available current price. They don't guarantee a price but do guarantee the execution. The risk you face here is of "slippage", which refers to the difference between the expected price of a trade and the price at which it actually gets executed. In fast and volatile markets, the price at which the trade is executed might differ from the last traded price.

2. **Limit Orders**: Now suppose, you walk into the restaurant and you say, "I want a pasta, but I won't pay more than $15 for it". Here you've set a limit to the price you're willing to pay. In finance, a limit order is an order to buy or sell a security at a specific price or better. This guarantees price, but does not guarantee execution (i.e., you might not be able to buy/sell if the market price doesn't reach your limit price). Limit orders are often used by traders who have a clear price at which they are willing to trade a security.

3. **Stop Orders (or Stop-Loss Orders)**: Let's change our scenario a bit. Imagine, you're already enjoying your pasta. You say, "I'm enjoying this pasta, but if it begins to get cold, take it away". Here, you've set a condition. In trading, a stop order (also referred to as a stop-loss order) is an order to buy or sell a security once the price of the security reaches a specified price, known as the stop price. When

the stop price is reached, a stop order becomes a market order. This doesn't guarantee the price but does trigger the sale/purchase. People use stop orders when they want to limit their losses or lock in their profits on a stock.

Hopefully that clears things up for you! Just like different situations in a restaurant might require a different approach, different trading strategies and market conditions lend themselves better to one kind of order or another.

2.12   How can iceberg orders be used strategically in algorithmic trading?

The strategic use of iceberg orders, also known as reserve orders, in algorithmic trading can be likened to an iceberg afloat the ocean – just as the greater portion of an iceberg remains underwater unseen, similarly, a large portion of an iceberg order remains hidden from market view.

For large institutional investors, making large transactions can majorly impact the market price, often not in their favor. Imagine yourself shouting at a bustling fish market that you are willing to buy a hundred boxes of fishes. Chances are, sellers might inflate the price seeing your high demand. So, instead, you would keep your demand discreet and buy gradually.

Similarly, an iceberg order is a large order that has been divided into smaller, limiting the market price from making unfavorable moves. The trader only shows a small portion of the order to the public, while the larger "iceberg" beneath the market surface remains hidden. For example, an investor wanting to buy 10,000 shares might only display an order for 1,000 shares to the market, and repeatedly buy 1,000-share parcels until the entire order is fulfilled.

In algorithmic trading, iceberg orders are strategically used in the following ways:

1. **Price Maintenance**: Iceberg orders help to prevent a large order from disrupting the market price, maintaining the per-share price closer to the value at the time an order was placed.

2. **Market Manipulation**: Advanced traders could potentially use iceberg orders for price manipulation tactics. For instance, a sell-side iceberg order at a certain level might scare off buyers, keeping prices lower than they would be otherwise.

3. **Reducing Market Impact**: Iceberg orders reduce information leakage into the market, which can help a buyer avoid driving up the cost of future purchases or a seller from driving down the price of future sales.

4. **Applying Game Theory**: Algorithms have been designed to spot other trader's iceberg orders for strategic advantages, creating a complex game of spotting and hiding iceberg orders.

Let's suppose we have a total volume V, which is to be traded in n parts (each publicly displaying only v_i). This process continues until all orders are executed ($i = 1, \cdots, n$ such that $V = \sum_{i=1}^{n} v_i$).

Overall, while iceberg orders provide benefits, they also require sophisticated trading algorithms, due diligence, and a good grasp of market dynamics to apply correctly. Misuse of iceberg orders or detection by other traders can sometimes lead to unfavorable trading outcomes.

2.13   How do algorithms manage slippage?

Slippage refers to the difference between the expected price of a trade and the price at which the trade is actually executed. It is a common issue in trading and it can affect the outcome of trading strategies, especially in the case of large orders or during periods of high market volatility. Slippage can occur due to several reasons such as market liquidity, bid-ask spread, and market volatility.

Algorithmic trading can be designed to manage and minimize slippage in several ways:

1. **Order Splitting (Slice and Dice)**: Large orders often cause market impact which can lead to slippage. To prevent this, trading algorithms can split a large order into many smaller chunks and execute them over a time duration. Think of it as climbing a staircase step by step rather than leaping several steps at once. By executing the orders bit by bit, the algorithm is able to mitigate the market impact.

2. **Smart Order Routing (SOR)**: Algorithms can be designed to route orders to different exchanges, choosing the one where the order can be executed at the best possible price. Consider it like choosing a grocery store - you would want to go to the store where you find the best possible deals.

3. **Minimal Market Impact Models**: Some algorithms are designed to operate in a way that minimizes the market impact. They dynamically adjust the trading speed by monitoring market conditions such as volume, volatility, and the stock's intraday price path. Think of this as driving a car - you adjust the speed based on the road conditions, traffic, and speed limits to ensure a smooth ride.

4. **Time Weighted Average Price (TWAP) and Volume Weighted Average Price (VWAP) Strategies**: These are commonly used algorithms in trading which can help manage slippage. VWAP, like an excellent tour guide, would consider the volume (popular spots) in its trajectory to ensure the journey (trade execution) matches the volume pattern of the market. TWAP, on the other hand, executes trades uniformly over a chosen time horizon, ensuring an average impact similar to the market's time pattern.

5. **Limit Orders**: Unlike market orders where a trade is executed at the current market price, limit orders are executed only at a specified price or better. It's like setting a budget for your shopping and sticking to it. This can help manage instances of slippage that occur due to market volatility.

Remember, while these algorithms can minimize slippage, they cannot eliminate it entirely. Just as one cannot completely eliminate the risk of delays while driving, slippage is an inherent risk of trading. The aim is to manage and minimize it as much as possible.

2.14   Why might a trader prefer a VWAP (Volume Weighted Average Price) order?

The VWAP (Volume Weighted Average Price) order type is a popular choice among traders in equity markets for a number of reasons, especially for those handling large quantities of shares.

But before diving into why VWAP is preferred, let's consider an analogy. Suppose you're an artist who needs to buy paints in bulk for your next project. You need a variety of colors (equivalent to shares in the market), and you want to get the best possible price. Commendingly, some paints are more expensive than others, and some are sold in larger quantities than others. You cannot directly compare the price tag on each tube of paint, as it doesn't tell you the cost per unit of paint, and you may end up overpaying for some colors while scoring a discount on others. What you really need is a method to compare these prices on a per-unit basis (equivalent to the VWAP in trading), which gives a more accurate and fair representation of the cost.

Coming back to trading, VWAP is used as a benchmark to ensure the trader is getting a good "average" price for their trades because it gives the average price of a security weighted by volume. In other words, it calculates the average price at which trades have been executed, taking into consideration the volume of trades at each price point, not just the price itself.

Using VWAP can prove to be very beneficial for traders, particularly for the following reasons:

1. **Minimizing Market Impact**: Large orders can significantly impact the market price. By breaking down a large order into smaller parts, and scheduling them according to the historical volume distribution pattern, the trader can work to minimize the "footprint" and market impact of their order, thereby helping to achieve better execution.

2. **Cost Efficiency**: VWAP helps ensure cost efficiency because it reflects both price and volume. If the trader's average execution price is better than the VWAP at the end of the day, they've bought or sold the security at a more favorable price than the average market participant — quite a win!

3. **Benchmarking Performance**: VWAP is often used as a benchmark to compare a trader's performance against the market average, which is critical for institutional investors. It provides a clear, defined metric by which to compare and assess the trader's skill at executing trades effectively.

Remember, VWAP is most effective for trading large orders incrementally throughout the day, and it's suitable when the main objective is to reduce market impact and achieve cost-effective trades. As each trading strategy has its unique strengths and weaknesses, it's important for traders to couple their understanding of VWAP with other market indicators to achieve their goals.

2.15   How do algorithms utilize order book depth?

Algorithmic trading systems employ order book depth as a key component of their decision-making process. The order book depth, which refers to the amount of buy and sell orders at each price level for a given security, is used by high-frequency trading algorithms to gauge the supply and demand dynamics of the asset.

Suppose you look at an order book depth and observe a large number of sell orders well above the current price, this may imply a resistance level for the price. On the other hand, a significant number of buy orders well below the current price may suggest a support level. Essentially, by examining an order book, algorithms can gain an understanding of where there might be price walls.

To make this clearer, consider the example of a popular online marketplace - Amazon. Imagine if you have the chance to see the number of units of an item that potential buyers are willing to purchase at various price levels, and the number of units that sellers are willing to sell at different price levels. This marketplace's order book will give you a picture of where prices might rise or fall based on current demand and supply. For instance, if there are 1000 units willing to be bought at a price of $10, but only 10 units available to sell at that price, you would expect the price to increase. This is a basic analogy for understanding how order book depth works in financial markets.

It's worth noting that algorithmic trading systems often have more sophisticated ways of interpreting the order book. For instance, the algorithm may not only look at the current order book depths but also analyze changes in the order book over time to detect patterns. They may also combine order book information with other market data, such as price and volume data, to make trading decisions.

For example, an algorithm may use what is called a volume-weighted average price (VWAP) strategy, that aims to execute orders at a better average price by considering both volume and price. The formula for VWAP is:

$$VWAP = \frac{\sum_{i=1}^{n}(Price_i \times Volume_i)}{\sum_{i=1}^{n}(Volume_i)}$$

By combining the insights from VWAP with the order book depth, algorithms can strategize their buy and sell orders to maximize their potential return and minimize their market impact.

Chapter 3

Quantitative Analysis & Statistics

3.1 Why is understanding the distribution of returns crucial for a trader?

Understanding the distribution of returns is absolutely critical for a trader for several reasons, primarily due to the insights it provides about risk and return expectations. This can be likened to understanding the weather patterns before deciding to venture into the sea; just as seafarers interpret these patterns to predict stormy seas or calm waters, traders analyze the distribution of returns to anticipate risk levels and potential gains.

The distribution of returns aids in estimating two fundamental elements: 'expected return' and 'risk.'

- The 'expected return' is akin to the average water temperature - it gives us our baseline expectation, or what we would anticipate under normal conditions. More technically, it is the mean of our distribution.

- The 'risk', on the other hand, can be likened to the range of possible weather conditions - it's one thing to know the average temperature, but we also need to understand how wide the range of possible temperatures could be. In trading terms, this is typically measured as the 'standard deviation' of our return distribution.

Risk and return are two sides of the same coin, and the distribution of returns provides crucial insights about both. Essentially it helps us answer the following questions:

- What is the average return we might expect (mean of the distribution)?

- How much might returns deviate from this average (standard deviation of the distribution)?

- Are returns skewed towards gains or losses (skewness of the distribution)?

- Are there potential for extreme outcomes (kurtosis of the distribution)?

For instance, in normal distribution (or bell curve), the returns are symmetric around the mean, with the stable predictability of both positive and negative outcomes. But the world of trading doesn't always follow the "normal," real-world data can have fatter tails (higher probability of very high or very low returns), or could be skewed (more gains than losses or vice versa).

So, by understanding the distribution of returns, a trader can make more informed decisions about their trading strategies, such as how much to wager on each trade (money management), or when to cut losses and take profits (exit strategies).

In summary, to sail the unpredictable seas of the market, understanding the distribution of returns is an essential navigational tool for every trader.

3.2   How can skewness and kurtosis impact a trading strategy?

Skewness and kurtosis are essential statistical measures in the field of quantitative finance; they help in comprehending the characteristics of the return distribution of a trading strategy. Let's dive in a bit deeper to understand each concept and their implications.

Skewness measures the asymmetry of a probability distribution about its mean. It can indicate the potential direction of 'risk'. Positive skewness signifies that you will have many small losses and a few large gains; conversely, negative skewness signifies many small wins but a few large losses.

To put it in a more familiar context, let's imagine playing a game of darts. Positive skewness could be like a skilled player aiming for the bullseye but occasionally hitting the outer margins - a number of small losses but occasional large wins when the bullseye is hit. On the other hand, negative skewness may be like an inconsistent player hitting the board all over but occasionally hitting the bullseye - many small wins but occasional substantial losses.

An algorithmic trading strategy that exhibits a negative skewness may have a more consistent return, however, it might also present a significant risk of huge losses. This is akin to tail risk and is one reason why investors must not only consider the average return (mean) but also the skewness of their investment strategy.

On the other hand, kurtosis measures the "tailedness" or the extreme values in one versus the other tail, of the probability distribution of a real-valued random variable. In simpler words, it is an indicator of the presence of outliers. High kurtosis suggests a high probability of outlier returns; low kurtosis suggests a low probability of outlier returns.

To provide an analogy for kurtosis, consider two lakes: one with a flat, wide bed, and the other with a narrow bed but deep in the middle.

If the flatness or depth of the lake represents the return distribution, a lake with a vast, shallow bed represents a distribution with low kurtosis - return outcomes are spread and have less extreme values. On the other hand, a narrow and deep lake indicates a distribution with high kurtosis - most returns are close to the mean, but there's a high likelihood of extreme values or outliers.

High kurtosis in a trading strategy can imply fat tails, which associated with the higher likelihood of extreme price movements. While it may mean higher profits, it simultaneously increases the risk of heavy losses. Therefore, while formulating a trading strategy, ideally you would like to strive for one with lower kurtosis, meaning a lower risk of outliers.

Ultimately, managing skewness and kurtosis is another way to manage risk in a quantitative trading strategy. Skewness provides an understanding of the risk in one direction over the other, and kurtosis gives an insight into the risk of extreme outcomes. Both allow a trader to better understand and manage the distribution of their returns, and enable a more informed risk management strategy.

3.3   How do traders use correlation and covariance?

In financial trading, correlation and covariance are invaluable statistical tools used to measure how two variables move in relation to each other. They provide quantitative traders, or "quants", with crucial information regarding the relationship and interactions between different asset prices or market indicators.

Correlation is a statistical measurement that describes the degree to which two variables move in relation to each other. A correlation of +1 indicates a perfect positive correlation (i.e., if one variable moves up or down, the other does the same); a correlation of -1 indicates a perfect negative correlation (i.e., if one variable goes up, the other goes down, and vice versa); and a correlation of 0 suggests no relationship.

Similarly, covariance is a measure of the directional relationship between two asset returns. If the covariance is positive, the assets' returns move in the same direction; if it's negative, they move inversely.

To visualize this, imagine two dancers. Correlation would represent whether they move together or against each other, while covariance would represent how the same or different their movements are—the 'strength' of their dance, if you will.

Traders use this to their advantage in various ways:

1. **Portfolio Diversification**: Traders can use the correlation matrix to diversify their portfolio by selecting assets that are less correlated or negatively correlated, aiming to mitigate risk. If one asset falls, the other might remain stable or even increase, cushioning any potential losses. This can be seen as a wise gambler spreading his bets across different games to minimize losses should one outturn be unfavorable.

2. **Pairs Trading**: Some traders seek out pairs of stocks that are highly correlated. They go long (buy) the underperforming stock and short (sell) the overachieving one. The idea is that eventually, the "gap" will close, and they can profit from it.

3. **Risk Management**: By understanding the covariance of different assets, traders can better predict how their portfolio will behave in different market conditions. If the market takes a sudden downturn, knowing your assets' covariance could help you estimate your potential losses.

An important reminder is that while correlation and covariance are powerful tools, they are based on historical data and thus, like using your car's rear-view mirror to drive, they should only be part of a comprehensive trading strategy. It's also crucial to update your measures regularly, as relationships between assets can change.

Correlation and covariance are often denoted as $\rho(X,Y)$ and $\sigma(X,Y)$ or Cov(X,Y), respectively. They are calculated as follows:

Correlation:

$$\rho(X,Y) = \frac{Cov(X,Y)}{\sigma(X)\sigma(Y)}$$

Covariance:

$$Cov(X,Y) = E[(X - E[X])(Y - E[Y])]$$

Where:

- $\rho(X,Y)$ = correlation between X and Y
- $\sigma(X,Y)$ or Cov(X,Y) = covariance of X and Y.
- $E[X]$ = expected value (mean) of X
- $\sigma(X)$ = standard deviation of X.

3.4   Why is the concept of stationarity important in time series analysis?

The concept of stationarity is crucial in time series analysis, similar to the way stable foundations are necessary for building a skyscraper.

Just as architects and builders need to know that a building's foundations won't suddenly change or shift over time, quantitative analysts and statisticians need to be certain that the mean, variance, and autocorrelation of their data will remain consistent or "stationary" over time.

In formal terms, a time series $\{X_t\}$ is said to be stationary if its statistical properties do not change over time. That is, the mean $E(X_t)$, variance $Var(X_t)$, and autocorrelation function $\rho_X(h) = Cov(X_{t+h}, X_t)/Var(X_t)$ are all invariant to time shift.

This has far-reaching implications in using historical data to forecast future outcomes. This is because if the statistical characteristics of the underlying dataset are continually changing, using past data to predict future outputs would be as uncertain as building a skyscraper on moving sands.

Furthermore, many of the statistical tools and models that we use for forecasting (like ARMA, ARIMA, etc.), assume stationarity. These models wouldn't give us accurate or reliable results if the series are not stationary.

Therefore, to increase the reliability of the analyses, statisticians often modify non-stationary time series through differencing, transformation, or detrending to achieve stationarity.

In short, the concept of stationarity forms the bedrock of robust, reliable forecasting tools in time series analysis; without it, the tools and models would be built on shaky ground.

3.5 How can algorithms handle non-normal distribution of financial returns?

Quantitative analysis and statistics entail a broad array of methodologies, of which normal distributions are included. However, as many of you already know, real-world financial returns often tend not to follow a Gaussian or normal distribution.

Financial return distributions frequently exhibit 'fat tails' (greater likelihood of extreme outcomes) and 'skewness' (asymmetry), which are not characteristics of a normal distribution. Seeing as this is the case, it begs the question, how can algorithms handle these non-normal distributions?

Clearly, it does not suffice to simply apply algorithms assuming normal distribution at all times. That would be like trying to fit a square peg on a round hole. It might do the job in certain scenarios but cannot provide accurate results consistently.

To address this issue, algorithms can adapt in several ways:

1. **Use of Non-Parametric Models**: Non-parametric models do not make any preconceived assumptions about the underlying data distribution. As a matter of fact, non-parametric models can be thought of as free spirits moving along the rhythm of the data rather than trying to force the data to align with any set rhythm. For example, Kernel Density Estimation (KDE) is often used to model the probability distribution of financial returns.

2. **Inclusion of Higher Moments**: Instead of solely considering the mean (first moment) and variance (second moment), which is adequate in case of a normal distribution, algorithms can take into account higher moments. This is akin to adding more color gradients to a painting: while a grayscale offers some information, a full-color picture provides greater depth and detail. The third moment (skewness) and fourth moment (kurtosis) can provide further insights into the data.

3. **Robust Statistics**: Algorithms can also employ techniques of robust statistics, which attempt to provide accurate estimates even when the data contains outliers or does not follow an expected distribution. It's like a bulldozer plowing straight ahead, regardless of the kind of terrain it encounters.

4. **Extreme Value Theory (EVT)**: EVT is specially designed to measure the risk of extreme events, such as financial crashes. This is the metaphorical umbrella the algorithms can use when the financial weather turns stormy, which isn t predicted well by normal distribution.

5. **Monte Carlo Simulations**: Using these simulations, analysts can conduct numerous trials with varying inputs each time, producing a wide range of potential outcomes. It's like playing a video game over and over again to figure out all the possible endings.

In short, although the normal distribution provides a convenient model for many statistical analyses, financial trading algorithms need to incorporate additional tools when it comes to dealing with non-normal distributions. Methods like robust statistical models, higher moments, non-parametric models, EVT, or Monte Carlo simulations can help handle these real-world, irregular, and often unpredictable financial data distributions.

3.6 What challenges are unique to time series data in finance?

Dealing with time series data in finance is like navigating through a dark forest filled with numerous and murky challenges. Here are some of the main challenges unique to financial time series data:

1. **Non-stationarity**: Imagine you're trying to hit a moving target while you yourself are riding a roller coaster. That's the problem of non-stationarity. In a stationary process, properties such as mean and variance stay constant over time, unlike in financial markets where variables such as stock prices, interest rates, etc., keep changing and are influenced by numerous factors.

2. **Seasonality**: It's somewhat like dressing up according to the weather. You don't wear a jacket in summer because you know it tends to be warm, based on your past experiences or data about seasons. Financial time series data often demonstrates seasonality - patterns that repeat at regular intervals, like higher retail sales during the holiday season. Detecting and adjusting for these patterns can be rather challenging.

3. **Volatility clustering and varying volatility**: You can think of it like walking on a terrain that changes from flat to hilly frequently and unpredictably. Volatility of financial time series tends to demonstrate these clusters - periods of high volatility follow similar periods, and the same goes for low volatility. This leads to heteroscedasticity, a statistical phenomenon where the variability, or volatility, of a

variable is unequal across range of values.

4. **High dimensionality**: If handling one variable is like juggling one ball, high dimensionality is like juggling multiple at the same time. Financial time series data can have many dimensions, including different financial instruments, market indicators, economic indicators, etc. This increases computational complexity and can lead to the curse of dimensionality.

5. **Noise**: Imagine trying to have a conversation in a room full of other loud conversations. Financial data contains considerable noise that can drown out subtle signals. Teasing out true signal from the noise is not just difficult but also crucial to making accurate predictions.

6. **Non-normality**: Unlike a well-behaved bell-curved normal distribution, financial returns often demonstrate 'fat tails' and skewness. That's akin to expecting the queue for ice-cream to be evenly spread on a hot day but finding much more crowd at your favorite flavor. This violates assumptions of many standard statistical models and requires usage of more complex techniques for analysis.

An understanding of these unique challenges can significantly improve the robustness and accuracy of quantitative models used in finance. In this ever-evolving field, skills in time series analysis are worth their weight in gold. Or should I say, in Bitcoin!

3.7   Describe the concept of cointegration and its relevance in trading.

Cointegration is a critical statistical concept in quantitative analysis, particularly in pairs trading strategy. To grasp the importance of cointegration, let's first understand it in a simple way.

Imagine you take your dog for a walk to a nearby park. You both start from the same house (initial point). You stroll at your own pace, and the enthusiastic dog makes quick, random dashes here and then, drawn by the exciting stimuli around. Now, you and the dog represent two separate time series (read: stocks). Though you both enjoy relative freedom, there's an invisible "leash" (cointegration!) that restrains the dog from wandering too far from you. No matter where the dog goes or how much it darts around, it reverts back to you - a central tendency.

In financial parlance, cointegration between two stock prices means that though individual stock prices may freely wander driven by market conditions, there's a statistical relationship binding them together in the long run, ensuring they do not diverge too much from each other. This is different from correlation where the focus lies on the directional movement rather than the gap between the series.

Now, how does it matter to trading? Let's say you identified a cointegrated pair of stocks, Apple and Microsoft. If Apple's stock goes up while Microsoft's stock remains stagnant, you can assume that sooner or later Microsoft's prices will also rise to restore the equilibrium, or that Apple's will fall. So, you may decide to either short Apple or go long on Microsoft banking on the cointegration principle. This is the crux of pairs trading.

However, there's a cautionary note. Like your dog tugging hard on the leash spotting a squirrel (read: market shock), stock prices too can diverge significantly from the equilibrium in the short term, and it may take longer time to revert back which poses serious risks. Hence, understanding, testing for cointegration, and carefully managing the associated risks is vital while constructing algorithmic trading strategies.

In a mathematical way, if two time series X and Y are both $I(1)$ — they are non-stationary and have a stochastic trend — but a linear combination of them, say $\alpha X + \beta Y$, is stationary or $I(0)$, then X and Y are said to be cointegrated, representing a long-run equilibrium relationship. The cointegration vector (α, β) importantly determines the trade ratios in pairs trading.

3.8 How do you test for stationarity in a financial time series?

Testing for stationarity in a financial time series is a critical step in the quantitative analysis and modeling process. Stationarity implies that the statistical properties of the process generating the series do not change over time, allowing easier modeling and prediction. This assumes that means, variances, and covariances are not time-dependent.

Here are a few commonly used methods for testing stationarity:

1. **Visual Inspection**: This is a basic initial check where you plot the data and look for trends, seasonal patterns, or other systematic changes over time that might suggest non-stationarity.

2. **Summary Statistics**: Here, you divide your data into separate segments and compute descriptive statistics for each one. If there are large differences in mean or variance, the series might not be stationary.

3. **Augmented Dickey-Fuller (ADF) Test**: This is a formal statistical test for stationarity. The null hypothesis assumes that the series is non-stationary. A low p-value (typically 0.05) indicates that we can reject the null hypothesis in favor of stationarity.

The ADF method can be described using the following regression equation:

$$\Delta y_t = \alpha + \beta t + \gamma y_{t-1} + \delta \Delta y_{t-1} + \epsilon_t$$

where $\Delta y_t = y_t - y_{t-1}$. The null hypothesis is $\gamma = 0$, meaning the series is a unit root and is non-stationary. The alternative hypothesis is $\gamma < 0$, implying the series is stationary.

4. **Kwiatkowski-Phillips-Schmidt-Shin (KPSS) Test**: This test has a null hypothesis that the series is stationary (opposite of the ADF test). Here, a low p-value (typically 0.05) indicates non-stationarity.

It's like asking your two friends, Bob and Alice, who always disagree with each other, to check if a vegetable that you don't recognize is a tomato or not. If they both agree on the answer, then it's highly likely they are correct!

5. **Phillips-Perron (PP) Test**: This is another test for stationarity, which addresses some problems of small sample sizes in the ADF test. The null hypothesis is also that the series is non-stationary.

Depending on the type of series, its properties, and the specific application, one approach might be more suitable than another and provide a more reliable conclusion.

Keep in mind that tests like ADF, KPSS, and PP tests have assumptions and conditions for their implementation which should be satisfied to avoid misleading results. For example, a series should be sufficiently long and display autocorrelation for the ADF test to be valid.

Consider transforming the data (e.g., differencing, logging, deflating) or changing models (e.g., using ARIMA models) if the series is not stationary.

3.9 Why are autoregressive models frequently used in financial forecasting?

Autoregressive models, often abbreviated as AR models, have risen in popularity for financial forecasting primarily due to their ability to capture and model time-dependency in data. In finance, data points (such as stock prices or forex rates) are not isolated events; rather, they are time-series sequences where the current value often depends on the previous values.

Think of it like trying to predict the flow of a river. If you can observe how fast the river flowed in the past (previous values), you can make a reasonable estimate of how fast it will flow in the future (prediction). The autoregressive model encapsulates this concept mathematically.

The AR model description in terms of mathematics goes like this. If we're considering an AR(p) model, where p is the order of model, then it is described by

$$X_t = c + \sum_{i=1}^{p} \phi_i X_{t-i} + \varepsilon_t$$

where:

- X_t is the current value

- X_{t-i} are the previous values

- ϕ_i are the parameters of the model that we need to estimate

- c is a constant

- ε_t is the current error term, which is assumed to have constant variance and be normally distributed with zero mean

This mathematical model gives us a structured way to encapsulate the influence of past performance on future values.

The AR models have numerous advantages, they:

- Incorporate the time-dependent structure present in many financial datasets

- Are relatively straightforward and computationally light to estimate

- Have established theory and well-defined properties, making them reliable and understood

- Can capture a wide range of behaviors, from randomness to high predictability, depending on the coefficients ϕ_i

All these factors make autoregressive models a powerful tool for financial forecasting. However, it's worth noting that no model is a universal solution. It's important to validate your model using out-of-sample testing, compare various model options, and consider the business context when deciding which model to use.

3.10 How do traders use moving averages in algorithmic strategies?

Moving averages are one of the most used tools in quantitative analysis and traders find them especially useful due to their simplicity and effectiveness. The primary usage of moving averages in trading strategies is to identify the direction of a trend and to smooth out fluctuations in price to prevent false signals.

Before we delve into how traders use moving averages in algorithmic strategies, let's understand what moving averages are.

A moving average (MA) is used to analyze a set of data points by creating a series of averages of different subsets of the full data set. In the context of the trading environment, these data points usually represent the closing price of a stock for each day over a certain period of time.

There are mainly two types of moving averages:

1. Simple Moving Average (SMA): it simply averages the price over a certain number of periods. It's expressed as: $SMA = \frac{sum\ of\ n\ periods}{n}$

2. Exponential Moving Average (EMA): it gives more weight to the latest data, thus it reacts more quickly to price changes than the SMA.

Now, let's see how traders use these moving averages in algorithmic strategies:

1. **Crossover Strategy**: This is the most common strategy using MAs. A buy signal is generated when a short-term MA crosses above a long-term MA, indicating an upward trend. Conversely, a sell signal is generated when the short-term MA crosses below the long-term MA, indicating a downward trend.

2. **Price Level Strategy**: Here, the MA is used as a support or resistance level for the price. If the price drops towards the MA but then bounces back, the MA is acting as a support. If the price rallies towards the MA but then falls back, the MA is acting as a resistance.

3. **Confluence Strategy**: In this strategy, multiple moving averages are used and a trader looks for areas where different MAs converge (i.e., come together). These confluence zones can act as strong areas of support or resistance.

To better illustrate, think about moving averages like a summary of the previous episodes of a TV series. If you've missed the past few episodes, the summary (MA) can provide you an understanding of what's going on and what can be expected in the future. Similarly, MAs help traders understand where the price is likely to go based on historical data.

Finally, it's important to stress that no technical indicator, moving averages included, will work all the time, and they should be used in conjunction with other analysis tools and methods for building a robust algorithmic trading strategy.

3.11   Why is hypothesis testing crucial in the development of trading strategies?

In the world of quantitative trading, a trading strategy is akin to a scientific theory. Much like a theoretical physicist may propose a theory about why and how black holes form, as quants, we may hypothesize about market behaviors and propose trading strategies to capitalize on those behaviors.

Developing a trading strategy revolves around formulating a hypothesis and then testing its validity. This is where hypothesis testing becomes the cornerstone. You might think of it as the process of vetting your trading ideas and ensuring they're robust and consistently profitable, almost like quality assurance for our trading algorithms.

A central part of this process is the null hypothesis, denoted as H_0. This typically assumes that your trading strategy has no predictability and any observed gains resulted from pure chance. The alternate hypothesis, H_1, is that your strategy does possess predictability and the gains are not merely a product of luck.

Now imagine you're in a house of mirrors - confusion and uncertainty everywhere. Hypothesis testing, in this case, could be considered as your reliable friend who helps you discern between a real exit and a mirrored illusion. Your null hypothesis is that all the doors are illusions, while the alternate hypothesis suggests that a real door exists.

Now you statistically test your hypothesis, and if the p-value (probability of getting the observed data if H_0 is true) is less than a threshold (say 0.05), you'll reject the null hypothesis, concluding that you've indeed found an exit (i.e., your strategy is effective).

The beauty of this approach is that it reduces the risk of "overfitting", which is making decisions based on noise that we, in error, perceive as a pattern. Consider looking at clouds and seeing shapes. While your friend might see a unicorn, you might see a bunny, but it's all random formations. Hypothesis testing is the seatbelt that helps to prevent such overinterpretation of randomness in financial markets.

Therefore, by providing a mathematical framework to evaluate the probability of a strategy's success due to chance versus skill, hypothesis testing helps quants build more robust and reliable trading strategies.

3.12   How do you interpret p-values in the context of a trading strategy's performance?

In the context of a trading strategy's performance, a p-value can be used to measure the significance of the strategy's returns or its predictive power.

We can think of the p-value like an umpire in a baseball game. The umpire's job is to decide if a player is safe or out based on the rules of the game. Similarly, a p-value helps us decide if the trading strategy's performance is statistically significant or just due to chance.

Let's break this down a bit:

Let's say you have developed a trading strategy and you want to test if the returns generated by this strategy are statistically significant, meaning that the returns aren't due to mere luck. In this case, you would set up a null hypothesis (H0) that states "the strategy's returns are equivalent to random chance". The alternative hypothesis (H1) would be "the strategy's returns are not due to chance".

Then, you would conduct a statistical test (e.g. t-test) on the strategy's returns. This test would generate a p-value.

The p-value tells you the probability of observing the returns that your strategy has generated (or returns even more extreme), assuming the null hypothesis is true.

- If the p-value is small (typically   0.05), it means there is strong evidence against the null hypothesis, so you reject the null. This suggests that your strategy's performance is statistically significant and not due to chance. You can be pretty confident that your strategy is doing something more than just getting lucky.

- If the p-value is large (typically > 0.05), it means there is weak evidence against the null hypothesis, so you fail to reject the null. This suggests that the performance of your strategy could just be due to luck.

Remember, just like the baseball umpire, the p-value isn't perfect. It doesn't tell you the size or importance of the effect, and it's not a measure of the evidence for the null hypothesis. Furthermore, statistical significance doesn't always translate to practical significance. Even if a strategy has a low p-value, it should still be carefully and realistically evaluated before being used for actual trading.

In the end, keep in mind – statistics in quantitative trading are tools, not decision makers. They can guide us like a compass, but it's still up to us to navigate the uncertain seas of the market.

3.13   What are the dangers of multiple hypothesis testing in finance?

In quantitative finance, problems can arise from multiple hypothesis testing, which is also referred to as data "snooping" or "mining". This practice involves executing many statistical tests on a single dataset, then selecting the most profitable or successful results. However, this can lead to incorrect conclusions due to a few critical issues:

1. False positives: One of the key drawbacks of multiple hypothesis testing is the increased likelihood of Type I errors, also known as false positives. This scenario is analogous to fishing with a very wide net in a lake teeming with various aquatic species. If you cast your net wide and large often enough, you're bound to catch something - occasionally even a rare fish. However, the fish (in this case, financial patterns) that you catch may not represent the true distribution of what's in the lake, i.e., the market. Just because you've found a pattern doesn't mean it's a consistently repeatable one or one that holds water statistically. In the realm of statistics, that would mean rejecting the null hypothesis when it's actually true.

2. Overfitting: Multiple hypothesis testing can also lead to overfitting. In overfitting, a model is tailored so closely to past data that it performs poorly on new data. This scenario is akin to memorizing answers for previous test questions so thoroughly that when you are given a new question, you find it difficult to answer because the context or phrasing has changed. Overfit models "memorize" the noise or randomness, not just the signal, in historical data.

$$Overfitting \rightarrow Low\ Bias + High\ Variance$$

3. P-value interpretation: P-values can be misleading in multiple hypothesis testing. A p-value of 0.05, for example, means there's a 5% chance of observing a result as extreme as the one you got if the null hypothesis were indeed true. Now, let's say we do 20 tests. The probability of getting at least one statistically significant result just by chance is over 64%, not 5%! We can compute this using the formula for at least one success in Bernoulli trials:

$$P(\text{at least one significant result at 5\% level}) = 1 - (1 - 0.05)^{20} \approx 0.64$$

4. Ignoring these dangers can lead to spurious results: For instance, you might find a trading algorithm that seems to generate excellent returns based on historical data. However, this could be a product of overfitting or false positives from multiple hypothesis testing. If deployed, such a system could perform poorly on new data, leading to unforeseen losses.

It's essential to use proper methodology, like Bonferroni correction or the False Discovery Rate (FDR), to adjust the significance level when dealing with multiple comparisons. This will help control the rate of Type I errors and provide a more realistic view of the algorithm or strategy's actual performance.

3.14   Explain Type I and Type II errors in the context of trading.

In algorithmic trading, decisions are frequently made based on statistical analyses. To understand the implications of these decisions, it's crucial to understand the concept of Type I and Type II errors, which are regularly used in hypothesis testing, a common method in quantitative analysis.

To illustrate these error types, let's use the analogy of a courtroom trial. In this analogy, the null hypothesis (H0) is that the defendant (a particular trading strategy) is innocent until proven guilty.

A Type I error happens when we falsely reject the null hypothesis. In other words, it's like convicting an innocent trading strategy. In a practical trading scenario, suppose we reject a profitable strategy erroneously. This mistake is very costly because it could cause us to miss a great investment opportunity. The probability of committing a Type I error is denoted by α, also known as the significance level.

A Type II error occurs when we fail to reject the null hypothesis when we should have — much like setting a guilty person free. In trading, this would mean sticking to a strategy that's unprofitive. The consequences of such an error could be severe, as we continue investing in a losing proposition. The probability of making a Type II error is often denoted by β.

Minimizing Type I and Type II errors is a balancing act. Generally, as we reduce the likelihood of one type of error (say, Type I), we inadvertently increase the chance of the other (Type II), and vice versa. This is why it's necessary to determine a threshold, or significance level, that strikes a balance between these two types of errors based on the strategy risk tolerance.

Both Type I and Type II errors play a crucial role in algorithmic trading. For example, in backtests, we use historical data to test if a particular trading strategy would have been successful in the past. Therefore, understanding these error types can help us to avoid overoptimistic or overpessimistic estimations of a strategy's success.

3.15 Why is the concept of statistical significance crucial in algorithmic trading?

Statistical significance is a critical concept in algorithmic trading and here's why: At its core, algorithmic trading is all about making informed decisions based on an analytical, quantifiable approach. All trading strategies, including algorithmic ones, are built on the premise that certain patterns or behaviors of the market or specific securities can indicate future movements, thus opening opportunities for profitable trades.

Consider algorithmic trading as a grand Cooking Show. Chefs – or in our case, traders and algorithms – use various ingredients – our tradeable assets – to create tasty and satisfying dishes – trades that yield profit. Now, just as the Cooking Show would need to find out how reliable different ingredients are in making a tasty dish, traders also need to know how reliable their indicators are in predicting market movements.

Statistical significance comes into play here. Just as the chefs need to test their ingredients, traders use statistical significance to test how likely their patterns/indicators are due to a real connection or simply due to chance.

Suppose you have an algorithm that shows that every time the weather is rainy in New York City, a particular stock goes up. The algorithm might have discovered this pattern after observing it happens 10 times in a row. However, before you risk your money, you'd like to know whether this pattern is a 'real' effect or just a random coincidence.

With a statistical test, you can calculate the probability that this correlation between NYC weather and the stock's price happened by chance. The result of this test is known as the p-value. If the p-value is very low, typically below the 0.05 threshold (or 5%), you can reject the hypothesis that the observations occurred by random chance. This is what it means to reach statistical significance.

The smaller the p-value, the stronger the evidence that you should reject the null hypothesis. In other words, the stock is indeed influenced by the weather.

By assessing the statistical significance of various indicators, algorithmic traders can better understand which elements are most likely to lead to successful trades. This enables them to focus on strategies that are statistically sound, rather than relying on chance or anecdotal evidence. Through quantifiable evidence, traders can build, refine, and validate their trading strategies, making statistical significance indispensable in algorithmic trading.

3.16   What is overfitting, and why is it a concern in algorithmic trading?

Overfitting is a concept in statistical modeling and machine learning, reminiscent to wearing a tailored suit that fits one person perfectly, but may not fit another person due to individual differences in physique.

In mathematical terms, overfitting occurs when a statistical model or machine learning algorithm captures the noise instead of the underlying process. It's like trying to find patterns in the stock market using extreme precision, you might end up exceedingly fine-tuning your algorithm to perfectly fit historical data, but fail when applying it to new data.

Here's how it would look:

Imagine fitting a straight line ($y = mx + c$) to a set of points in a 2D space. If the points appear to form a somewhat straight line, a linear regression model would be a good fit. Now, consider you have a 10th-degree polynomial ($y = a_{10}x^{10} + a_9x^9 + ... + a_1x + a_0$). You can, in theory, adjust the coefficients to fit every point perfectly, leaving virtually no errors. While it may seem tempting, this approach is usually a bad idea because although the model perfectly fits the training data, it will likely perform poorly using new data. The polynomial is excessively tweaked to fit the given data (i.e., it's overfit), failing to generalise for new inputs.

In algorithmic trading, overfitting is a major concern. Let's say your model uses several parameters. If you fine-tune these parameters to get the best results from historical data, you might end up with an overfit model. You'd have a model that works greatly on historical data but fails in live markets - akin to having a map of yesterday's weather, which is not very useful for predicting today's climate.

A good trading strategy, like a well-tailored suit, should have a good fit but also some generalizability. It should work reasonably well under diverse market conditions, rather than just fitting perfectly to the past. Balancing this specificity-generalizability trade-off is one of the major challenges in algorithmic trading.

3.17   How can cross-validation be used to mitigate the risk of overfitting?

Cross-validation is a very useful technique in quantitative analysis and particularly in the field of machine learning, where it can be utilized to mitigate the risk of overfitting. The concept can be best explained through an analogy.

Imagine you're a teacher preparing a class for a final exam. You have a textbook full of problems that you can use to train the students, but you don't want the students to merely memorize the answers to those specific questions. Instead, you want to ensure they understand the underlying concepts and can generalize them to new, previously unseen questions. This is the same problem we face in machine learning. Overfitting is like a student who has memorized all the problems in the textbook but fails at the exam because he or she cannot apply the concepts to new problems.

Cross-validation, in this case, is akin to you choosing a subset of problems from the textbook for your students to practice with (the training set), and keeping some other problems secret to test their understanding later (the validation set). Repeat this procedure multiple times with different problems for practice and testing, and you have a system in place that ensures the students can handle all kinds of problems, not just the ones they've practiced with.

Mathematically speaking, this process involves partitioning our dataset into 'K' distinct subsets (or 'folds'). We then iteratively train our model on K-1 subsets, and test the model's performance on the subset we left out. This gives us a more robust estimation of model performance as each data instance gets to be in the testing set exactly once and gets to be in a training dataset K-1 times.

This approach effectively uses a more comprehensive section of our dataset to train the model, and another fresh section to objectively validate its performance. It helps us to avoid overfitting, as we're constantly testing our model on unseen data.

3.18   What are the signs that a trading strategy might be overfit to past data?

Overfitting is a statistical phenomenon that occurs when a model is attuned so precisely to data from the past performance that it becomes less effective at predicting future outcomes. When a trading strategy is overfitted, it performs exceptionally well on historical data but fails miserably in real-time trading.

Here are a few signs that a trading strategy might be overfit:

1. **Low Out-of-Sample (OOS) Performance**: A prominent sign of overfitting is an especially divergent difference between in-sample and out-of-sample performance. If the strategy performs flawlessly on historical data but has a drop in performance with new data, it may be overfitted. It's like reciting a poem perfectly in your room but stammering on stage.

2. **High Parameter Sensitivity**: If the performance of your strategy changes dramatically with minor changes to a parameter, it might be a sign of overfitting. Imagine tuning a radio for the perfect sound, a small twist left or right shouldn't make everything fuzzy.

3. **Complex Models with Many Parameters**: If the model is highly complex with numerous variables or parameters, it could be overfitted.

More parameters lead to higher chances of overfitting. It's like trying to hit a bullseye by drawing circles around every past spot you've hit before. When there are too many, you essentially create a target where you can't seem to miss. But when you aim at a new target (future data), you may find that you miss by a wide margin.

4. **Rules Tailored to Specific Cases**: When your model has trading rules tailored to specific times and situations in the past, it has likely been overfit.

The model is focusing too much on the noise rather than the signal of the data. It's comparable to basing a city's annual weather forecast solely on last year's whimsical weather behavior.

5. **Too Good to be True Results**: If the results look too good to be true, well, they probably are. Huge returns are typically a big red flag.

This is akin to cheating on a school test by memorizing answers from an answer key. You may score 100% on that particular test but will likely perform poorly in a situation where the questions change even slightly.

To mitigate the risk of overfitting, one can use methods like cross-validation, regularization, and out-of-sample testing. Also, starting with simpler models and gradually adding complexity as justified by improved predictive power can help.

Remember, a good trading strategy is one that walks the fine balance between being well-fitted to past data and being adaptive enough for future data, just as a good piece of clothing should be neither too tight-fit that it's uncomfortable, nor too loose that it doesn't serve its purpose.

3.19 How does the curse of dimensionality relate to overfitting?

Excellent question. When it comes to the curse of dimensionality, I often like to imagine it as a rapidly expanding universe. The concept refers to the phenomena where, as we add more dimensions to our data set (or in other words, include more variables for analysis), the volume of the data space expands so quickly that the available data becomes sparse and it becomes increasingly difficult to achieve statistical significance.

Similarly, overfitting is like trying to map this expansive universe with a super detailed star map. Overfitting in machine learning models happens when we design our model with an excess of parameters, hence it becomes highly sensitive to the peculiarities and noise of the training data set. When such models are exposed to unseen data in the future, their performance often drops, as they fail to generalize from the specific to the unseen, somewhat like a star map that works brilliantly in one part of the universe but utterly fails in an uncharted region.

Now, imagine linking these two scenarios together - The curse of dimensionality and overfitting. By continuously adding features (dimensions) to your model, you're likely to end up in a situation where the model is too complex and has learnt the 'noise' rather than the 'signal'. This contributes to overfitting because, in this high dimensionality situation, even a complex model might appear to perform well on training data due to the model fitting itself onto the noise rather than the underlying patterns in the data. Therefore, the curse of dimensionality exacerbates overfitting, especially when not enough representative data is available for the multitude of dimensions being considered.

In mathematical notation, if n denotes the size of our dataset and p represents the number of features (or dimensions), then there is a high chance of overfitting when $p >> n$. In such situations, we might get misleadingly good results on the training set, but the model will likely perform poorly on future unseen data.

Therefore, it's important to keep in mind the balance between the number of parameters (complexity) of your model and the number of dimensions in your data to get better generalization performance.

3.20   What practices can be employed to reduce overfitting during the development of a trading algorithm?

Overfitting is a phenomenon that plagues many areas of quantitative analysis and it is especially risky in the realm of algorithmic trading. Imagine you have a pair of shoes that fits perfectly on your feet, but then you try to wear the same pair on different terrain - cobblestones or snow, instead of a smooth road. It might not fit as well anymore, and you may end up stumbling. It's the same with overfitted models, they fit perfectly on the data they've been tailored to, but may stumble when exposed to unseen market scenarios.

To reduce overfitting while developing a trading algorithm, there are few practices you can adopt:

1. **Use of Cross-Validation**: Cross-validation is a statistical method used to estimate the skill of machine learning models. It essentially involves running the analysis multiple times, on sub-parts of your data, rather than on the full set. You can think of it like running a rehearsal for a play with one set of cast members at a time, instead of the whole ensemble at once.

2. **Regularization Techniques**: These techniques work effectively to prevent overfitting by adding a penalty term to the loss function. The two widely used techniques are Lasso (L1 regularization) and Ridge (L2 regularization). This is akin to adding a 'leash' to your model, reining it in when it tries to fit the data too perfectly, preventing it from running 'wild' on unseen data.

3. **Simplify the Model**: A model which is too complex can easily capture noise instead of the underlying pattern. So, use a simpler model or reduce the number of features used in the model. You wouldn't want to clutter your trading desk with too many indicators, each flashing different signals, right? A cleaner, unhurried approach often works better.

4. **Out of Sample Testing**: Reserve a part of your data for testing and train the model on the remaining data. This gives a clearer idea of how your model will function on unseen data – it's like the final performance on the stage, after all the rehearsals.

5. **Use of Ensemble Methods**: These methods combine predictions from multiple models thereby reducing variance and improving generalization. The wisdom of the crowd can often exceed an individual, right?

Remember, in trading, you're not looking for a model that can replay history with perfect accuracy. Instead, you want a model that can, more often than not, predict the future correctly.

Chapter 4

Trading Strategies

4.1 Describe the basic premise behind momentum trading strategies.

Momentum trading strategies are built on the notion of "the wind in your sails", drawing from Newton's first law of motion: an object in motion tends to stay in motion with the same speed and in the same direction. In the realm of trading, this translates to the idea that stocks exhibiting strong trends, either upwards or downwards, are likely to continue to do so in the near-term future.

Conceptually, you can think of a momentum trading strategy like surfing: surfers catch the wave and ride it until it loses power. In the stock market world, traders buy stocks that are on an upswing and sell them before the momentum fades.

For example, suppose an algorithm identifies a stock whose price has been steadily and significantly increasing in the past few days or weeks - more importantly, at an accelerating rate. This may indicate that there is strong buyer interest and sentiment is bullish, and such a scenario could trigger a buy signal in a momentum strategy.

The algorithm would then hold the stock until signals indicate that the upward momentum is slowing or reversing (i.e., the 'wave' is about to break), at which point it would execute a sell order to exit the position.

One common approach to quantifying momentum is to use the rate of change (ROC), defined as:

$$ROC = \frac{CurrentPrice - Price\_n\_periods\_ago}{Price\_n\_periods\_ago} \times 100$$

Where n is a predetermined period. A higher ROC indicates stronger momentum.

While effective, the momentum strategy isn't without risks. Sudden market reversals can lead to substantial losses. Plus, knowing precisely when to enter and exit the market is challenging. Therefore, practitioners often employ stop-loss measures and closely monitor market conditions to adapt their strategies as necessary.

But, much like skillful surfers who can read waves and weather conditions, adept traders backed with strong algorithms can ride the market waves for considerable gains using momentum strategies.

4.2 How do momentum algorithms handle periods of market consolidation or sideways movement?

Momentum algorithms, often referred to as "trend-following" strategies, basically aim to capitalize on the continuation of an existing market trend. They work best in times of sustained market uptrends or downtrends, buying when prices are going up, and selling when prices are going down.

However, during periods of market consolidation or sideways movement, these strategies generally have a harder time achieving profitable results. This is because, in a sideways market, the momentum is neutral, and therefore, price movement can be random and less predictable.

To visualize this, imagine trying to roll a ball down the hill (this is when the momentum trading algorithms work best). Now, instead of a hill, if you're trying to roll that same ball on a flat surface, it wouldn't really go anywhere as there is no existing momentum to carry it forward. That's kind of how these algorithms behave in a neutral, "sideways" market.

Despite this, good momentum algorithms employ techniques to mitigate the effects of market consolidation periods. One common technique is to use stop-loss orders. Stop-loss orders serve as a form of insurance, where a trade is automatically exited if the price goes beyond a pre-defined level, thus limiting the potential loss on a stock that isn't maintaining its momentum.

Another strategy is to utilize different signals or indicators that can suggest a potential breakout from the consolidation phase. For instance, volume analysis can be used to identify increased activity, which could precede a breakout.

Applying diversification is yet another effective approach to handle periods of market consolidation. By diversifying the portfolio among different asset classes, the algorithm can continue to find momentum in other markets even if one particular market is going through a consolidation phase.

So, while the momentum algorithms might not be at their peak during market consolidation, they are not entirely helpless either. Just like a savvy surfer, who not only rides the big waves but also knows how to navigate the quiet waters, waiting for the next big wave (market trend) to roll in.

4.3 What are the main risks associated with momentum trading?

Momentum trading is a strategy that aims to capitalize on the continuance of existing trends in the market. It involves going long stocks, futures, or market ETFs showing upward-trending prices, and short the respective assets with downward-trending prices. Despite its potential for profits, this type of trading strategy involves several key risks.

1. **Systematic Risk:** Like driving a sports car, momentum trading can be fast-paced and exhilarating but can also quite easily lead to a crash if you aren't careful. The equivalent of a crash in trading is a sudden, broad market downturn, sometimes called a "systemic risk". This type of risk is inherent to the entire market and cannot be eliminated through diversification.

2. **Trading Psychology Risk:** This risk is akin to the behavioural pitfalls one might encounter on a weight loss journey. Just as someone might be tempted to over indulge in a cheat meal, jeopardizing their diet, a trader might fall prey to fear or greed, leading to impulsive decisions that can dramatically impact their financial health. If a trade starts to fall, there may be the tendency to hang on and hope it will bounce back, leading to potential significant losses.

3. **Estimation Risk:** Identifying a momentum is like trying to catch a wave while surfing. Sometimes, it might look like a big wave is forming, but in reality, it could just be a smaller ripple. In the same way, identifying an asset's momentum can be tricky. The momentum might be about to decline or it could be stronger than it appears. This uncertainty can make it difficult to always accurately estimate the best point of entry or exit in a trade.

4. **Execution Risk:** Just as there may be a delay between the moment you decide to jump off a cliff into a pool and the moment you actually do it, there can be a delay from the time you decide to make a trade until the moment it is actually executed. Sometimes,

during this time gap, the market can move against you and the price you thought you were getting isn't the price you actually get. This is called slippage and is an execution risk.

5. **Overfitting Risk:** Overfitting is like trying to fit a round peg in a square hole, but then chipping the peg until it fits, and declaring "It fits perfectly!". In trading, overfitting happens when a model is excessively complex and captures the noise in the data rather than the signal. While this model might work well on historical data, it often performs poorly on new, out-of-sample data.

Overall, while momentum trading can provide significant prospects for profit, it's critical to understand and manage these risks in order to be successful in the long-term. A key to managing these risks is having a solid trading plan and sticking to it, much like having a GPS in a car during a long journey.

4.4   How do momentum strategies identify and validate trends in the market?

Momentum trading strategies essentially attempt to profit from market volatility. They aim to identify and participate in trades that are likely to continue in a particular direction, based on the established momentum in the price change.

To identify trends, momentum traders use a mix of data analysis tools and indicators that help quantify the underlying momentum of a security. One of the most common tools used in this analysis is the "Moving Average" which is represented mathematically as:

$$MA(T) = \frac{1}{T} \sum_{t=1}^{T} P_t$$

Where P_t is the price at time t, and T is the chosen time frame for the moving average (e.g., 50 days, 200 days, etc.). When the price of a stock is above its moving average, it is considered in an uptrend and vice versa.

Next, they might use the "Relative Strength Index" (RSI), an oscillator that measures the speed and change of price movements and provides a value between 0 to 100. High values (typically above 70) suggest that an asset is overbought, which could signify the upturning of the bulls; whereas low values (typically below 30) indicate that it is oversold, which could suggest a downturn of the bears.

$$RSI = 100 - \frac{100}{1 + RS}$$

where RS is the average of N days' up close divided by the average of N days' down close.

Another common tool is the "Moving Average Convergence Divergence" (MACD), which calculates the difference between two Exponential Moving Averages (EMA) – usually the 12-period and 26-period EMAs. The trigger or 'signal' line is then a 9-period EMA of the MACD.

To validate the identified trend, momentum traders look for confirmation signals, such as increased volume during the trend, or the alignment of multiple analysis tools pointing to the same conclusion. Sometimes, they sustain the trade until they see a trend reversal or when other pre-existing exit rules get triggered.

However, just like cooking a perfect dish doesn't always guarantee it will be loved by all guests, these indicators, meant to identify and validate trends, don't always predict a winning trade. Market forces are affected by a multitude of unpredictable factors, just as meal preference can be influenced by personal tastes or dietary restrictions. So the use of these trading strategies requires skillful interpretation, proper risk management, and continuous learning.

4.5 Can you provide an example of a technical indicator commonly used in momentum trading?

A common and widely used technical indicator for momentum trading is the Relative Strength Index (RSI). The RSI is a momentum oscillator that measures the speed and change of price movements. It is used to identify overbought or oversold conditions in a market, which can give an indication of an impending reversal.

Let's explore the RSI a bit more in depth. It is typically calculated over 14 periods and can range from 0 to 100. The formula to calculate RSI is:

$$RSI = 100 - \frac{100}{(1 + RS)}$$

Where RS is the average gain of up periods over the specified time frame divided by the average loss of down periods over the specified time frame:

$$RS = \frac{Average\ Gain}{Average\ Loss}$$

Values of 70 or above indicate that an asset is becoming overbought and may be primed for a trend reversal or corrective pullback in price. An RSI reading of 30 or below indicates an oversold or undervalued condition.

Consider RSI as a speedometer for a car. When a car is going too fast (over 70 on the RSI), it might be an indication that it's time to slow down or risk a speeding ticket (price correction). Conversely, if the car is going way too slow (under 30 on the RSI), it might be time to speed up a bit (price increase).

However, just like a speedometer, the RSI is merely a tool. It doesn't drive the car or determine where it's going. It only reflects current conditions. As with all trading strategies, risk management and careful interpretation of indicators is key. It's important to consider the RSI alongside other technical analysis tools and market indicators.

4.6   What is the underlying assumption of mean reversion strategies?

Mean-reversion strategies, one of the key trading strategies, are based on a fundamental assumption that prices of assets or financial instruments naturally tend to revert to their average or mean over time.

Imagine a youthful puppy on a leash as it explores its surroundings during a walk. No matter how energetic or curious, the leash (our mean price) limits the puppy's meandering. Assuming the leash holder (the mean) walks at a regular pace, the puppy (our price) will always return closer to the leash holder (the mean) after it has pulled away, no matter how far it seems to initially stray.

In mathematical terms, it implies that if an asset's price fluctuates significantly away from its mean, it's expected to eventually return back to that mean price. Traders use this to predict when to buy or sell, assuming a higher probability of price movements returning to the mean.

Consider a stock whose price, for ease of illustration, has historically hovered around $100. There are occasional spikes and dips, but overall, the price has an apparent gravitational pull towards $100 — you could say, $100 is the mean price. In a mean-reversion strategy, if the price happened to spike up to $110, the trader would notionally short the stock, betting on the price falling back towards the mean.

Similarly, if the price dipped to $90, the trader would typically buy, predicting the price to rise back toward the mean.

Mathematically this could be represented by the equation

$$\Delta P = -\alpha(P - \mu)$$

where

ΔP denotes the change in price,

α is the speed at which prices revert to the mean,

P is the current much deviated price,

μ is the historical average price.

The minus sign indicates the 'reversion' towards the mean.

This fundamental assumption, like all statistical generalizations, is not without its caveats. Although it has its empirical successes, mean-reversion strategies can be disrupted by sudden market shifts or external influences, and it's not guaranteed to hold true over all time periods or asset classes. Further, the mean itself might not be stationary and could evolve over time. It is the trader's responsibility to account for these standpoints and manage risk accordingly.

4.7   How do mean reversion strategies determine the "mean" or equilibrium price?

A mean reversion trading strategy operates on the assumption that prices will move towards their average over time. Mean reversion traders try to identify and capitalize on price deviations from the perceived 'mean' or 'equilibrium' price.

Determination of this "mean," however, isn't always as straightforward as simply calculating the average price over a certain time period. In fact, it can be quite complex and can involve a range of statistical methods. Moreover, the mean is dynamic and will change as new prices emerge and old prices age out of the relevant time period you are focusing on.

One common approach is to use rolling averages, where this mean value is the average of the security's price over a specific number of previous bars or periods. Traders then seek opportunities where the stock price deviates significantly from this average with the expectation that it will revert back. Another method is to use exponential moving averages, which weigh more recent prices heavier than distant prices.

Another way to determine mean involves the use of statistical methods like regression analysis. In this method, the traders develop a regression line that best fits the historical data points, and that line (or the function generating that line) is taken to represent the mean.

To visualize, think of the price movement as a drunk man walking home. The equity price is the drunk man, and the 'home' is the mean price. He may stumble left or right (deviate from the path), but he will eventually steer towards his home (mean).

Remember, different strategies and different time horizons might require different methodologies for determining the mean. If the time horizon is very short, some traders might use high-frequency data and econometric models. On the other hand, some traders might prefer a longer-term approach, using fundamental analysis to decide if a security is over or undervalued relative to its "fundamental value" (calculated based on factors like earnings, book value, etc.)

However, it's important to note that all these strategies assume the existence of an equilibrium price to which prices will revert. This assumption itself, while practical, is at some level a simplification of the complex dynamics of financial markets. Events like significant changes to company fundamentals, or to the broader economy, can permanently shift the equilibrium price.

4.8 What are potential risks or challenges in deploying mean reversion strategies?

Mean reversion strategies are like boomerangs. They're based on the statistical concept that the price or returns of an asset will tend to move to the the average over time, just like how a boomerang that you throw will aim to come back to you. However, the risk is that unlike a boomerang that you have control over, you can't control the market. Therefore, like a boomerang gone astray, a mean reversion strategy may not always perform as expected.

Here are a few risks and challenges associated with deploying mean reversion trading strategies:

1. Non-return to the mean: The biggest risk is the assumption that the price will revert to the mean. Prices may not revert in the expected timeframe, or possibly won't revert at all, due to any number of fundamental changes in the associated asset or marketplace. It's like expecting a boomerang to come back when it has been caught by a gust of wind and thrown off its course.

2. Extended losses: Mean reversion strategies are prone to experience large losses during periods of sustained price trends opposite to the assumed eventual direction. If stock prices or other trading metrics continue to trend away from the mean, you can post significant losses.

3. Market changes: Market conditions can change rapidly. Changes in trends or shifts in market regime could affect the effectiveness of the strategy. Like if suddenly the shape or weight of our boomerang changes, it surely is not going to have the same flight pattern.

4. Timing: Timing is crucial for these strategies. Entering or exiting a position too early or too late could significantly impact the performance of the strategy. If you throw your boomerang too hard or too soft, it may not return correctly.

5. Structural breaks: In statistics, a structural break is an abrupt

shift in a time series. If such a shift occurs, it can drastically distort the mean and make mean reversion strategies unprofitable. It's as if the wind direction changed suddenly; our boomerang, designed for a different wind direction, falters.

6. Execution risk: Even if the strategy is sound in theory, the practical application, which includes trading costs, can erode assumed gains or even lead to losses. It's as if our boomerang is perfect, but every time we throw it, we have to pay a fee. If the fee outweighs the joy of throwing the boomerang, it's pointless, isn't it?

Always remember, fruitful intraday trading involves a lot more than just picking a strategy. One still needs to consider the trading platform, trading fees, regulatory norms, market conditions, and many other factors. Or in boomerang terms: know the weather, know the field, know your strength, watch for trees, and keep practicing!

4.9 How can algorithms determine if an asset has deviated significantly from its mean?

An algorithm can determine if an asset has deviated significantly from its mean using various statistical methods, among the most common of which is the concept of a "standard deviation."

If we use the analogy of a Greek procession, the mean (or average) is the center of the procession while the standard deviation would represent people straying away from the center. The bigger the standard deviation, the more "wild" or "chaotic" the procession is with people straying farther from the center. In trading terms, a larger standard deviation means more volatility and more price dispersion.

If we represent the asset prices as a statistical distribution, typically assuming a normal distribution (also known as Gaussian distribution), the mean would represent the average price of the asset, and the standard deviation would provide an indication of the volatility of these asset prices. Standard deviation measures the extent of variability or dispersion from the average.

In the world of finance and trading, a one standard deviation move from the mean usually covers 68% of all price movements; two standard deviations cover roughly 95

A general technical algorithm to determine if an asset price has deviated significantly from its mean would look similar to this:

1. You compute the mean μ of the price for a given period using the formula:

$$\mu = \frac{1}{N} \sum_{i=1}^{N} p_i$$

where p_i represents the price at time i, and N is the total number of prices within the period under consideration.

2. Then you compute the standard deviation σ with the formula:

$$\sigma = \sqrt{\frac{1}{N} \sum_{i=1}^{N} (p_i - \mu)^2}$$

3. Having both μ and σ, what's left is to compare the current price p_t of the asset to the range defined by the mean plus or minus a certain number of standard deviations. Let's say we consider three standard deviations for our significant deviation:

If $p_t > \mu + 3\sigma$ or $p_t < \mu - 3\sigma$, then we would consider the price to have deviated significantly from the mean.

By adjusting the number of standard deviations, we set our threshold for what we consider being significant deviation. The larger the

number, the more unique the event is, but it will also occur less frequently. Conversely, a smaller number will give more frequent signals,
but these signals will be less distinctive. This, like many decisions
when building trading strategies, is a trade-off that each algorithm
developer needs to consider.

4.10   How do mean reversion strategies manage sudden market shocks or news events?

Mean reversion is a financial term for the assumption that a stock's
price will tend to move to the average price over time. This is similar
to a rubber band that, when stretched, will place an increasingly
powerful force to pull back to its original position. In the trading
world, a stock price would be this metaphorical rubber band.

Mean reversion strategies can indeed become vulnerable during sudden market shock or news event. The key point here is the unpre-
dictability that comes with them, which may result in a situation
known as a 'regime shift'. This is where the conditions which enable
the mean reversion strategy to perform optimally suddenly change,
thereby skewing the logic applied in the trading model.

One common way to manage this risk is to use 'stop-loss' orders, a tool
that automatically closes an open position if the price moves against
the trade beyond a certain degree. By setting a stop-loss order, a
trader can limit their downside risk, which works like a safety net
that catches your financial 'fall', preventing further losses once the
price hits a certain level.

Also, traders often apply different risk management techniques such
as position sizing (not trading more capital than you can afford to
lose in a particular trade), capping exposure to any one market, and
others.

Moreover, there is the incorporation of 'news analysis' into the trading algorithm. This involves taking into consideration significant news events that could impact market prices. Sophisticated algorithms analyze text in real-time for news articles, social media posts, and economic reports, allowing for the trading system to react to new information as soon as it becomes available.

Ultimately, like other trading strategies, mean reversion has its risks and isn't foolproof. The best traders blend mathematics, instinct, and a deep understanding of the markets to guide their decisions, while simultaneously preparing for the times when they are wrong.

4.11 Define statistical arbitrage and its main components.

Statistical arbitrage, often referred to as StatArb, is an investment strategy that applies complex mathematical models to exploit statistical anomalies or price patterns in financial markets. It is a type of quantitative trading strategy, which makes trading decisions based on rigorous quantitative analysis of the data.

Think of statistical arbitrage as playing a game of "spot the difference". If you have two very similar pictures, you might find small differences where things are not in perfect alignment; these disparities are the opportunities that statistical arbitrage aims to exploit.

The main components of statistical arbitrage are:

1. **Securities Selection**: Just as in our "spot the difference" game where you need two similar pictures, in StatArb, you need securities that are similar or related in some manner. These securities can be related by industry, geographical region, or some other factor. StatArb often involves trading pairs or portfolios of securities.

2. **Modeling and Prediction**: The heartbeat of StatArb is the use of advanced mathematical models to predict future price move-

ments. These mathematical models, often based on historical price data, identify price deviations that will likely converge in the future. This is similar to predicting where the differences between our two pictures will disappear in the future based on past transformations of the images.

3. **Automated Trading**: An important component of statistical arbitrage is the use of automated trading systems. These systems can react quickly to changes in market conditions and capitalize on trading opportunities that can disappear in milliseconds. Returning to our analogy, these would be the high-speed tools that spot and flag the differences between the two pictures instantly.

4. **Risk Management**: Lastly, but notably, no trading strategy is complete without proper risk management. These controls minimize the potential for large losses. In our game, this would be akin to a fail-safe that stops the picture comparison when the differences become too significant, suggesting the images aren't as similar as initially thought.

5. **Quantitative Techniques**: Some statistical arbitrage strategies also make use of sophisticated machine learning techniques to predict changes in market sentiment, market movements, etc. effectively, which are further used to inform trading strategies.

Remember, statistical arbitrage is not guaranteed to always be profitable as it relies on the assumption that the identified statistical patterns will continue into the future. But, historical data can't predict future events or changes in market conditions, just as spotting past changes between two pictures can't predict future transformations.

4.12   How do traders identify pairs or groups of assets for statistical arbitrage?

In statistical arbitrage, we aim to exploit pricing inefficiencies between related securities. The first step in this process is to identify these "related" securities, which could be pairs or larger groups of assets.

The most common way to identify these is through a process known as cointegration. Essentially, if two (or more) time series are cointegrated, this signifies that, even though the individual prices may wander, there is a certain stable, long-term relationship between them.

More specifically, two time series X and Y are said to be cointegrated if some linear combination $Y - \beta X$ is stationary, i.e., its statistical properties such as mean, variance do not change over time.

Imagine a man walking his dog in a park. The man is strolling along a path while the dog is running all around. However, there is a leash tying the dog to the man's hand. Even though both are moving around in what may seem like random directions (just like our price series), the leash (think β) ensures that there is a certain relation between them.

To test if a pair of securities are cointegrated, traders usually make use of statistical tests like the Augmented Dickey-Fuller test (ADF), Johansen test, etc. ADF, for example, tests the null hypothesis that a unit root is present in a time series sample. If we can reject this hypothesis for the series $Y - \beta X$, then we can say that the series are cointegrated.

However, it's not always as simple as testing for cointegration. The policy of how pairs are formed can widely vary, and there are numerous other factors taken into consideration such as transaction costs, liquidity, market factors etc., which makes the process of pair selection more of a combination of art and science.

The key, however, is to always remember to look for securities where there is a statistical evidence of some long-term relationship, just like the leash between the man and his dog. Without this, the pricing errors will not tend to revert to the mean and the strategy may result in losses.

4.13   What role does cointegration play in statistical arbitrage?

Cointegration plays a pivotal role in certain types of statistical arbitrage, most notably pairs trading. The core concept behind statistical arbitrage is that price discrepancies between related financial instruments are temporal and will converge over time. The basic notion is similar to a rubber band stretching apart then snapping back together.

Cointegration is a statistical property of time series data which indicates how closely two financial instruments are related to each other in a long-run equilibrium, despite prices diverging from each other in the short run. Think of it like two friends walking their dogs in a park. While the dogs may wander off in different directions in the short term (representing short term price differences), they always end up near their owners at the end of the walk (representing the long-term equilibrium relationship).

In pairs trading, the use of cointegrated pairs has a distinct advantage. If two stocks are cointegrated, it implies that there exists a certain linear combination of their prices which is stationary i.e., the difference in prices have a constant mean and variance. When this price difference diverges significantly from the mean (like the dogs wandering away), a trader can go long on the underpriced stock (betting on the dog that's behind) and short on the overpriced stock (betting against the dog that's wandered too far). The expectation is that the price difference will eventually revert to the mean (both dogs coming back near their owners), which would result in a profit.

To translate this into mathematical terms, if Y_t and X_t are the price series of two cointegrated stocks, their cointegration is represented as:

$$Y_t = a + bX_t + \epsilon_t$$

where a is the intercept, b is the cointegration vector or hedge ratio, and ϵ_t is the error term.

With a well-defined strategy and risk management, cointegration and reversion to the mean can be used effectively as a basis for profitable statistical arbitrage strategies, such as pairs trading.

4.14 How do statistical arbitrage strategies manage risk?

Statistical Arbitrage strategies, often referred to as "StatArb," manage risk in several ways that can be analogous to having multiple safety nets to protect a tightrope walker. Allow me to explain.

1. **Diversification:** Similar to placing several eggs in different baskets, rather than relying on a single trade, statistical arbitrage strategies spread risk across many different trades. This is done by creating a broad portfolio of several hundred to several thousand securities. The idea is to mitigate idiosyncratic risk (specific to a particular security) with portfolio diversification, assuming that not all securities will move in the same direction at the same time.

2. **Market Neutralization:** Market neutralization is akin to wearing a belt as well as suspenders, ensuring that the pants (the portfolio) stay up even if one fails. StatArb strategies are designed to be beta-neutral, i.e., they have zero correlation with market movement. This strategy takes both long and short positions, which theoretically reduces exposure to systematic market risk.

3. **Risk Models:** Risk models in StatArb act as the safety harness for the tightrope walker, predicting and adjusting for potential falls. StatArb uses sophisticated risk models to identify and manage different types of risks, such as market, sector, and style risks. The strategies adjust positions or dynamically hedge to mitigate these risks, based on the models' predictions.

4. **Limiting Leverage**: Leverage is like a rod for the tightrope walker, it helps to balance, but too much of it could make things tricky. While leverage can amplify profits, it can also amplify losses.

Hence, maintaining a prudent leverage level is crucial for risk management in StatArb strategies.

It's important to remember that no risk management mechanism can completely eliminate risk. Market conditions, shifts in correlations and volatilities, model errors, and unforeseen events (known as black swan events) still pose risks. Therefore, continuous monitoring, adjustment and refinement of the strategies, based on quantitative and qualitative assessments, are essential in statistical arbitrage risk management.

4.15   What are the limitations or potential pitfalls of statistical arbitrage?

Statistical arbitrage, in essence, is a quantitatively driven trading strategy that leverages statistical methods and big data analytics. However, like any strategy, it does come with its own set of limitations and potential pitfalls.

1. **Model Risk**: Take the example of creating a Lego structure with a few missing pieces. In the world of statistical arbitrage, these 'missing pieces' could be the wrong assumptions or inappropriate statistical models. The performance of a statistical arbitrage strategy is heavily dependent on the assumption that the chosen mathematical models correctly represent the behavior of financial markets. Model risk emerges if this assumption proves wrong. This could stem from models using outdated data, inappropriate models being used, or mathematical errors during model construction.

2. **Market Risk**: Imagine you're playing a game of chess but the rules keep changing every now and then. Financial markets can be equally unpredictable. They can suddenly change due to macroeconomic events, market sentiments or unexpected news, thereby invalidating the statistical arbitrage strategy.

3. **Execution Risk**: Think about trying to catch a rabbit in a

garden. In principle, it's straightforward, but in practice, it's difficult to execute. Similarly, in algorithmic trading, there's always a risk that the trades may not execute as intended due to various factors such as high volatility, sudden change in liquidity, or technical issues with the trading platform.

4. **Data Snooping Bias**: Consider a scenario where you try to predict lifestyle-related health outcomes based on data solely from gym-goers. Your predictions may hold fairly accurate for gym-enthusiasts but fail drastically for others who don't engage in gym activities. Similarly, statistical arbitrage strategies present a risk of "overfitting" or "data snooping bias". It's when the strategy performs well on past data (the data it was tested on) but potentially fails to predict future trends accurately.

5. **Competition and Market Efficiency**: If everyone is trying to find the same hidden treasure in the same place, the value of that treasure decreases. Owing to its profitable concept, there is fierce competition in statistical arbitrage. As more traders start employing similar strategies based on the same or related sets of information, opportunities decrease, 'correcting' the market, and the arbitrage opportunities may quickly evaporate, leading to rapidly diminishing returns.

To sum up, while statistical arbitrage can provide significant advantages by using sophisticated mathematical models and algorithms to exploit market inefficiencies, it's vital to be aware of these limitations and risks. Traders should ensure they back-test their models with caution, use up-to-date datasets, and diversify their strategies where possible.

4.16   Explain the concept of pairs trading and the rationale behind it.

Pairs trading is a form of statistical arbitrage trading strategy that is designed to profit from the deviation in price of two highly correlated securities. Trading pairs require strong understanding about the fundamental properties of the securities, statistical modeling, and the use of algorithmic trading systems.

Let's understand this with a simple analogy. Let's consider two athletes who usually run at the same speed, comparable to two stocks that are highly correlated. One day, one of the runners is temporarily slowed down due to some minor injury, similarly as one stock price lower due to some short term negative news. Given both athletes' historical performance, we expect the slowed athlete to catch up once he recovers, just as the undervalued stock's price is expected to rise back to its 'fair value'. In pairs trading, this is the rationale we use to make profit.

Mathematically, if we consider two assets S_1 and S_2, both priced X and Y respectively, the strategy suggests we short the overpriced asset, S_1, and long the underpriced asset, S_2. This means:

- If X increases and Y decreases, we will gain on S_1 and lose on S_2.

- If X decreases and Y increases, we will lose on S_1 and gain on S_2.

- If X increases and Y increases, but X increases at a slower rate than Y, then we lose on S_1 and gain on S_2.

- If X decreases and Y decreases, but X decreases at a faster rate than Y, then we gain on S_1 and lose on S_2.

So irrespective of market movements, the aim is to make profit out of the convergence of the two securities' prices.

The rationale behind this strategy lies in the 'Law of One Price', which states that two identical assets should sell for the same price. If the prices diverge (which can happen due to a range of factors such as liquidity, specific investor demand, or even temporary price shocks), then a pairs trade can be profitable. These divergences can often be identified via quantitative techniques such as cointegration tests.

One of the key advantages of pairs trading is that it is market neutral. This means that the direction of the overall market does not affect the outcome of the strategy – it's only the relative performance of the two stocks that matters. That makes it an attractive option in a variety of market conditions. However, one needs to consider the costs of trading and ensure the potential profit is attractive after these costs.

4.17   How do algorithms identify and validate tradable pairs?

Algorithmic trading entails high-speed, automated execution of trades on a trading platform. In pairs trading, two assets that are historically correlated are operationally traded. The primary goal of this strategy is to capture the spread between the pair of assets when they diverge from their historical mean reversion trend. For validation purposes, factors like cointegration, correlation, and stationary time series are used to identify tradable pairs. Once tradable pairs are identified, they are validated by using methods like half-life of mean reversion, Hurst Exponents, and running certain statistical tests.

Identification of Tradable Pairs: Suppose that we have a pair of sneakers (Asset 1) and a pair of high heels (Asset 2). If a marked trend shows that the increase in the price of sneakers always corresponds with a rise in the price of high heels and vice versa (due to, say, a general growth in the footwear industry), they could be seen as a potential tradable pair. This is evaluated using a statistical measure called correlation.

A high correlation, closer to 1, indicates that the assets tend to move in the similar direction. However, correlation alone is not sufficient.

To ensure that the spread between the pair is mean-reverting i.e.,
it fluctuates around a historical average and tends to revert to the
mean, we use cointegration tests like the Augmented Dickey Fuller
Test.

Validation of Tradable pairs: Let's consider the previous example,
but replace sneakers and high heels with stocks A & B. The spread
(the difference in prices) between these two stocks over time can be
thought of as a rubber band that can stretch to an extent (when
prices of the stocks diverge) but eventually snaps back (revert to the
mean).

Therefore, to validate the tradable pairs, we look at:

1. **Half-life of mean reversion:** It gives an estimate of how quickly
the spread reverts back to the mean. It's like the time it takes for that
"rubber band" to snap halfway back.

2. **Hurst Exponents:** This provides the degree of mean reversion or
trendiness in a time series. The closer the Hurst exponent is to 0, the
more mean-reverting it is; closer to 1, it's more trending.

3. **Statistical Tests:** Engle-Granger test is most commonly used to test
cointegration between the pairs. Other statistical tests like Johansen test
or Phillips-Ouliaris test can also be used depending upon the complexity
and requirements.

The above methods are some of the ways through which algorithms
identify and validate tradable pairs but remember that market structures constantly change and what works today might not work tomorrow. Hence, continuous monitoring, testing, and diligence are
key attributes of a successful pairs trading strategy.

4.18   How can pairs trading be considered a market-neutral strategy?

Pairs trading, also known as Statistical Arbitrage or Relative Value
Arbitrage, can indeed be considered a market-neutral strategy. The

concept of "market-neutral" implies that the strategy's success is independent of the direction of the market. It doesn't necessarily mean generating profits in all market conditions but rather not being directly affected by the overall market movements.

The components of a pairs trading strategy enable it to be market-neutral. The strategy involves taking offsetting positions in two highly correlated securities. That is, you go long (buy) on one security that you expect to perform well and go short (sell) on another security that you expect to perform poorly.

It's much like pedaling a tandem bicycle with your friend. You're trying to keep the bicycle (your portfolio) moving smoothly on a flat road (market-neutral). Your friend up front (the long position) pedals hard (performing well), while the friend at the back (the short position) does less work (performing less well). If both pedal equally hard, the bicycle still moves smoothly. If both slack off, it still remains upright—albeit moving slowly. The performance of the bicycle and your journey is less affected by whether the road is going uphill or downhill (market ups and downs), and more by the difference in effort between your two friends (the difference in the performance of the two securities).

So, let's put this in a more mathematical form. The pair trading strategy creates a portfolio which is a linear combination of two assets A and B. That is,

$$\Pi = \alpha A - \beta B$$

where A is the asset you long, B is the asset you short, α and β are certain weights computed based on various factors such as price, volatility, etc.

Now, both assets A and B are chosen such that they are highly correlated. When the market moves up or down, both assets are going to increase or decrease approximately by the same amount. Hence, the portfolio value Π remains approximately stable, thus making the strategy market-neutral.

The profit in pairs trading comes from the discrepancy in the price relationship between the two securities, and not from the overall market movements. For a successful pairs trade, it doesn't matter if both securities increase or decrease in value; it matters that the long position outperforms the short.

It's crucial to note, though, that while pairs trading is a market-neutral strategy in theory, it's subject to implementation risk and market anomalies in practice, potentially leading to non-neutral outcomes. So, it's always important to manage the risks associated with the positions.

4.19   What are the risks associated with pairs trading?

Pairs trading is a type of statistical arbitrage trading strategy that involves matching a long position with a short position in two stocks that are statistically correlated. This strategy attempts to take advantage of the fact that the prices of the two stocks will maintain a similar movement pattern over the long term.

However, like any trading strategy, pairs trading comes with its unique set of risks. Here are a few of them:

1. **Convergence Risk:** This is akin to trying to catch two racing horses with a single lasso. You bet on the presumption that the two stocks, which have diverged, will eventually converge. However, there's always the risk that they might not. The stocks might continue to diverge due to various factors such as industry trends, market volatility or company-specific news.

2. **Model Risk:** The risk associated with the model used to identify the pairs. If your model is not robust enough or suffers from overfitting, underfitting or other statistical issues, your pairs trading

strategy may not yield the desired results. It's like using an inaccurate map to get to a destination, the chances are you might get lost or end up in the wrong place.

3. **Execution Risk:** This arises from delay or failure in executing a trade. For example, you might be able to buy one stock at the desired price but not sell the other, leaving you exposed.

4. **Liquidity Risk:** Pairs trading often involves dealing with stocks that aren't very liquid. Sometimes, you might not be able to offload a stock at the price you want, leading to losses.

5. **Regulatory Risk:** Last but not least, regulatory changes can affect your pairs trading strategy. For example, if short selling is banned, you cannot open any pairs trading positions that involve short selling.

In conclusion, while pairs trading offers a good risk mitigation strategy by hedging, it is not without its own set of risks. Just like driving a car, you might mitigate the risk of an accident by wearing seat belts and obeying traffic rules, but you can't eliminate all risks because there are always factors beyond your control.

4.20 How have advancements in technology impacted the profitability of traditional pairs trading strategies?

Advancements in technology, specifically in areas such as computational power and data management, have had a significant impact on the profitability of traditional pairs trading strategies.

Let's first establish what pairs trading is. Pairs trading is a strategy that involves matching a long position in one stock with a short position in another. The goal is to find two stocks that move in relation and take advantage of any deviations. However, the efficiency of this strategy is deeply tied with the speed of execution and accuracy of prediction.

Imagine it like a high-stakes game of Ping-Pong. The more skilled and quick you are, the more likely you'll win. In the past, with older technology, we were playing this game with a paddle and a slow-moving ball. But with advancements in technology, the game has evolved into a super-fast, skills-driven contest. It's like the paddle has upgraded to an ultra-responsive racket and the ball can move at lightning speed.

One of the most noticeable impacts of technology advancements has surfaced in the form of high-frequency pairs trading. High-frequency trading (HFT) techniques utilize powerful computers to transact a large number of orders at very fast speeds. Pairs trading in the HFT world implies the algorithm needs to process the pairs' relationship, calculate the spread and its mean-reverting tendencies, and execute trades all within milliseconds.

Vast improvements in data collection, storage, and analysis mean traders have access to more data than ever before. This avalanche of data aids in creating more accurate and robust statistical models around pairs trading. For instance, you can scrutinize the relationship between two assets with unprecedented granularity, improving your ability to predict and react to changes, like a weather forecaster with a supercomputer versus a handheld thermometer.

To put it into context, let's assume a pairs trading strategy where we trade on Coca-Cola and Pepsi. We believe that any significant divergence in the pair's typical behavior represents an opportunity for arbitrage. By leveraging powerful machine learning algorithms, for example, we could predict the catch-up behavior more accurately and thus execute trades more efficiently.

However, advancements in technology aren't exclusively an advantage. They have also resulted in increased competition. Just as the fastest runners benefit most in a race, in pairs trading, firms that can process information and execute trades the quickest often see the most profit. Barriers to entry for new traders have also been significantly raised with the cost of relevant technology.

In summary, while advancements in technology have provided pairs traders with tools to better predict and capitalize on marketplace inefficiencies, they also upped the competition and the challenge's intensity. It has become an arms race of who can tap into better technology, maintain more robust data sets, and execute trades faster.

4.21 Describe the principles of trend-following strategies.

Trend-following strategies are a type of trading strategy in which attempts are made to capitalize on the continuation of existing trends in the market. The principle is straightforward: "Buy low, sell high" if the trend is upward, or "Sell high, buy low" if the trend is downward.

Consider a surfer waiting for the perfect wave to ride. Trend-followers are like surfers, they wait patiently and when the right trend (wave) comes along - based on their analysis - they ride it till they believe it has run its course. They essentially aim to "go with the flow" of the market.

Underpinning trend-following strategies are a few core principles:

1. **Market Trends:** Markets tend to move in trends. Individual market variables (like a stock price, forex rate, etc.) rarely remain static; they often move in a particular direction over a period of time, creating a trend.

2. **Technical Analysis:** Trend-following strategies rely heavily on technical analysis, a discipline that involves analyzing chart patterns, moving averages, market volume, etc., to identify potential trading opportunities.

3. **Mechanical Rules:** Trend-following strategies usually employ

mechanical trading rules so that entry and exit decisions aren't influenced by human emotions. These mechanical rules might encompass aspects such as moving average crossovers, breakout levels, etc.

4. **Defensive Money Management:** This pertains to the principle of preserving capital and limiting risk through tools such as stop-losses and carefully calculated position sizes. This prevents a single bad trade from significantly impacting the trading capital.

5. **Timeframes:** Trend-following strategies can be deployed across various timeframes. Some traders might focus on short-term trends (days to weeks), while others might be more interested in medium to long-term trends (months to years).

In a mathematical format, a simple and classic trend-following strategy can be looked as:

If $P_t > M_t$; Buy

Else Sell

Where, P_t is the Price at time t and M_t is the moving average at time t.

While trend-following strategies have proven successful over time, it's important to note that they tend to perform well during trending markets and may experience losses during non-trending, choppy markets. Further, these strategies might also face difficulties during sudden market reversals and can give false signals in volatile markets.

4.22 How do trend-following algorithms differentiate between short-term noise and a genuine trend change?

Trend-following algorithms generally make use of statistical and mathematical models to observe historical price trends and try to predict future price movements. The challenge is to accurately distinguish between short-term noise, which is often just temporary fluctuations in prices, and genuine long-term trend changes.

So how do they do this? Let's use an example to illustrate. Imagine you're standing on the shore of a beach, watching the waves come in. If you watch a single wave, you'll see it grow, crest and then fade away. However, this single wave doesn't tell us much about the overall trend or direction of the tide (either incoming or outgoing). But, if you were to watch many waves over a longer period, you'll start to notice a pattern - the tide coming in or going out.

Finding trends in algorithmic trading is similar, where price fluctuations are like these individual waves. The algorithm uses different indicators to confirm if these waves form part of a bigger tide, i.e., a genuine trend change.

Some common methods algorithmic trading strategies utilize to smooth out 'noise' and detect longer term trends are:

1. **Moving Averages** (MA): A moving average helps smooth out random price fluctuations and thus helps in identifying the direction of the trend. Prices above the moving average indicate an upward trend, and prices below suggest a downward trend.

2. **Exponential Moving Averages** (EMA): EMA is a type of moving average that gives more weight to recent data points. This makes it more responsive to new information, and hence more capable of identifying sudden trend changes.

3. **Relative Strength Index** (RSI): The Relative Strength Index is a momentum oscillator that measures the speed and change of price movements. Generally, RSI is considered overbought when above 70 and oversold when below 30.

4. **Bollinger Bands**: Bollinger Bands consist of a middle band (which is a moving average) and two outer bands that are standard deviations away from the middle band. When the price breaks through the upper band, it's considered bullish (upward trend) and when it

breaks through the lower band, it's considered bearish (downward trend).

Remember though, while these methods can help differentiate between noise and genuine trend changes, they are not foolproof, and are most effective when combined with other forms of analysis. Algorithmic trading is like meteorology, the use of various indicators ensure a more accurate forecast but cannot guarantee it. Identifying false signals and adapting to market changes is an ongoing challenge in this field.

4.23 What are common technical indicators used in trend-following algorithms?

Trend-following algorithms often leverage a variety of technical indicators to predict price movements and to define entry and exit points. Here are some common technical indicators that are typically used.

1. **Moving Averages (MA):** Perhaps the most common amongst trend-followers, the moving average smoothens out the price data by continuously updating an average of the price over a specified period. An analogy would be measuring the average speed at which you're travelling during a road trip, it provides an idea of your overall pace.

The Simple Moving Average (SMA) takes the arithmetic mean of prices over the lookback period, while the Exponential Moving Average (EMA) gives more weight to the recent data points.

2. **Bollinger Bands (BB):** This is a volatility indicator which consists of a SMA (Middle Band) and an upper and lower band. Much like the elasticity of a rubber band, these 'bands' expand when volatility is high and contract when low. Prices tend to revert when they touch these bands.

3. **Moving Average Convergence Divergence (MACD):** This is a trend-following weighted momentum indicator, that shows the rela-

tionship between two moving averages. Think of it as a fuel gauge in
a vehicle, indicating whether it's picking up speed or running out of
momentum.

4. **Average True Range (ATR):** It measures the volatility of a
price over a certain period which can be applied to modify the size
of a position according to the instrument's volatility. Again, we can
liken it to a road trip: it measures how much "bumpy" the journey
is.

5. **Relative Strength Index (RSI):** This is a momentum oscillator
that measures the speed and change of price movements. It can signify
overbought and oversold levels and often traders might look for price
divergences with the RSI for potential reversals.

Remember, no single indicator can provide the entire picture, a combination of these indicators (like the instruments on a vehicle's dashboard) gives better results. For example, if RSI indicates overbought
levels, volatility is low (i.e., Bollinger bands are narrow) and price is
above a certain moving average, a trader might consider it as a sell
opportunity.

Remember to backtest and stress test your algorithmic strategies before going live as market conditions continually evolve.

4.24   How do trend-following strategies man-age false breakout signals?

Trend-following strategies are generally known for their robustness,
but one of the critical challenges they face is handling false breakout
signals. A false breakout happens when the price seems to move
beyond a level of resistance or support, hinting at a new trend, only to
reverse and return within the previous range, hence 'falsely' breaking
out.

A typical way to manage this risk is by deploying various techniques designed to filter out potential false signals.

Here are a few examples:

1. **Time Confirmation**: It's like waiting for the paint to dry. A trend-follower may wait for the price to close beyond the breakout level for a certain number of periods (e.g. days or weeks) before considering it a genuine breakout. This can help filter out short-term price fluctuations.

2. **Volume Confirmation**: This is similar to checking if there's enough water in a river before deciding to swim in it. The idea is to confirm that there's sufficient volume (trading activity) supporting the breakout. Higher trading volume during a breakout can be interpreted as stronger market conviction, reducing the likelihood of a false breakout.

3. **Moving Average Filters**: It can be thought of like using a pair of glasses to see clearer. A frequently used technical indicator is the moving average, which smooths out short-term fluctuations and highlights longer-term trends. Many trend-followers will only consider breakouts that occur in the direction of the moving average.

4. **Market Sentiment/ Fundamental Analysis**: It's like listening to what people are saying at a party. In addition to technical analysis, trend-followers might use market sentiment indicators or consider material fundamental economic indicators to identify whether a breakout is likely to be false or not.

5. **Risk Management**: Perhaps the best analogy here is wearing a seatbelt while driving a car. Despite every careful calculation and filtering, it is impossible to eliminate the possibility of a false breakout entirely. So, trend-followers often employ risk management practices, such as setting stop-loss levels or limiting the size of any single trade, to mitigate the impact of potential false breakouts.

It is important to remember that there's no "one-size-fits-all" approach to filtering out false breakouts. Different trend-followers will likely employ different techniques based on their trading style, asset class, investment horizon and risk tolerance.

4.25 What challenges do trend-following strategies face in choppy or sideways markets?

Trend-following strategies generally perform well in markets with consistent and persistent uptrends or downtrends. However, they do face several challenges in choppy or sideways markets.

1. **False Signals**: In a choppy market, small movements can often trigger trading signals. For instance, let's liken this to a cat chasing a laser pointer. The cat (as the trend follower) might overreact to small, insignificant movements of the laser, just as a trend-following strategy might to minor price fluctuations, resulting in false signals. This can lead to more trades being made, increasing transaction costs and potentially misleading the strategy.

2. **Lack of Persistent Directional Movement**: Trend-following strategies thrive in environments where there is a clear upward or downward movement. Without these trends, it can be difficult for such strategies to generate significant profit. Imagine if you were trying to ride a bike uphill or downhill, you'd have the gravitational pull aiding you in both cases. In a flat terrain, however, you'd have to put your effort into pushing the pedals without any external aid - this is somewhat similar to applying a trend-following strategy in a sideways market.

3. **Whipsaws**: These occur when the price of a security sharply reverses direction in a short period of time, and are common in choppy or volatile markets. Whipsaws can create a high degree of false trading signals, leading to increased transaction costs and potential losses. Imagine being on a roller coaster, twisting and turning quickly in different directions. Now imagine that ride is the stock price - a trend following strategy might likely struggle to accurately keep up with

the abrupt changes.

4. **Low Volatility**: Sideways markets often have lower volatility levels, and lower volatility often means lower returns for trend-followers. If we liken the market to an ocean, and price changes to waves, then a trend-follower is like a surfer who thrives on big, powerful waves (high volatility). When the sea is calm, the surfer can't ride much - just like a trend-follower can't gain much in a low volatility environment.

To overcome these challenges, many traders may incorporate different strategies for different market conditions, or use additional tools to filter out market noise and minimize the impact of false signals. These can include using higher time frames, incorporating additional filters or conditions into their algorithms, and using strict risk management rules.

Chapter 5

Algorithm Design and Development

5.1 Outline the typical process of developing a trading algorithm from concept to deployment.

The development process of a trading algorithm can be likened to the process of designing and constructing a magnificent skyscraper it starts with a concept and ends with an actualization of that vision. Just like in architecture, this process involves key steps each with its own significance.

Just so we're clear, a trading algorithm, also known as algo-trading or black-box trading, uses complex formulas combined with mathematics and computer programming to make high-speed, high-frequency decisions for trading.

Here's the typical step-by-step process:

1. **Conceptualization:**

Like a skyscraper, our algorithm begins on a blueprint— in this case, a theoretical basis that aligns with the trader's objectives. This is translation of an investment thesis into structured ideas that can be coded. The concept must be clearly defined, testable, and practical.

2. **Modeling and Preliminary Analysis:**

The next step involves developing a mathematical model of the concept that we've derived. We might use a variety of mathematical components here such as probability theory, statistical analysis, and calculus to build a model that adequately represents our idea. This is akin to selecting the best materials to give life to our architectural plan.

We'd also perform a preliminary backtest using historical data. It's basically a dress rehearsal, testing the efficiency and effectiveness of our algorithm   a foundation stress test if you will.

3. **Coding:**

After sketching the blueprint and choosing the right 'materials', it's time to start building... or in algorithmic trading, start coding. The efficacy of the model depends on how well it's translated into a program or software that a computer can understand and execute efficiently. High level programming languages like Python, Java, and C++ are often used.

4. **Backtesting:**

Think of backtesting as structural integrity tests for skyscrapers. For trading algorithms, we run simulations using historical data under various market conditions to assess the algorithm's performance, reliability, and risk. Sometimes there might be overfitting where algorithms work splendidly on historical data but fall flat on the real-world data, so this phase is quite critical.

For the math whizzes, the standard metrics we often measure include the *Sharpe ratio, Sortino ratio, Maximum Drawdown,* and some others.

5. **Validation:**

No architect would allow an unsafe skyscraper to be accessed by the public. In the same way, before launching a trading algorithm, we must validate it using out-of-sample testing. This helps us confirm whether the algorithmic parameters, which may have been overfit during backtesting (working well only on specific datasets), are actually valid on new, unseen data.

6. **Implementation:**

When the model has been tested, validated, and approved, it's ready to be deployed into the real-world markets – just like opening the doors of a brand new skyscraper to bustling city life. But accommodation doesn't end there...

7. **Monitoring & Adjusting:**

Just as a skyscraper requires regular maintenance, so too do trading algorithms. Market dynamics evolve, bringing about changes in trends, volatility and liquidity. As such, we continuously monitor the algorithm's performance and adjust its parameters/strategy accordingly when need be.

That was a long trip from start to finish, but that's how we ensure our trading algo-skyscraper stands tall and resilient in the financial skyline!

5.2   How do you determine the success criteria for a trading algorithm?

Determining the success criteria for a trading algorithm involves several quantitative and qualitative factors. Let's consider these factors as being elements of a soccer match, where the algorithm is a player with specific roles and tasks:

1. **Profitability (Scoring Goals)**: The most direct measure of an algorithm's success is its profitability. In our soccer match analogy, this is equivalent to the number of goals scored. However, similar to a striker who targets to score but might also miss, algorithms can generate losses. Hence, average profitability or expectancy per trade are more precise indicators.

In quantitative terms:

$$E[Profit] = p(winning)*average(profit) - p(losing)*average(loss)$$

where $p(winning)$ and $average(profit)$ represent the winning probability and average profit of winning trades, and $p(losing)$ and $average(loss)$ represent the losing probability and average loss of losing trades.

2. **Risk Management (Defence Setup)**: Scoring goals is not the only task in a match, a good defence setup is similarly important. The same applies to trading algorithms. Drawdown is an important measure of risk, it represents the decline from a historical peak in the capital of a trading account. Such losses need to be recovered, often requiring greater profitability due to the asymmetric nature of profit and loss. Therefore, algorithms with smaller drawdowns are usually considered more successful.

3. **Sharp Ratio (Efficiency Rating)**: This is akin to the player's efficiency rating in the game. The Sharpe ratio evaluates how much excess return you receive for the additional volatility you endure for holding a riskier asset.

The Sharpe Ratio formula is defined as:

$$SharpeRatio = \frac{(MeanPortfolioReturn - RiskFreeRate)}{StandardDeviationPortfolioReturns}$$

Higher Sharpe ratios are usually better. They denote either higher returns for the same risk or the same returns for lesser risk.

4. **Stability (Consistence in Performance)**: A team doesn't want a player who performs brilliantly in one match but poorly in the next. Similarly, the consistency of a trading algorithm is crucial. Algorithms that exhibit steady returns over different regimes of the market are preferred. Various statistical measures, like standard deviation of returns, can be used to measure stability.

5. **Adaptability (Versatility on Field)**: Market conditions change, just as field conditions and opposing teams change in a soccer match. An algorithm should be robust and adaptable to different market conditions to be successful.

Designing a successful trading algorithm is a complex and iterative process, just like training a soccer player. It involves considerations of profitability, risk, efficiency, stability and versatility. Therefore, the success of a trading algorithm should not only be judged by the profits it generates, but also by how it manages risk, its efficiency, stability, and adaptability to different market conditions. Each of these factors represent a crucial part of the algorithm's overall performance in the challenging field of algorithmic trading.

5.3   What considerations come into play when choosing data sources for algorithm development?

Choosing data sources is critical in algorithm development. The correct choice can make the difference between a successful and unsuccessful trading algorithm. Below are the considerations you need to have in mind when selecting data sources:

1. **Reliability:** You need to select a data source that is well-maintained and reliable. Imagine going to a supermarket to find that

sometimes there are products available and sometimes not. Over time, you switch to a more reliable source for your groceries. The same applies to data sources.

2. **Data Quality:** Like a chef prioritizes high-quality ingredients in their cooking, you need high quality, clean, and accurate data to design your trading algorithm. Poor data quality could introduce bias, errors in your models and impair your trading algorithm.

3. **Scope of the Data (completeness):** The scope of the data refers to the width and depth of it. A wider scope, in the context of trading, could mean having data about more asset classes, stocks, etc. and a deeper scope could mean having more historical data. Like the geographical scale of a map, the more coverage it has, the more beneficial it could be to your discovery journey.

4. **Format of the Data:** The data structure and format should fit your needs. It can range from structured data like CSV or Excel files to unstructured data like news articles. Imagine trying to assemble a Lego set with Duplo blocks - it just doesn't work.

5. **Refresh Rate:** The frequency of updates can play a key role in the type of trading strategy you're looking to implement. For high-frequency trading, you would need real-time or tick-level data. It's like watching a sports game: watching it live versus reading about it in the newspaper the next day — the information's currency dramatically affects how you react to it.

6. **Cost:** Data can be expensive, especially high-quality and specialized data. It is vital to assess the cost-benefit ratio to see if the investment is worthwhile. It's like buying a Ferrari just to do a weekly shop at the local supermarket — overkill, unless your requirement warrants the cost.

7. **Legality and Compliance:** Last but not least, ensure the data source complies with all relevant data protection and privacy laws. The repercussions of using non-compliant or illegal data are significant.

Remember, the choice of data source will heavily impact your model's ability to generate accurate predictions, much like a car's performance heavily depends on the quality of fuel you put into it.

5.4   How do you account for transaction costs and slippage in algorithm development?

Modeling transaction costs and slippage accurately is a crucial aspect of the development and backtesting phase of an algorithm. Not accounting for them can result in misleadingly optimistic results. Let's discuss how we incorporate them in algorithm design.

Firstly, we have transaction costs which are quite straightforward. They are usually a fixed fee per traded unit or a percentage of the total trade volume. These costs can be directly subtracted when computing the net result of an executed trade. For instance, if you're working with a broker that charges $0.01 per share, and your algorithm is executing 1000-share transactions, you'd include a $10 cost in your P&L calculations.

Slippage, on the other hand, is a bit more complex. Slippage occurs due to the difference between the expected price of a trade, and the price at which the trade is actually executed. This can be due to market fluctuations in the time between the decision to trade and the trade execution.

To include slippage into your algorithm, let's consider the following analogy:

Imagine you're at a fruit market and you see apples being sold at a dollar each. You decide to buy 100 apples. But when you ask for this quantity, the seller increases the price a bit because he realizes he might run out of stock sooner than expected. Slippage in financial markets is similar, as increasing market orders can affect the stock price.

To account for slippage, you can use historical market data and statistical measures. one simple method is to assume a fixed slippage per trade. For example, you might assume that slippage costs will account for 0.05% of each trade. This approximation is straightforward, but not very realistic.

A more advanced method to account for slippage is to model it based on the trade size and market liquidity (for instance, using the bid-ask spread as a proxy). You could assume that the slippage is proportional to the square root of the trade size divided by the average daily trading volume. In formula terms:

$$\text{Slippage} = k \cdot \left(\frac{\text{Trade Size}}{\text{Average Daily Volume}} \right)^{0.5}$$

where k is a constant factor that can be defined per asset or calibrated using historical executions.

Here, if you trade smaller sizes relative to the market liquidity, your slippage would be smaller, and vice versa.

Important to keep in mind that these will always be approximations, and the goal here is to align these models as closely as possible to the actual transaction costs and slippage observed in live trading.

5.5 How do you handle missing or erroneous data during algorithm development?

Handling missing or erroneous data during algorithm development is a critical challenge that is often confronted in algorithmic trading and other data-intensive areas. Algorithmic trading primarily depends on granular data for buy/sell signals, and any deficiency or lack of accuracy can lead to significant financial risks.

A common approach for dealing with missing data is called imputation. It's analogous to filling in a jigsaw puzzle where some pieces are missing - you use the information you have with the surrounding pieces to estimate what's missing. In the context of data, you might estimate the missing value based on the mean, median, mode or a regression model derived from the available data.

Let's focus on 3 common techniques:

1. **Mean/ Median / Mode Imputation**: This method computes the mean, median, or mode of a particular feature column and uses that value to fill in the missing data. Let's imagine you are reading a book but a page is missing. If the book is a repetitive poetry or a song, you might fill in the missing page with the most common lines.

2. **Last Observation Carried Forward (LOCF) and Next observation Carried backward (NOCB)**: These strategies are often employed in time-series data like in trading. In LOCF, we fill an 'NA' with the last observed data point, while in NOCB, we fill the 'NA' with the next observed valid data point. It's like repairing a broken video sequence by replacing the missing frame with the previous or subsequent frame.

3. **Model-Based Imputation**: It involves more complex methods like regression imputation or machine learning algorithms like k-Nearest Neighbours (kNN) to predict and impute missing values based on other data points. Going back to our jigsaw puzzle analogy, if the missing pieces are part of an image of a sky with clouds, instead of just filling them with more "average" sky, you could predict that there might be a cloud there based on the other data you have.

Regarding erroneous data, the first step is anomaly detection. Erroneous data often present themselves as statistical outliers in your dataset. Anomaly detection would be like identifying misprinted puzzle pieces that are not fitting despite being supposed to.

Once the anomalies are detected, there are several ways to deal with them which could be as simple as removing them, or if they are not substantial, one could cap them to a certain maximum or minimum value (a process is known as "winsorizing").

Error handling strategies are context-specific and can affect the performance of the trading algorithm. Therefore, this task requires careful consideration, and often a combination of techniques will provide the best results.

To sum up, handling missing or erroneous data is like trying to piece together a puzzle with some missing or misprinted pieces. It requires logic, intuition, and trial-and-error to complete the picture (predictive model) as accurately and completely as possible.

5.6   Why is backtesting essential in algorithmic trading?

Backtesting is an absolutely crucial element of algorithmic trading system design and development. You can think of backtesting as a dress rehearsal before a big play debut. It's where we test our strategies and make any necessary revisions.

In a more engaging way, imagine you're trying to invent a new board game. You've come up with a set of rules and winning conditions. They feel right in your head, but you won't know if it's enjoyable, too easy, or even playable until you gather some friends for a few rounds. That's exactly what backtesting does for trading strategies. Instead of friends, we use historical data; instead of rounds of games, we simulate trades.

Backtesting in algorithmic trading is the process of applying a trading strategy or analytical method to historical data to see how accurately the strategy or model would have predicted actual results. In mathematical terms, you'd be testing your algorithms against your dataset, akin to

$$\int f(X)_{\text{historical}} \, dx_{\text{algorithm}}$$

.

You're basically integrating your algorithm over your historical data.

This allows you to:

1. Verify the efficacy of your strategy: The primary objective of backtesting is to prove that your trading strategy is better than just blind guessing.

2. Refine the strategy: Backtesting can help you fine-tune the parameters of your strategy to maximize your profits and minimize potential losses.

3. Evaluate performance and risks: Backtesting helps determine the likelihood of profit and the risk of loss. It can also generate measures such as maximum drawdown and Sharpe ratio, that allow you to measure the risk-adjusted return of the strategy.

However, keep in mind that backtesting, while indispensable, is not without its pitfalls. The common problems include overfitting, lookahead bias and transaction cost bias which could give a false sense of security. That's why any experienced game designer will not only playtest their game in controlled environments but also consider blind playtests and other forms of testing. So, backtesting should never be the sole factor when determining a trade strategy's viability, but it's nonetheless an excellent starting point.

5.7 Describe the concept of "look-ahead bias" in backtesting and how to avoid it.

Look-ahead bias is a term used often in the world of financial trading, particularly in algorithmic trading, to describe errors that can sneak into your backtesting results when you include information that wouldn't have been available during the time period you're backtesting.

Imagine you're trying to predict tomorrow's weather. You use a sophisticated prediction algorithm, and when you test it using yesterday's weather data, it accurately predicts today's weather. It might seem like your algorithm is spot on. However, if the algorithm had access to data from today when making its prediction—a "sneak peek" into the future—then you've got yourself a clear case of look-ahead bias. This tends to make our model look incredibly accurate and predictive, but it's actually flawed because when it's time to predict the real "tomorrow", there would be no way to have information about that day.

In the context of trading, an example could be testing a moving average crossover strategy, where you generate a buy signal when the short-term moving average crosses above the long-term moving average. A common look-ahead bias mistake is to include the price of the day where the crossover happens as part of the long-term average. At the start of that day, you wouldn't have the closing price available to know whether the crossover will happen.

To avoid look-ahead bias, make sure data is lagged appropriately, so your model is only using information that would actually be available at the point in time when you're making the trading decision. For every data point at time t in your backtest, only use data from time $t-1$ and earlier. Frameworks such as 'pandas' in Python are beneficial to manage the chronological sequence of data, while backtesting libraries such as 'bt', 'pyalgotrade', or 'backtrader' take care of this to avoid these pitfalls.

Additionally, be cautious when constructing indicators with rolling windows. Always ensure that the day for which you calculate the indicator does not include information from the "future".

Remember, in trading, just like in predicting the weather, it's critical to create models and strategies based on the information "you'd actually have" at the decision-making moment. Future paint is invisible today, no matter how badly we wish we could see it.

5.8 How do you ensure the reliability and robustness of backtesting results?

Ensuring the reliability and robustness of backtesting results is like trying to ensure that the medicine you're testing will work consistently across a wide array of patients. It involves testing over different market conditions, investigating outliers, validating hypotheses across various timeframes, and more. Let me break this down further:

1. **Out-of-Sample Testing**: In-sample data is used for creating the model, while out-of-sample data is used for testing it. This emulates the method doctors use to test a new medicine — first, they test it in a lab, then experiment on a control group (in-sample), and finally use a separate group to validate the results (out-of-sample). Similarly, part of the historical data is used for strategy development and a different part, which the model hasn't seen before, for testing.

2. **Modifying Parameters**: You shouldn't only rely on the model's 'best' parameters. It's like having a football team only play against the same type of opponent over and over again. To see how robust your team is, you need to see how it performs against a variety of oppositions. So, testing a model over a range of parameters (Parameter Sensitivity Analysis) helps check how it performs in various conditions and provides an insight into the potential for parameter tweaking in the future.

3. **Variable Market Conditions**: The market is an unpredictable beast, sometimes it's calm and gentle, other times it's volatile and fierce. Your trading model should be able to weather all these situations, thus testing across different market regimes (bullish, bearish, sideways, high volatility, low volatility, etc.) is important to ensure reliability.

4. **Statistical Significance**: To ascertain if your model's perfor-

mance is due to skill or just pure luck, you have to delve into statistical tests. If a coin lands on heads 9 times out of 10, it may be just luck, but tossing a coin 10,000 times and having it lands on heads 9,000 times, you'd suspect the coin is biased. Similarly, statistical measures such as Sharpe ratio, Sortino ratio, standard deviation of returns, maximum drawdown, and other statistics can numerically state the model's reliability.

5. **Hypothesis Testing**: This is like having a theory about the moon's movement and then checking how it holds up with actual data. If you hypothesize that your trading algorithm makes money because it successfully exploits a certain seasonal trend, for example, test this specific hypothesis by simulating trading only within the season (Time Series Data) or compare its performance with random entry and exits.

6. **Stress Testing**: This is asking the "what if" question. What if the largest stock in your portfolio were to lose half its value overnight, or what if there was a flash crash like in 2010? It's about simulating unlikely but plausible scenarios to see how your model fares.

There's no single foolproof way to ensure absolute reliability and robustness of backtesting results, but combining these multiple methods will certainly organize out the weak arguments and reinforce the strong ones, just as multiple experiments ensure the robustness of a scientific theory.

5.9 What are the limitations of backtesting using historical data?

Backtesting an algorithmic trading strategy might initially sound like a surefire way to gauge performance – a bit like reverse walking a well-tread path to see if you made any mistakes along your journey. However, it comes with its own set of challenges and limitations. Let's walk through a few key ones:

1. **Overfitting**: Overfitting is like trying to guess an artist's taste by looking at one specific painting. You tailor your assumptions so narrowly that while they might perfectly depict that one piece of work, they may fail to generalize to any other works. In terms of backtesting, you run the risk of twisting your strategy so minutely to perfectly align with historical data that it fails to perform efficiently in real markets.

2. **Look Ahead Bias**: Look-ahead bias occurs when you use data in a backtest that would not have been available at the time of trading. This can lead to overly optimistic backtest results. It is like knowing the plot twist of a movie before it comes, it can lead you to think you have an uncanny ability to predict scripts!

3. **Survivorship Bias**: Survivorship bias is the possibility of significant skewing due to considering only entities which 'survived' a certain period. For instance, if you backtest using current S&P 500 constituents, you disregard companies that may have existed, but eliminated over the backtest period. It's like only studying the habits of successful people and assuming adopting their habits would make you successful, ignoring the fact that unsuccessful people might have had similar habits.

4. **Data Snooping Bias**: The problem arises when the same set of data is used repeatedly in order to evolve the trading strategy. The more you 'snoop' around in the data, greater the chances that you find patterns that simply occurred by chance. It's like continually digging into the same bag of tricks, it tends to yield decreasingly novel results.

5. **Regime Change**: Economic conditions – or "regimes" – change over time. Backtesting assumes that historical reactions to market stimuli would always hold in the future, but it is not guaranteed. For example, you are watching an old horror film and you predict the next action based on current scene. But the movie takes an unexpected turn because a new character was introduced. These unexpected turns in markets are hard to predict and can affect the algorithm's performance.

6. **Limitations of the Model**: The mathematical and statistical model used for the backtesting itself may have its limitations. Assumptions regarding normal distribution of returns, constant correlations, or volatility can lead to inaccurate and misleading backtesting results. Notably, it's like believing the world is flat because that's all you observed, it crumbles apart once new evidence arises.

7. **Liquidity Constraints**: Most backtests typically ignore liquidity constraints and assume that the strategy can trade any volume without significantly affecting the market price. However, in reality, trading large volumes can skew the market price. It is like an elephant trying to blend into a group of mice, it might still cause a ripple regardless of efforts!

In summary, while backtesting is a critical part of developing an algorithmic trading strategy, it's always important to be aware of its limitations to ensure you make informed and realistic strategy assessments.

5.10   How do you account for changes in market conditions during backtesting?

Backtesting is like time travel. It lets you rewind and replay market events and see how your algorithm would have performed if it were running during those previous conditions. It can provide significant insights, but it also conversely highlights a major limitation: Markets change, and past behavior may not predict future outcomes.

Taking care of changing market conditions is crucial while backtesting trading algorithms. Here are some ways to account for changes in market conditions:

1. **Sliding Windows**: Imagine you are looking through a long telescope, the telescope's view represents your data point, and you're

continually moving it such that you are always viewing the most recent data points. This technique is used to ensure that the model gives more importance to the recent market conditions rather than the old ones.

2. **Walk-forward Optimization**: Think of this like training for a marathon. You progressively increase your stamina over the weeks (the optimized parameters), keeping hindsight of your past performance (past data), to prepare for D-Day (real trading). This approach involves optimizing parameters over a segment of historical data, then testing those parameters in the next segment, and repeating it.

3. **Use of Dynamic Models**: Remember the storms in the movie 'The Day After Tomorrow'? What forecasted these were dynamic models, taking into account all the volatility and immediate changes in weather patterns. In a similar vein, dynamic models account for shifts in market conditions. These models adapt their parameters to the market conditions, tweaking and refining them over time.

4. **Robustness Tests**: Picture this like a car crash safety test. Cars (or in our case, strategies) are put through extreme conditions to see how they hold up. In backtesting, perform stress-testing to extreme market conditions (rapid rise/fall, high volatility periods) to ensure that the algorithm performs well during market swings.

5. **Including Various Market Conditions in Test Set**: The world soccer championship is played in different countries every time, having varying weather conditions, which is a great leveler challenging the teams in different ways. Similarly, ensure that your test set includes varied market conditions - that covers bull markets, bear markets, high volatility periods, crises etc. This increases the chances that the algorithm can handle most future scenarios.

Paying special attention to these points during backtesting is like a traveler preparing back-up plans considering all possible variables - a storm, a flight cancellation, a sudden local strike, or even hotel reservations falling through.

Utilizing a blend of various techniques will help in developing a robust strategy that can withstand the test of changing market conditions. However, it's also imperative to take into account that no model (or backtesting strategy) can completely eliminate market risk. Past performance is not an indicator of future results. Hence, keep refining and adapting your algorithm to the ever-changing market dynamics and don't rely solely on backtesting to dictate future trading decisions.

5.11   What is walk-forward analysis, and why is it important?

In algorithmic trading, walk-forward analysis is a sophisticated method of testing the robustness of your trading algorithm or strategy. If we were to relate it to something widely understandable, it'd be similar to running a dress rehearsal before the actual play; you get a chance to see how well your prepared plan will fare in conditions very close to the live event.

Technically, the walk forward analysis involves two significant steps for iterative periods on your data: the first is the 'In-Sample' period where you optimize your parameters, and the second is the 'Out-of-Sample' where you test those fixed optimized parameters.

It's akin to practicing a recipe using a small portion before you serve it to others. Think of 'in-sample' data as your practice run where you'll tweak the recipe, varying the ingredients until you find the perfect mix. The 'out-of-sample' data represents cooking with the fixed recipe for guests. Tasting the dish after it's been cooked would give you an honest feedback on how well you executed the recipe.

Mathematically, if you have market data for a period of 10 years, you could, for instance, use the first 2 years as your 'In-Sample' period. In this period, you obtain the 'optimal parameters' for your trading system. You then test or "walk-forward" these parameters on the next six months of data - this is your 'Out-of-Sample' period. Post this, you roll forward, i.e., you again optimize on the next 2 years, and test on the six months after that. Repeating this process lets the system learn and adapt to more recent data while testing its performance on unseen subsequent data.

The importance of walk-forward analysis lies in its validation of a trading system's real-time performance in unseen market conditions, thus providing a more realistic view of its likely future performance. By checking the performance of the model on out-of-sample data, i.e., data that has not been used in optimizing the parameters, we get a valid measure of how well our trading system might perform in real-world, unseen conditions. Without walk-forward analysis, we risk falling into the trap of "curve fitting" or over-optimization, where our model looks perfect on the data used to create it, but performs poorly in real-world trading.

In summary, you might have designed the perfect algorithm on paper (or rather, on backtest), walk-forward analysis is the reality check it needs. It is the ticket that allows your algorithm to graduate from great theory to tool ready-for-use.

5.12   How does walk-forward analysis mitigate some of the shortcomings of traditional backtesting?

Walk-forward analysis is like a rolling test where each iteration uses a different subset of data for the 'in-sample' parameter optimization and the 'out-of-sample' testing period. While traditional backtesting relies on analyzing past data, walk-forward analysis introduces a forward-looking element with "moving windows" of backtesting.

To help visualize what's happening, think of how a rolling pin flattens dough into a uniform, flat surface. Traditional backtesting would be like a snapshot of this dough at one point in time, while walk-forward analysis would be akin to the rolling action of the pin, constantly testing and adjusting over the duration of the process.

Walk-forward analysis mitigates some of the shortcomings of traditional backtesting in several ways:

1. **Parameter Robustness**: The key advantage of walk-forward analysis is its ability to test for parameter 'robustness'. It is able to ensure that your trading algorithm doesn't just perform well on one historical test, but that it adjusts well over multiple tests (in various market conditions). In comparison, traditional backtesting might 'overfit' an algorithm to a particular historic dataset.

2. **Adaptability**: The dynamic nature of walk-forward analysis allows an algorithm to adapt to market changes over time. Traditional backtesting may bias towards favorable (or unfavorable) market conditions which exhibit different trends and behaviors. In contrast, walk-forward analysis potentially includes a more diverse range of conditions, making the output more reliable and robust.

3. **Validation**: Walk-forward analysis reinforces the validity of the strategy by continually testing on unseen data. If a strategy works well in the in-sample period and also perform well in the out-of-sample period, it raises the confidence in the strategy. Such a form of cross-validation provides a stronger safeguard against overfitting than a single instance of backtesting.

4. **Future Insights**: Walk-forward analysis provides insights into how the algorithm might perform in the future under similar market conditions. Traditional backtesting only provides a one-off snapshot of algorithm performance against past market conditions. In algorithmic trading, the goal is to create an algorithm that can navigate future market conditions effectively. By its very nature, walk-forward analysis is closer to this objective.

By combining asset allocation, multiple samples of in-sample and out-of-sample testing periods, and deploying a walk-forward analysis, one can mitigate a great deal of the risks associated with the standard backtesting methods used in algorithmic trading.

5.13 What challenges might arise during walk-forward analysis?

Walk-forward analysis is a method used in algorithmic trading to optimize and validate a trading strategy. It can provide a realistic simulation of how a certain strategy would have performed over a specific period of time. However, several challenges might arise during the implementation of walk-forward analysis.

1. **Overfitting**: This is similar to wearing a pair of jeans that only fit you and no one else because they're designed to your exact measurements. In trading, a model overfits during the testing phase when it's tailored to perfectly predict past market data but fails to perform well on new, unseen data. Walk-forward analysis tries to combat overfitting by iterating the optimization and testing process, but it's not completely immune to it.

2. **Parameter Stability**: This might be likened to adjusting the seat and mirrors in your car every time you drive. Ideally, you want to make these adjustments once and have them work for all future drives. Similarly, in trading, the parameters of your model should remain stable over time. However, during walk-forward analysis, you may find that optimal parameters may change with each "walk" iteration, leading to instability in the model's performance.

3. **Length of the In-Sample and Out-of-Sample Data**: Deciding how much data to use for the training (in-sample) and testing (out-of-sample) periods can be challenging. It's like deciding how much time to train for a marathon: train too little, and you won't be prepared; train too much, and you might end up overtrained and exhausted. Using too little data might lead to poor strategy optimization, while using too much data can lead to resource-intensive computation or your model being trained on redundant information.

4. **Computational Demand**: Walk-forward analysis demands significant computational resources as it iteratively optimizes and validates the trading strategy over multiple in-sample and out-of-sample

periods. If we relate this to baking, it would be like repeatedly baking batches of cookies with small adjustments each time to find the best recipe - with the added challenge of not having a high-powered kitchen.

5. **Market Regime Shifts**: This refers to a significant change in one or more characteristics of a market. A trading strategy developed during a bull market, for example, may not perform well when the market turns bearish. Thus, a model that performs well during the walk-forward analysis may not perform well in the future if the market conditions drastically change. This is similar to practicing to play football on a dry, sunny day but having to play the actual match in heavy rain and mud.

In summary, while walk-forward analysis is indispensable in validating and optimizing a trading strategy, it is not without its challenges. Thus, meticulous care ought to be taken when developing, testing, and interpreting the results.

5.14 How frequently should walk-forward analysis be conducted for a live trading algorithm?

The frequency at which you conduct a walk-forward analysis largely depends on various factors related to your trading algorithm and market conditions. It could range from every week to a few months. Let me use an analogy to explain this better - consider your trading algorithm as a ship navigating through the ocean (the market). The ocean's conditions keep changing - there could be calm days, stormy days, days with high winds, etc. Now, how frequently would you check your compass and navigation charts?

Similarly, the financial markets are ever-changing - with different conditions such as heightened volatility, periods of stability, market news, earnings season, and so on.

If your trading algorithm was designed with a certain market condition in mind and these conditions change significantly, then it is wise to perform a walk-forward analysis more frequently. For instance, if your model was trained with data during a calm market period and suddenly the market turns volatile, the algorithm may start underperforming.

You could also set performance benchmarks with drawdown limits, hit rate, etc. If you notice the algorithm is underperforming for a predetermined period or is missing out on the set benchmarks, then a walk-forward analysis should be conducted.

In more steady states of market, you can perform the walk-forward analysis on a monthly or a quarterly basis.

Lastly, the frequency of walk-forward analysis also depends on the trading time frame of your algorithm. For high-frequency trading, you would need to do this analysis more frequently, perhaps even daily since the market conditions can change drastically within short time periods. For lower frequency systems such as daily or weekly, a less frequent update cycle can be appropriate, like bi-weekly or monthly.

In conclusion, there is no set rule, and the frequency should be tuned based on the robustness of your model, the nature of the markets your algorithm trades in, and how quickly market conditions change. It's all about ensuring that your "ship" is sailing correctly in the changing waters.

5.15 How does walk-forward analysis help in parameter optimization?

Walk-Forward Analysis (WFA) is a key player in the game of algorithmic trading, serving as a simulation technique that helps us overcome the limitations of traditional "out-of-sample" testing when it comes to parameter optimization. It's like the natural evolution of the "train and test" strategy in a machine learning model.

Imagine we are trying to improve a race car's performance. We could experiment with different tuning setups and see what works best on our home track (the "training" track). However, we could not be 100% sure if the best setup will perform equally well on other race tracks with different conditions (the "out-of-sample" tracks). Similarly, to optimize trading parameters, we usually split our data into a training set and a test set. We find the best parameters on training set and validate them on the test set.

The problematic part here is that these parameters often lack adaptability as the market changes over time. That's where our hero WFA steps in.

WFA is like a travelling racing engineer who constantly tweaks the car's setup according to the characteristics of each new track. In trading terms, WFA involves the process of optimizing a trading system using a certain period of time (the "in-sample" period), and then testing it over the following (the "out-of-sample" period). This walk-forward period is then rolled forward in time, and the process repeats.

Mathematically, it can be expressed as follows:

1. Optimize the parameters using the training data from T_1 to T_2.

2. Apply the optimized parameters to the test data from T_2 to T_3.

3. Repeat the process from T_2 to T_3 for optimization and from T_3 to T_4 for the out-of-sample testing.

By building and rebuilding the model at different intervals, we are training our model to be adaptable, as the market conditions change. This provides a more robust parameter optimization and makes our model more resilient to the dreaded curse of overfitting.

In essence, walk-forward analysis is like teaching our model to sail, allowing it to adjust its sails in response to the shifting winds (market conditions), rather than relying on a fixed rudder setting (fixed optimized parameters). For a successful algorithmic trading strategy, enabling the model to adapt to the ever-changing sea of the financial market is crucial.

5.16 Why is it crucial to integrate risk management directly into trading algorithms?

Integrating risk management directly into trading algorithms is much like installing an advanced braking system in a race car. A race car driver goes at maximum speed, pushing the car to its limits to win the race. However, without an effective braking system, the driver is at constant risk of a catastrophic crash.

In much the same way, algorithmic trading allows traders to execute trades at maximum speed and efficiency. However, without incorporating risk management directly into these algorithms, the potential for significant losses or even a catastrophic event in a portfolio is always high.

So, why is risk management integration so crucial?

1. **Volatility Tolerance:** Markets are inherently volatile, with prices fluctuating rapidly in short periods of time. Directly integrating risk management into the algorithm allows it to account for this volatility, ensuring that trades are only executed when they align with the risk parameters set by the trader. For example, an algorithm may be designed to halt trading when certain volatility thresholds are exceeded.

2. **Automation & Speed:** The nature of algorithmic trading resides on its speedy order placement, execution, and capacity of handling vast amounts of data. Leaving risk management outside the algorithm's execution process can lead to a considerable time gap as risk checks are typically slower. This time gap could allow the algorithm to execute trades that no longer meet the risk criteria.

3. **Risk-Reward Balance:** Every investment carries a certain level of risk. Risk management tools ensure that the potential rewards outweigh the risks. It is thus crucial to integrate this directly into the trading algorithm to uphold the risk-reward balance set by the trader in real time.

4. **Market Impact Control:** A key part of risk management in trading is understanding and controlling the market impact of trades. If market impact is not properly managed, large trades can significantly move the market, leading to unfavorable prices. By integrating risk management into the algorithm, the market impact of trades can be minimized to keep prices favorable.

5. **Regulatory Compliance:** Regulatory authorities impose various risk management requirements that trading firms must adhere to. An algorithm that incorporates risk management strategies can help ensure compliance with these standards.

In conclusion, just as a race car driver needs an advanced braking system, or a typesetter needs error-checking tools, traders require risk management strategies to be incorporated directly into their trading algorithms. This ensures they navigate financial markets efficiently, swiftly, but also safely.

5.17   How can an algorithm dynamically adjust position sizes based on volatility?

To dynamically adjust position sizes in algorithmic trading based on volatility, one common approach is to implement a concept known as 'Volatility Targeting'. The central idea is to adjust the size of your positions according to the volatility of the market.

Let's consider an analogy to make it easier to understand: Think of volatility as a roller coaster ride. When the ride (or the market in this case) is quite smooth and predictable, you're somewhat comfortable and can afford to carry a large backpack (a large position size). But when the ride gets wild (i.e., the market becomes more volatile), you need to lighten your load (reduce your position size), to reduce the risk of getting tossed out of the ride (suffering large losses).

To put this into practice, we first need to define the measure of volatility. The most common measure used is the Standard Deviation of returns. We denote it as σ.

Let's say the size of your position for a particular asset is represented by w. w is what you call as 'weights'. Normally, weights should sum to 1 for a portfolio.

You can dynamically adjust this weight w using the formula:

$$w = \frac{T}{\sigma}$$

In this equation, T is your target volatility level, and σ is the current volatility level of the asset.

If market volatility is higher than your target, the current σ is larger and thus, the weight w for the asset decreases. Conversely, if the market volatility is lower than your target, the weight w increases.

This is how an algorithm can dynamically adjust position sizes based on volatility. It continuously measures volatility and adjusts the position size to maintain a balance between risk (volatility) and return.

Extra factors can also be added to the formula to account for other elements like liquidity, transaction costs, etc., based on specific needs and strategy. Nonetheless, the core concept remains the same: keep adjusting position sizes based on the measure of volatility.

5.18   What mechanisms can be used by an algorithm to detect and react to abnormal market conditions?

In algorithmic trading, the detection and reaction to abnormal market conditions rely on using a variety of mechanisms generally based on statistical models, technical indicators, machine learning methods, and risk management protocols. Here are some of the commonly used approaches:

1. **Moving Averages**: Moving averages can be used to detect abnormalities in price movements. For example, if the current prices deviate significantly from the moving average, it may signal abnormal market conditions.

2. **Standard Deviation and Z-Scores**: By calculating the standard deviation of a price and comparing it to historical standards, an algorithm can detect abnormal volatility. Abnormal conditions could be interpreted when the price moves more than n standard deviations from the mean $(Z > n)$, where n is often set to 2 or 3.

3. **Statistical methods such as GARCH and EGARCH models** can be used to model and forecast volatility. Significant divergences from these predictions could indicate unusual market behavior.

4. **Machine Learning Techniques**: Advanced machine learning methods such as Reinforcement Learning, Neural Networks, and Anomaly Detection algorithms can be employed to detect anomalies based on historical data patterns.

5. **Market Depth Analysis**: Consider an analogy where the market is a ship on the sea. The market depth is the sea's depth under the ship. A normal sea allows the ship to sail smoothly, but when the depth (liquidity) decreases suddenly, the ship (market) may behave unpredictably. Algorithms can monitor the order book or Level II market data for sudden changes in market depth, indicative of abnormal conditions.

6. **Risk Management Protocols**: Just like guard rails on a winding mountain road, risk controls serve to prevent disastrous outcomes of trading algorithms reacting wrongly to abnormal market conditions. For example, value-at-risk (VaR) measures the risk of extreme losses, and an algorithm could be programmed to reduce exposure if VaR exceeds a certain threshold.

Each of the above mechanisms presents its own strengths and limitations. Proper design and testing of an algorithm to handle abnormal market conditions is a crucial aspect of algorithmic trading and fundamentally influences the algorithm's overall performance and risk exposure.

5.19 How do algorithms handle stop-loss and take-profit levels?

In the world of algorithmic trading, stop-loss and take-profit levels are key elements that algorithms leverage to automatically execute trades according to the trader's strategy.

1. **Stop-loss levels:** A stop-loss level is akin to a safety net. It is a predetermined price at which an algorithm is programmed to sell a security if the price begins to fall below that level. It's like going rock climbing, and you set a safety rope (stop-loss) at a certain height to prevent a painful fall (huge financial losses).

The basic structure of the stop-loss function in an algorithm could look something like this:

```
if security_price <= stop_loss_level:
    sell(security)
```

This is a quintessential example of a 'threshold-based action' where the algorithm compares the current security price with the stop-loss level, and if the price drops and hits that threshold, the algorithm executes a sell operation.

2. **Take-profit levels:** A take-profit level is like the summit of a mountain that a climber aims to reach. It is a predetermined price at which an algorithm is programmed to sell a security if the price begins to rise and reaches that level. It enables the trader to capture profit automatically.

The basic structure of the take-profit function in an algorithm could look something like this:

```
if security_price >= take_profit_level:
    sell(security)
```

In this case, if the financial security's price rises and hits the intended take-profit level, the algorithm sells it off, securing the anticipated profit for the trader.

These two paradigms are integrated into trading algorithms to ensure that trading strategies have pre-defined risk and reward parameters. Trading algorithms regularly monitor market prices and autonomously execute trades when these stop-loss or take-profit levels are hit.

It's important to note that these are simplistic representations of the functions for illustrative purposes only. In reality, algorithmic trading incorporates many more factors. For example, it includes checks for market volatility, checks to avoid false signals, and applying principles of money management and position-sizing to determine exactly how many units of security to buy or sell. Further, different types of stop-loss (fixed price, trailing stop loss etc.) and take-profit (fixed price, multiple take-profit levels) strategies can be implemented for different types of trading strategies.

Algorithmic trading reduces the necessity for constant vigilance by the trader, and aids in minimizing emotional responses to market movements, thus promoting a more disciplined and consistent approach to trading.

5.20 Discuss the balance between risk and return in the context of algorithm design.

When designing trading algorithms, it's imperative to strike a balance between risk and return. This comes down to the fundamental principle of finance, which is the trade-off between risk and return. In order to achieve higher returns, one often has to accept higher levels of risk.

Let's venture down to how this principle impacts algorithm design and optimization for trading. We can think of it as walking on a tightrope. On one side, we have the potential for high return, and on the other, lies the risk.

Formally, the algorithm's goal will mostly be to maximize some sort of expected reward. This may be the expected end-of-day portfolio value, often defined as R. One way to do this could involve placing highly leveraged bets on very volatile stocks, which could indeed have a high expected return. However, it goes without saying that this would be incredibly risky, akin to walking on a thin, unsteady tightrope.

Often, we want not only to maximize R, but also to minimize risk. This optimization problem is hence multicriterial in nature and is essentially about finding a compromise between multiple conflicting objectives. The two most common measures for risk are variance and Value-at-Risk (VaR). Variance measures how much the portfolio's returns can vary, and VaR measures the worst expected loss over a given time period at a given confidence level.

Our optimization problem can be illustrated as:

$$\max_{w} \quad E[R_p] - \rho\sigma_p$$

where, $E[R_p]$ is the expected return, σ_p is the standard deviation of the portfolio, and ρ is the risk aversion coefficient. Here, we are trying to maximize our expected return while simultaneously penalizing higher levels of risk. ρ in the equation determines the trade-off between risk and return.

However, this optimization problem suffers from a drawback: it assumes that returns are normally distributed. In reality, returns usually have fat-tails, which mean they are more likely to experience extreme values than the normal distribution can account for. Therefore, a measure like Conditional Value-at-Risk (CVaR) often better quantifies risk in the tails of the distribution.

To bring it back to our tightrope analogy: walking directly in the middle may be the "safest" but slow. Leaning too much either way ends up in a fall (heavy loss). So, the trading algorithm, like an experienced tightrope walker, needs to smartly balance between risk (falling off) and return (reaching the end).

In conclusion, balancing risk and return is an elegant dance in the world of algorithmic trading. One misstep could lead to potentially dire financial consequences, while an adept maneuver could lead to high returns. The algorithm designer should focus on creating this balance by taking into account the investor's risk preference and the risk properties of the asset classes being traded.

Chapter 6

Technology and Infrastructure

6.1 Which programming languages are most prevalent in algorithmic trading and why?

Algorithmic Trading is fundamentally about developing and testing trading strategies that are executed by computers with high precision and speed. So, the technology and infrastructure of algorithmic trading require programming languages that rate highly on parameters such as speed of execution, ability to handle large data sets, mathematical capabilities, and ease of use for algorithmic design, testing, and execution.

Below are some of the most popular programming languages used in Algorithmic Trading:

1. **Python**: Python is one of the most widely used programming

languages in algorithmic trading due to its simplicity, robustness, and the wide range of libraries it offers for scientific computing, like NumPy, pandas, and SciPy. If we drew an analogy, Python would be like a Swiss army knife, offering functionality and flexibility for a range of tasks. Although it isn't the fastest language per se, it's 'fast enough' for many scenarios in trading and its versatility and user-friendly nature often outweigh the pure speed concerns.

2. **C++**: C++ is preferred in instances where extreme low latency and high speed are paramount. This is the language that runs Formula 1 cars of the trading world. It is used in 'High Frequency Trading' (HFT) where even a microsecond speed advantage can mean a significant profit. The trade-off with C++, however, is that it has a steeper learning curve and requires more stringent management due to its low-level nature.

3. **Java**: Java's 'Write Once, Run Anywhere' (WORA) capability makes it a good choice for large, complex, distributed trading systems. Its Object-Oriented nature comes handy while building large-scale systems. It's like a massive shipping vessel – not as quick as a speedboat, but able to hold and manage a vast array of functionalities and manage them well. It falls middle-of-the-pack in terms of speed.

4. **R**: R is typically used for designing, testing, and executing statistical and predictive trading strategies, owing to a large number of packages it offers for statistical analysis. Think of it as your specialized research lab where you can test and validate hypotheses with relative ease.

5. **MATLAB**: MATLAB, like R, is utilized for its powerful mathematical and statistical modeling capabilities. It is used for backtesting models and for risk management purposes.

6. **JavaScript/HTML5**: Frontend languages like JavaScript combined with HTML5 are often employed for creating user-friendly, interactive trade visualization and analytics dashboard.

It's also worth noting that a multi-language set-up is popular in many trading firms where Python/R could be used for model research and prototyping, which is then ported to Java/C++ for production.

To sum up, the choice of a language depends on various factors like personal proficiency, part of the trading process it's being used for, speed requirements, scalability, and complexity. Like a toolbox, you choose the tool that's the most fitting for the task at hand.

6.2 How do compiled languages like C++ compare to interpreted languages like Python in the context of high-frequency trading?

The comparison of compiled languages like C++ and interpreted languages like Python essentially boils down to issues of speed, control vs ease of use, and community support. The choice of one over the other is heavily influenced by the specifics of the task at hand and the trade-offs one is willing to make.

Let's start by discussing speed, which is a significant factor in high-frequency trading. Imagine trading as a high-speed car race. Vehicles representing different trades are all racing to be first. In this metaphor, C++ is like a top-tier Formula 1 car while Python is more like a standard issue sports car. Both can get you to your destination, but in a straight race, the top-tier car unsurprisingly wins.

C++ is a compiled language. The source code written by developers is directly translated into a machine-readable format before execution. This allows the compiled code in C++ to run significantly faster. On the other hand, Python is an interpreted language. The Python interpreter reads and executes the code line by line, which, though it facilitates debugging, is considerably slower.

In high-frequency trading, where success is defined by being the quickest to execute trades, speed is crucial. For tasks like transaction cost

analysis, order routing or execution, where microsecond-level laten-
cies can have a significant impact, C++ is usually the preferred tool.

Now, let's talk about control versus ease of use. Using another analogy, C++ is like a manual-transmission car, while Python is more like
an automatic one. With C++, you have to manage memory manually and have a lot of control over system resources, but the learning
curve is steeper. Python, on the other hand, is easy to learn and use
but offers less control and is more resource heavy.

You have to weigh whether the time and effort spent optimising C++
code (and therein making it faster and more efficient) is feasible within
the project timelines, or whether quick prototyping, facile readability
and ease of debugging in Python may better serve you, even at the
cost of a few microseconds per transaction.

Lastly, community support and library availability are areas where
Python shines, sort of functioning like a pit crew in a race. Python's
extensive libraries such as pandas, scikit-learn and TensorFlow, combined with its strong community support, make it an excellent choice
for data analysis and predictive modelling tasks in high-frequency
trading. While C++ also has some libraries for mathematical com-
putations and machine learning, it generally lags behind Python in
this area.

So, in conclusion, while C++ presents an edge for real-time trade
execution due to its speed and control, Python may be more suited
for less time-critical tasks like backtesting, predictive modelling, and
strategy development. A common practice in financial institutions
and hedge funds is to use a combination of both - Python for high
level tasks and rapid prototyping, and C++ for low-level tasks and
finalised code.

6.3 What are the advantages of using a domain-specific language like R in quantitative analysis?

R is one of the popular domain-specific languages that is used in quantitative analysis. It uniquely caters to the needs and requirements of quant analysts and offers several benefits.

1. **Statistical Package Libraries**: Utilizing R is comparable to having a vast toolbox at your disposal, where each tool is thoughtfully designed for a specific function. Any statistical model that you can think of, from simple linear regression to the more complex machine learning models, has been implemented in one of the R packages. This breadth and depth in readily usable statistical tools make R highly advantageous for quantitative analysis.

2. **Data Visualization**: Imagine going on a journey where the data is your guide, R's data visualization capabilities are like a compass and map. It has great libraries, like ggplot2, that provide incredibly versatile, and high-quality graphical capabilities essential for data exploration, analysis, and presentation.

3. **Data Manipulation**: Sometimes data is like a puzzle. Pieces may be scattered, missing, or need some adjustment. R's data manipulation capabilities are like the magic puzzle-solving adhesive. Packages like dplyr make it easier to "clean," transform, and aggregate complicated datasets, reducing the chances of errors and saving time.

4. **Reproducibility**: R, like a hearty cookbook, enables reproducible research. This means that the entire process of data gathering, manipulation, analysis, and reporting is understandable, transparent, and replicable. This is important for increasing the reliability and validity of the quantitative analysis.

5. **Integrated Development Environment**: RStudio, the IDE for R, is like the fitting cockpit for a racer. It offers a user-friendly and powerful environment that includes features such as syntax highlight-

ing, code completion, and tabs, making R programming more efficient and enjoyable.

As you can see, using a domain-specific language like R in quantitative analysis is like packing a Swiss Army knife for a camping trip. It has a wide range of built-in capabilities and functionalities that are essential for the unpredictable wilderness of data crunching, manipulation, modeling, and analysis. It's the perfect companion for explorations in the world of quantitative analysis.

6.4   How important is parallel processing and multi-threading in algo trading?

Parallel processing and multi-threading are incredibly important in algorithmic trading - they can be likened to the difference between having one cook or several cooks in a kitchen.

In algorithmic trading, every microsecond matters. Calculation more often than not involves complex mathematical models and algorithms that need to process large volumes of data in real time and to make decisions in a fraction of a second. Without parallel processing and multi-threading, an algorithm could only process one piece of data after the other, not unlike a single cook preparing a multi-course meal on his own.

On the other hand, with parallel computing (several cooks), you can process multiple tasks (dishes) concurrently with each task being handled by a separate processor (a cook), thus significantly reducing the overall processing time. For example, if you can split your algorithm to execute on 4 cores instead of 1, you can theoretically reduce your computing time by up to 75%.

Multi-threading plays a similar role by effectively managing and optimizing the use of these processors or cores. It allows a single process to have multiple threads of execution, just like assigning each cook to handle a specific task (chopping veggies, stirring the soup, and baking the bread simultaneously).

However, keep in mind the complexity that parallelism and multi-threading introduce. Going back to the cooking analogy, if not properly organized, cooks might run into each other, mix up the dishes, or mess up the timing. In parallel programming, difficulties arise from condition race, deadlock and resource starvation, which if not handled well, can cause more harm than good. Therefore, a well-structured code and finely tuned architecture are critical when implementing these features.

In short, imagine operating a bustling restaurant during the dinner rush. To serve your customers timely and efficiently, you would need multiple cooks working in parallel and each cook multi-tasking. That's exactly what parallel processing and multi-threading do for algorithmic trading.

6.5   How do modern trading platforms accommodate various programming languages?

Modern trading platforms are extremely versatile, just like a Swiss Army knife designed to accommodate multiple tools in a compact form. They are built in such a way that they can accommodate programming in various languages, through mechanisms like APIs (Application Programming Interfaces), SDKs (Software Development Kits), and language-specific wrappers.

Let's consider an API as a universal electrical adapter. When you travel internationally, with gadgets that have different plug designs than the country you're visiting, you need a universal adapter to connect your device to the electricity supply. Similarly, APIs help a program written in one language to communicate and interact with a platform written in another. They define the methods and data formats that a program can use to communicate with the platform, allowing developers to use their preferred language while still being able to interact with the platform.

Most algorithms in the trading world are implemented in C++, Python, Java, R, and MATLAB. So modern trading platforms come with Software Development Kits (SDKs) for these languages. An SDK is like a pre-packed suitcase with all the bits you need for your trip. It provides the libraries and tools necessary for developers to create software for specific devices or platforms using their preferred language.

Furthermore, some platforms also provide wrappers for different languages. A wrapper is essentially a bridge between two programming languages, making it possible to write code in one language, and then wrap it in another language so it can be executed there. Consider a wrapper like a translator at the United Nations who translates the speech of a representative into a language that everyone attending can understand.

In conclusion, modern trading platforms are designed to be language-agnostic, accommodating various programming languages by offering mechanisms like APIs, SDKs, and language wrappers. Just as international facilities accommodate various languages and cultures, in a similar fashion, these trading platforms accommodate various programming languages to ensure seamless and efficient trading.

6.6 How do APIs play a central role in algorithmic trading?

APIs, or Application Programming Interfaces, are the bedrock of modern algorithmic trading, acting like a universal translator, undertaking the critical job of facilitating communication between different software systems.

You can think of an API as a waiter at your favorite restaurant. When you sit down to order a meal, you need the waiter (API) to express your needs (requests) to the kitchen (server). The chef (program, exchange, database, etc.) then gets your orders, prepares the food (data or services), and hands it back to the waiter (API), who finally presents it to you (the user or another application). The beauty of this system is that you (the user) don't need to know how the kitchen works or the recipe of your ordered dish. You only intermingle with the waiter (API).

In the context of algorithmic trading, APIs interact with trading platforms to retrieve real-time price quotes, historical data, execute trades, and write algorithms for smart order routing, risk management, etc. Here is how they operate.

1. **Data Retrieval:** APIs allow algorithmic trading systems to access real-time trading data from the market. Via APIs, algorithms can fetch price quotes, fundamental data, macroeconomic figures, and even news updates. Without this interface, gathering all this information would be a tedious and time-consuming task.

2. **Placement of Orders:** APIs don't just retrieve information but also deliver instructions. When an algorithm decides to execute a trade, it sends this instruction via the API to the broker's trading platform. The trade is completed transparently and rapidly without any manual intervention.

3. **Automation of Tasks:** The ultimate goal of algorithmic trading is the automation of trading tasks. APIs facilitate the automation of tasks like technological analysis, portfolio rebalancing, and risk management. With specified algorithms, APIs can conduct these tasks significantly faster and more accurately than a human trader.

4. **Integration with other Systems:** APIs allow applications to communicate with one another, allowing algorithmic trading systems to integrate with other algorithms or custom-built software. This integration is crucial in forming a robust and synergistic trading system that can interact with multiple markets, news feeds, and modeling tools.

In summary, APIs act as a critical cog in the machinery of algorithmic trading, integrating various software components into a seamless information and transaction processing conduit. Without APIs, algorithmic trading systems would be akin to an orchestra without a conductor.

6.7 What are the key features you would look for in a trading API?

When looking for a trading API, you would want to consider several key elements. Think of it as selecting an orchestral conductor - you need someone who can interpret the musical score (trading strategy), handle the different musical instruments (different asset classes), and ensure that everything is perfectly timed.

1. **Breadth of Asset Classes**: Different APIs can facilitate trading in different asset types like stocks, bonds, futures, options, forex, etc. Based on your trading strategy, you'll need an API that can effectively support your chosen asset class. If your investing strategy is a symphony, your chosen instruments are the asset classes - you need a conductor who can handle them all!

2. **Order Type Handling**: Different trading strategies would require different types of orders, such as limit orders, market orders, stop orders, trailing stops, etc. It's important that the trading API supports a variety of order types.

3. **Real-time Access to Market Data**: Like a conductor needs to be attentive of each instrument's sound in real-time, an API needs to provide real-time access to market data. Access to real-time data feeds that include price quotes, order book details, and trade execution details are crucial.

4. **Reliability and Speed**: Ideally, a trading API would be extremely reliable, capable of handling multiple concurrent trades, and executing them in milliseconds. Fast and reliable execution is like a conductor ensuring that the orchestra keeps tempo and doesn't miss a beat.

5. **Cost**: Some APIs come with fees. This could be per-trade costs, monthly or annual costs, or based on the amount traded (volume-based fees). Analysing the cost versus the benefits provided can help choose the right one for your needs.

6. **Technological Compatibility**: The API should be compatible with the programming language you wish to use like Python, Java, C++, etc. It should offer a well-documented, supportive developer's guide to answer any potential queries one might have.

7. **Security**: A secure API ensures that your trading strategy remains confidential and is resistant to malicious attacks. It's like making sure the conductor's music score can't be stolen or tampered with.

8. **Customer Support**: An active and responsive customer support team can be really helpful, especially if you encounter any technical difficulties or need assistance with the API at some point.

So, to continue the analogy, if you choose your 'conductor' wisely, your orchestral masterpiece, the trading strategy, will have the best chance to shine and provide the audience (you, the trader) with beautiful music (profits).

6.8 How do you handle rate limits and potential disconnections when interacting with trading APIs?

Dealing with rate limits and potential disconnections is a common challenge when interacting with trading APIs. Here are some ways to handle these problems:

1. **Handling Rate Limits**:

Rate limits are like the number of free samples that a shop allows you to take in a given hour. If the shop only permits 100 free samples an hour, it means you can only take 100, not 101. Similarly, an API might limit the number of requests you can make in an hour.

To manage rate limits effectively:

* **Understand the limit**: Read the API's documentation to understand the limit imposed. It might be a per-minute, per-hour, or per-day limit.

* **Intelligent Requests**: Make requests intelligently. For example, if the limit is 100 requests per hour, it means approximately 1.67 requests per minute. You can program your script to make requests at this pace.

* **Caching**: Cache the responses from the API. This is like taking a snapshot of the free sample before tasting it, so you can refer to it later without needing another sample.

* **Bulk Requests**: If the API allows, make bulk requests. Instead of asking for one piece of information in each request, you can ask for several. This is like asking for all 100 samples at one go.

2. **Handling Potential Disconnections**:

Internet disconnections are like interruptions in a phone conversation. Just like you would call back the person after an interruption, similarly, your script should be able to reconnect and continue from where it left off.

To tackle disconnections:

* **Auto-reconnect**: Implement a mechanism to automatically re-establish a connection if there's a disconnection. Libraries like 'requests' in Python provide options to do this.

* **Timeouts**: Implement generous timeouts while making API requests. This is similar to waiting patiently for the other person to respond in a phone conversation.

* **Retries**: Implement a retry mechanism with backoff strategy. If a request fails, wait for some time and then retry. This waiting time should increase with each failed attempt. For example, on the first failed attempt, wait for 1 minute. If the second attempt also fails, wait for 2 minutes, and so on.

Lastly, it is always good practice to log all interactions with the API. In the event that something does go wrong, these logs can provide valuable insight into what happened and help fix the issue.

Remember, while trading, time is money. So, being efficient and fault-tolerant in the interaction with trading APIs could mean the difference between making a profit and incurring a loss.

6.9 Why is data consistency crucial when using third-party APIs?

When dealing with third-party APIs in algorithmic trading, data consistency can be compared to the foundation of a house. A solid and consistent foundation ensures the house (our algorithm) stands strong and performs effectively. Similarly, in algorithmic trading, reliable and consistent data is necessary for an algorithm to make accurate predictions and execute successful trades.

Let's consider a simple algorithm that relies on the closing price of a particular stock. Suppose, one day, the subscribed API suddenly changes the format in which this data is returned or maybe it starts giving the opening price instead of the closing price without informing us. Our algorithm may stop understanding this crucial input or start making trade decisions based on the wrong data. Worst case scenario, it could lead to significant financial losses.

On an even more technical level, here's where data consistency becomes essential:

1. **Accuracy of Calculations:** Most trading algorithms perform complex calculations, often involving summations, multiplications, and divisions. Any inconsistency in the data can result in inaccurate results and further erroneous decisions.

2. **Persistent Database Record:** Many algorithms store the retrieved data for future use and analysis. Inconsistent data can mess

with your database schemas and cause problems with data retrieval.

3. **Compatibility with Other Systems:** Trading firms usually have a variety of systems in operation. For the smooth flow of operations, data consistency becomes crucial.

4. **Robustness of Machine Learning Models:** Machine learning tools rely on consistent data for training. These models can perform inadequately or inaccurately when fed with inconsistent data. This is like training your pet dog to fetch the newspaper with a bone and then one day giving it a ball instead. It will leave the dog confused and ineffective.

5. **Performance Metrics:** Inconsistent data can affect the performance measurement of strategies and algorithms, leading to a flawed understanding of their success rate.

The message here is crystal clear - data consistency is as important to your trading algorithm as a well-cooked, consistent recipe is to a master chef. Without it, things won't taste right and may fall flat.

6.10 How do websockets differ from traditional REST APIs in the context of trading?

Websockets and REST APIs both have their own unique roles in the world of online trading. Let's put on our technology caps and dive right in.

One way to look at the difference between Websockets and REST APIs is to compare them to different styles of conversation. Imagine you're at a party.

1. A REST API-based interaction is like having a series of individual conversations. You approach a person (server), ask a question (GET

request), they reply with an answer (response) and the conversation ends. If you have a new question, you start a new conversation. This is a request-response architecture, where client-driven requests are sent, and the server responds each time.

2. A Websocket-based interaction, on the other hand, is more like joining a group conversation that's ongoing. You mingle with a group (open a websocket connection) and as long as you're part of the circle (connection is open), you can listen to what everyone else is saying (streaming data) and chime in when you have something to say (send data). This is a bidirectional, full-duplex communication protocol.

Now, let's talk about how this applies to trading.

REST API in Algorithmic Trading:

REST APIs are useful when a trading strategy doesn't need to react in real-time. Every single time you want to know the latest stock price, you have to ask for it (send a GET request). For trade execution, you send a POST request.

For instance, if you use an algorithm that trades based on end-of-day prices, a REST API approach works because you only need the market data once per day.

WebSocket in Algorithmic Trading:

If you're working on a high-frequency trading strategy that needs real-time market data and fast execution, Websockets have an advantage. Once you open a websocket connection, you are continually streamed the trades, quotes, and other market data that you have subscribed to. This allows you to react to market events immediately as they occur. It also reduces network latency because you've an open connection with the server; you don't need to repeatedly open and close connections like in REST API model.

So, choosing between websockets or REST APIs will depend largely on the nature of your trading strategy. Both have valid uses and can even co-exist in a robust, flexible, and efficient trading platform.

6.11   What are some popular trading platforms used in algorithmic trading?

There are several popular trading platforms utilized in algorithmic trading, each with its own set of unique features and advantages. Here are some of them:

1. **MetaTrader 4 (MT4):** This platform, like the Swiss Army Knife for the outdoors lover, is the ultimate tool for many individual algorithmic traders and brokers. It's user-friendly, provides great charting tools, and has a built-in programming language, MQL4, for creating custom strategies and indicators.

2. **Interactive Brokers (IB):** It could be compared to a professional DSLR camera, providing a highly customizable platform with advanced functions that experienced algorithmic traders appreciate. It offers APIs to use with various languages including Python, a favourite among algorithm developers due to its readability and versatility.

3. **Quantopian:** It's a crowd-sourced hedge fund and algorithmic trading platform, kind of like a combination of GitHub and a traditional Wall Street firm. It allows users to write algorithms in Python, backtest against historical data, and participate in contests with real money prizes.

4. **TradeStation:** With EasyLanguage, its built-in scripting language, this platform is like LEGO set exclusively made for building algorithmic trading strategies. With Easylanguage, traders without extensive programming experience can also build their trading systems.

5. **NinjaTrader:** One of the more popular platforms, NinjaTrader provides extensive back-testing capabilities and advanced charting options. It's kind of like Minecraft for developers, with its tools offering you the freedom to construct complicated algorithmic strategies in an engaging environment.

These are just a few examples of the many platforms available for algorithmic trading. It's crucial to choose a platform that suits your unique trading needs and level of programming expertise.

6.12   How do institutional platforms differ from retail trading platforms?

In comparing institutional trading platforms to retail trading platforms, let's take an analogy of high-speed trains versus passenger cars.

Institutional trading platforms are like high-end high-speed trains built for power and speed and equipped to hold a large amount of freight (i.e., big trading volumes). They are also built for efficacy and accuracy, having the ability to stop exactly at the right stations (i.e., precise trade execution). To ensure smooth functioning, these trains operate on dedicated rails (i.e., specialized technical infrastructures) and have highly trained drivers (i.e., professional traders) operating them. It's important to note that high-speed trains require a huge investment of resources for their operation.

On the other hand, retail trading platforms may be compared to regular passenger cars. These cars do not have the same capacity as the train, nor can they reach the same speeds, but they are still very functional for the average individual. They are more affordable and accommodating for their users' comfort (i.e., user-friendly interfaces and features). They operate on everyday roads (i.e., public networks) and can be driven by anyone (i.e., retail traders) who possesses a driver's license.

Here are some key differences between the two:

1. **Speed and Capacity:** Institutional platforms are designed to execute trades at a much faster speed and handle higher trading volumes. They are equipped with advanced technology, such as high-speed networks, colocated servers, and algorithmic trading tools to

facilitate rapid trade execution.

2. **Access to markets/orders:** Institutional platforms often provide more extensive access to liquidity pools and advanced order types. They can also directly interact with an exchange's order book.

3. **Cost:** Institutional platforms generally come with a higher subscription cost or trade commission structure due to their advanced capabilities.

4. **Customization and Control:** Institutional platforms tend to offer a higher degree of customization and control, granting the ability to implement complex strategies, routing rules, real-time risk management, and more.

5. **Regulations and Reporting:** Given the volumes involved and the scale of transactions, institutional platforms are often subject to broader regulatory oversight and they have sophisticated reporting modules to comply with these regulations.

6. **Technology and Infrastructure:** Institutional platforms usually are built on robust and advanced technical infrastructures. This includes high-frequency trading algorithms, low latency, and fault-tolerance systems.

Remember, both institutional and retail platforms serve their specific purposes and are geared towards their target users accordingly. Determining which one is "better" will largely depend on the needs, capital, skills, and strategies of the end user.

6.13 What features are crucial for backtesting and simulation in a trading platform?

When designing a trading platform for efficient backtesting and simulation, there are several crucial features that must be considered.

1. **Historical and Real-Time Data**: The platform needs to have access to quality historical and real-time data. This is analogous to a time machine that allows us to go back and forth in time to test our strategies.

2. **Data Management Tools**: It's also important to have effective data management tools for ease in manipulating data before backtesting. It's like having a well-organized toolbox before starting a car's maintenance.

3. **Order Emulation**: This feature helps imitate real-life trading conditions during backtesting, such as the timing of trades and potential slippage. This can be compared to using a flight simulator where pilots simulate different flying conditions.

4. **Simulation Speed**: Speed is crucial when doing extensive backtesting over multiple periods and scenarios, and optimizing your strategies accordingly. Imagine trying to watch an entire movie on an old, slow projector. Wouldn't be very effective, right?

5. **High-Resolution Backtesting**: Key feature possible only with event-driven systems. It involves backtesting trading logic on each market event, not only based on end-of-day or in regular time intervals, rendering a greater precision.

6. **Backtest Reporting**: After all, you would need a detailed report of how your backtest performed, including maximum drawdown, Sharpe ratio, etc. This report is like your medical examination report, showing the health of your trading strategy.

7. **Interactive User Interface**: An efficient interface helps users to easily access the features of the platform, visualizing and understanding the backtesting result effectively. This is similar to the dashboard of your car where you can access all necessary controls and feedback mechanism.

8. **Programming Flexibility**: The platform should offer programming flexibility to the users to allow them to code their strategies. This could be compared to having a customizable robot at your disposal.

9. **Large Scale Parameter Testing**: This feature allows traders to test numerous scenarios by changing the parameters of their trading strategy. Think of it as having a 3D printer that can create different shapes and objects based on different software inputs.

10. **Risk Management Tools**: This includes functions for calculating key risk ratios, conducting stress tests, etc., much like what a civil engineer uses to ensure a building can withstand various loads.

These are some of the essential features a trading platform should have in order to perform efficient backtesting and simulation. Without these, you could land yourself in a situation similar to venturing into the sea without proper navigation tools.

6.14   How do trading platforms handle real-time data feeds and order routing?

Trading platforms face the enormous challenge of processing mountains of real-time data at lightning speed. They're like the world's busiest librarians rapidly sorting through countless books (data points) and ensuring each one swiftly reaches the right person (trading algorithm).

Let's break this down into two key tasks: handling real-time data feeds and managing order routing.

Real-time Data Feeds

Data is the lifeblood of algorithmic trading and trading platforms have to process vast data streams on things like stock prices, volumes, foreign exchange rates, and macroeconomic indicators. Imagine you're standing on the shore and need to analyze the entire ocean minute by minute, that's the scale of data a trading platform deals with.

To handle this, many trading platforms rely on mechanisms similar to Pub/Sub (Publish/Subscribe) models which are like exclusive clubs where members (subscribers) sign up to receive updates about new events (publications). Here, real-time data feeds can be thought of as publishers and the trading algorithms as subscribers.

Order Routing

The next challenge is order routing i.e., to swiftly and effectively relay buy/sell orders from the trading algorithm to the relevant trading venue. Think of it as a highly efficient postal service which not only delivers letters (orders) quickly, but also chooses the best route dynamically.

Order routing is highly dependent on the FIX (Financial Information eXchange) protocol, the 'Esperanto' of trading world, and widely used for communicating trade orders. Advanced trading platforms also implement 'smart order routing' which dynamically determines the best execution venue based on parameters like price, liquidity, and exchange fees.

Further more, all of this has to be done while maintaining robustness and fault-tolerance. After all, in the financial markets, even a delay of a nanosecond can mean the difference between profit and loss.

Using technologies like High Performance Computing (HPC), In-memory databases (like Redis), Batching etc., the platforms are designed as an intricate web of systems, ensuring that the library keeps functioning, even if one section is temporarily shut down.

For managing such a large scale complex operation, it's essential to continuously monitor and optimize system performance, liken to a Formula 1 pit crew constantly fine-tuning the car in a race where every millisecond counts. Therefore, the trading platforms are often a blend of the fastest hardware and the most sophisticated software, supported by advanced networking protocols and infrastructure. All of this technology and infrastructure work together, ensuring that the world of algorithmic trading can run smoothly, twenty-four hours a day, seven days a week.

6.15 Discuss the importance of security and encryption in trading platforms.

In the area of algorithmic trading, technology, and infrastructure, security, and encryption play fundamental roles just like the goal-keepers in a soccer match. Without them, the integrity of the game would be at stake, and the whole system would be prone to disrupt and chaos.

To break it down, let's consider security first. Imagine this as the coach who devises strategies to prevent the opposing team (hackers and malicious software) from scoring goals. The coach employs multiple strategies including having a robust defense line (firewalls), swift and agile defenders who can predict the next move of the striker (anti-virus and anti-malware software), and well-orchestrated communication between players (secure and updated software and systems). The same way, in a trading platform, security comprises of firewalls, intrusion detection/prevention systems, up-to-date applications, and systems free from known vulnerabilities.

On the other hand, encryption can be viewed as the secret language or codes that the team uses to communicate. It ensures that even if the opposing team intercepts the messages, they won't be able to comprehend unless they have the "key" to decipher the code. This is paramount in the trading world where sensitive data such as credit card information, personal identification information, order details, etc., are transmitted. Encryption ensures that even if someone could sniff the trafficking data, they would only observe gibberish, keeping sensitive data safe.

Trading platforms particularly need high levels of security and encryption because of the sensitivity and volume of the data they process. A single breach could affect millions of transactions potentially leading to significant financial loss and erosion of trust. Besides, financial regulators like Securities Exchange Commission (SEC), Financial Industry Regulatory Authority (FINRA), etc., have data protection standards which must be met by these platforms.

Thus, security and encryption are not optional but core requirements of technology and infrastructure in trading platforms. They are the custodians that ensure the trading field is safe, the game is fair, and players can focus on their strategies and transactions instead of worrying about security threats or data breaches.

6.16   Why is low latency crucial in high-frequency trading?

Low latency in high-frequency trading (HFT) is much like a sprinter needing quick reaction times for the starter's gun in a 100-meter race, except in this scenario, the race is happening at a speed far beyond human comprehension, and all participants are aiming for the same finish line: profit.

Let's break it down further.

In high-frequency trading, traders use powerful computers to execute thousands, if not millions, of trades within fractions of a second. These trades are driven by algorithms that are designed to detect small inefficiencies in the market and capitalize on them.

The "latency" in this context refers to the time it takes for information (like a trading signal or a price update) to travel from one point (say a stock exchange) to another point (like the high-frequency trader's system). When we talk about "low latency" in this context, we mean these instances of information transmission happening extremely fast – in the order of microseconds (1e-6 seconds) or even nanoseconds (1e-9 seconds).

Why is this so crucial? Well, imagine a setting where an inefficiency is present that allows a trader to buy a security at a lower price and sell it higher. This discrepancy won't last for long as other traders will catch up and the price inefficiency will vanish. Here, the HFT system with the lowest latency will get to the proverbial "cheese" first - executing both trades before the market has a chance to correct itself.

It's important to note that a low latency doesn't guarantee success by itself. The quality of the trading algorithms, the reliability of the infrastructure and the managing of trading risks are equally important. But without low latency, the best lap time of our previously mentioned sprinter wouldn't even count because the race would be over before he got his running shoes on.

In this environment, where milliseconds can mean the difference between profit and loss, having low latency infrastructure is a key asset for high-frequency traders.

6.17   How do firms achieve ultra-low latency in their trading systems?

Achieving ultra-low latency in algorithmic trading systems is akin to being a track athlete aiming for the fastest sprint times. Just as each stride and breath taken by the athlete influences their overall speed, every hardware component, software application, and network connection in a trading system contributes to its latency.

Let's dissect how firms tackle latency at different levels:

1. **Hardware Acceleration**: This is like a runner training to improve body strength and stamina. In the trading world, firms use high-quality essential hardware, such as top-tier servers and processors with enhanced processing capabilities. An advanced example is Field Programmable Gate Arrays (FPGA), hardware devices that can be programmed to execute specific tasks exceptionally quickly.

2. **Optimized Software**: This is akin to training the athlete's technique and improving their reaction time off the starting blocks. Trading firms utilize efficient algorithms and data structures, often written in low-level languages like C++ for maximum performance. This minimizes unnecessary processing delays and ensures faster order execution.

3. **Co-location**: Similar to the runner securing a lane closer to the inner circle of the track for an advantageous position, trading firms place their servers in the same data centers as the exchange's servers to minimize travel time for data, known as network latency.

4. **Network Optimization**: Like the athlete who maintains a clean diet to fuel their performance, firms use clean, direct network paths. Express optical routes such as dedicated fibre links or microwave connections are used where possible to ensure the fastest data transmission times.

5. **Reduced "Tick-to-Trade" Latency**: Firms design their systems to minimize the time it takes to act on market data, such as identifying a trading opportunity ("tick") and placing an order ("trade"). This process is similar to the sprinter's ability to respond quickly to the sound of the starting pistol.

So, achieving ultra-low latency in a trading system is a multidimensional task requiring careful optimization at each step. It's like the athlete's pursuit for the fastest sprint time—each component contributes to the whole, and perfecting the details is the key to success.

6.18   What are the potential sources of latency in an algorithmic trading setup?

There are several potential sources of latency in an algorithmic trading system, similar to the delay in delivering a package. Imagine like you're sending a package from point A to point B but instead of a package, it's an instruction to execute a trade and instead of dealing with physical distance, you're dealing with electronic and digital systems.

Just as the package could be delayed by several factors such as road conditions, traffic, or the speed of the delivery vehicle, your trading orders can be delayed by numerous technological and infrastructural factors. Here are some of them:

1. **Networking Issues**: This can be compared to the route your delivery vehicle takes. Is it the most optimized route? Is there traffic? Similarly, data packet transfer over network and bandwidth limitations can cause significant latency.

2. **Exchange Connectivity**: This is comparable to the conditions at the delivery pick-up and drop-off points. If your pick-up location (trading platform) or drop-off point (the exchange) are busy or poorly structured, this could delay the transaction.

3. **Hardware performance**: This can be compared to the condition and power of your vehicle engine. The better your hardware (processor speed, disk I/O, RAM), the faster your algorithms will run.

4. **Latency introduced in Software development**: This is like the technique of the person who prepares your package for delivery. If the processes are inefficient, it could delay the entire delivery. Inefficient or poorly coded algorithms can significantly increase the execution time.

5. **Data Fetching and Preprocessing Time**: This could be par-

alleled to the time taken to package your item for delivery. If your data needs a lot of cleaning or normalising, this could introduce extra time before analysis.

6. **Order Routing**: This is comparable to the way the delivery vehicle navigates through the streets. If the GPS system is not optimal, the delivery will be delayed. Similarly, if your broker cannot find the best and quickest path to execute your order, this will increase the time taken, thus increasing latency.

Remember, in algorithmic trading, every microsecond matters. A delay in the order of a few milliseconds could result in significant opportunity costs. Just like in our courier analogy, a delivery delay might mean failing to deliver an important document on time, therefore it's crucial to optimize these sources of latency in an algorithmic trading setup.

6.19   How can co-location services reduce latency?

Co-location services reduce latency by placing servers in the same physical location as an exchange's servers or as close to an exchange's servers as possible. This achieves two things - minimal physical distance for data to travel and the shortest possible path for the data.

To help visualize this, consider you have to deliver a letter to your neighbor. In terms of distance, clearly, delivering a letter to your next-door neighbor (co-located) is quicker than delivering it to a friend who lives across town.

First, by minimizing the physical distance, the transmission speed is increased since the data transmission is highly dependent on the speed of light. It's the same reason why talking with someone face to face (assuming no awkward pauses) tends to be quicker than over a phone call. Even though the conversation's content might be the same, the distance the sound (in case of a face-to-face chat) or the signal (in case of a phone call) needs to travel is different.

Secondly, by ensuring the shortest path, potential interference is reduced, as well as reducing the amount of hardware the data travels through. Each piece of hardware introduces delays, be these routers, switches, firewalls, etc. It's like taking a direct flight (co-located) versus a connecting flight (non-co-located). Even if you can fly at the same speed, the layover (hardware) at the connecting airport would add extra time.

However, it is important to note that while co-location can significantly reduce latency, it can be pricey. Smaller trading firms may not be able to afford these services, and there may also be ethical and fairness debates around the practice, especially in the field of high-frequency trading.

6.20 Discuss the concept of "latency arbitrage" and its implications.

Latency arbitrage is a high-frequency trading strategy that exploits the delay in the price feed provided by trading exchanges. It's like a cheetah exploiting its fast speed to capture an antelope: the cheetah represents the high-frequency trader with fast access to market information, while the antelope represents the slower trader trying to spot an opportunity.

To illustrate by mathematical notation, suppose that the true universal price of a stock at time t is $P(t)$. However, due to latency (i.e., delay), some market participants see the delayed price $P(t - \tau)$, where $\tau > 0$. Therefore, if $P(t) > P(t - \tau)$, a trader with access to the real-time price $P(t)$ can buy the stock at the delayed lower price $P(t - \tau)$ and expect to sell it at a higher price, making a profit.

The phenomenon is hence named "latency arbitrage" and is initiated by high-frequency traders (HFTs) who have invested heavily in technology to reduce latency to near zero.

In terms of its implications, latency arbitrage is highly controversial. While it greatly incentivizes technologically driven trading firms to invest in faster connections and infrastructures (which can improve overall market efficiency), it can also exacerbate market volatility and inequity.

Market volatility can occur as HFTs react to new information faster than their slower counterparts, executing aggressive trades that could potentially trigger rapid price changes. Moreover, the inequity issue arises because not every participant can afford the cost of reducing latency, thus creating an uneven playing field where the fastest players can consistently beat the slower ones.

Additionally, latency arbitrage can erode market liquidity. It can disincentivize market-making (where traders typically earn a spread between buying and selling prices) because HFTs can trade against these orders before prices update, and their profits would come directly at the expense of these liquidity providers. This depletion in turn could affect price discovery and market functionality.

So, while latency arbitrage is a natural outcome of technological advancement in trading, it merits careful regulation and consideration to mitigate its potential negative implications on the financial markets.

Chapter 7

Machine Learning in Algorithmic Trading

7.1 How has machine learning been integrated into modern trading strategies?

Machine learning (ML) has opened a lot of possibilities in the field of algorithmic trading. Particularly, it has enabled modern trading strategies to adapt and improve over time. Let's have a closer look into how this is happening.

1. **Prediction models:** These are the most obvious application of ML in trading. Prediction models are used to forecast prices, demand, volumes, etc. For instance, neural networks, a subset of ML, is used extensively for predicting future prices. These models are trained using a large dataset of historical prices. It's rather like using past weather patterns to predict tomorrow's weather.

2. **Signal generation:** ML algorithms can effectively dissect large sets of data to identify trading signals. These signals are cues to buy or sell. For instance, many algorithmic traders apply ML algorithms like Support Vector Machines (SVM) to generate investment signals.

3. **Portfolio Optimization:** ML's ability to handle multivariate problems serves as a boon in managing and optimizing portfolios. Covariance, returns and risks across an array of securities need to be balanced and ML can tackle these problems effectively. So, if you think of your investment portfolio as a meal, machine learning helps you combine ingredients to get the maximum flavor (returns) while minimizing unwanted effects like indigestion (risk).

4. **High-frequency trading (HFT):** High-frequency trading, where buy/sell orders are placed and processed within microseconds, leverages ML in multiple ways. Mainly, it uses ML for short term price predictions and order routing. It's as if ML is playing speed chess on behalf of the trader, making rapid decisions in response to the moves of the market.

5. **News scraping and sentiment analysis:** In trading, it's important to keep track of financial news. ML allows scanning the news, blogs, and forums, processing it to identify sentiments in the market. Like a seasoned politician reading a room, ML algorithms can sense dominant mood (bullish, bearish) in market chatter.

6. **Prevention of overfitting:** Overfitting, a common problem in algorithmic trading, arises when a model captures noise along with underlying pattern in data. It's like memorizing answers to specific questions for an exam instead of understanding the whole subject. ML techniques like Regularization, Cross-validation, and Dropout (in case of neural networks), help to combat overfitting in algo-trading models.

In addition to these, techniques such as reinforcement learning, where an agent learns to behave in an environment by performing actions and observing the results, are being used for dynamic allocation and portfolio management.

In conclusion, using ML in algorithmic trading is like having an extra pair of very powerful eyes that can see patterns, trends and signals which were earlier invisible or too complex to be spotted. It's not that traders cannot analyze data or generate signals, it's that machine learning algorithms can do it quicker, more effectively, and on a much broader scale.

7.2   What are the potential advantages of using machine learning over traditional algorithmic strategies?

Machine learning (ML), a subset of artificial intelligence, plays an instrumental role in algorithmic trading and has distinct advantages over traditional algorithmic strategies.

1. **Model Complexity:** Trading markets are complex, non-linear and frequently changing their behaviour. Traditional strategies often use assumptions which simplify the reality beyond recognition. On the other hand, ML algorithms are built by learning from the data and hence can automatically adapt to such complexity and non-linearity. If we compare this to cooking, the traditional methods are like having a static recipe without the ability to adjust to the taste preference of the individual, the availability of ingredients or the cooking conditions. Machine Learning, on the other hand, acts more like a seasoned chef, who tastes the dish, adjusts the recipe, checks the available ingredients, and even adapts to the equipment at hand.

2. **Adaptability:** Traditional algorithms are static; they do exactly what we tell them to do and they lack the ability to adjust to new trends or changing market conditions. In the other hand, ML models can continuously learn from the new data and auto-adjust to new trends. In terms of our cooking story, it's like our chef constantly trying new recipes, learning from customers' feedback, and improving his dishes over time.

3. **Feature Discovery:** ML can automatically identify and use a large number of features which can predict the trading signal. While in traditional trading strategies, feature design is manual and time-consuming. To relate this to a different kind of example, imagine you're trying to predict the weather. Traditionally, you'd have to identify relevant factors like humidity, wind speed, temperature, etc., yourself. But with ML, you can feed in all the information you have, and it can figure out what's important.

4. **Risk Management:** ML can model intricate dependencies and correlations between different assets, market indicators and macro-economic variables, which can make risk control and portfolio management more efficient than using traditional strategies.

5. **Noise Handling:** Markets are often subject to random fluctuations or 'noise'. ML algorithms, especially those based on deep learning, can handle and reduce the effect of noisy data, leading to better accuracy. Picture trying to have a conversation in a crowded, noisy room. Machine learning is like having a sophisticated, noise-cancelling headphone, able to separate the signal (your desired conversation) from the noise (all the other conversations buzzing around).

6. **Efficiency:** Once a ML model is trained, it can process data and make trading decisions in milliseconds, which is a distinct advantage in high-frequency trading where speed matters.

Remember, it's not all roses and rainbows. While the potential of ML in trading is huge, we also need to be aware of its limitations and problems such as overfitting, lack of transparency in decision making (also termed as black-box problem), and the substantial computational power ML models demand. It's important to have these in consideration when building a trading system.

7.3 How do you handle the risk of overfitting with machine learning models in trading?

Overfitting is indeed a crucial concern when using machine learning models in algorithmic trading. When a model is overfitted, it works well with the training data but fails to generalize well to unseen data. In the context of algorithmic trading, this means the model could perform poorly with real market data and potentially lead to financial losses. It's akin to acing performance rehearsals but stumbling during the live concert.

Here are some strategies to handle overfitting:

1. **Splitting Your Dataset**: The first essential step is to divide your data into training, validation, and test sets. The model learns from the training set, the validation set fine-tunes the model parameters, and the test set evaluates the model's performance on unseen data. Picture this as a student learning from textbooks (training), practicing with a study guide (validation), and finally taking the actual exam (testing).

2. **Cross-Validation**: In cross-validation, the data is split into 'k' number of subsets or 'folds'. Imagine a pie cut into several pieces. The model is then trained on 'k-1' folds while one fold is held back for validation. This process is repeated 'k' times for each fold serving as the validation set once. Making use of all available data for training and validation makes the model better equipped to perform on unseen data.

3. **Regularization**: You can apply penalizing complex models using methods like Lasso or Ridge, which add a cost to the loss function for overly complex models. These methods act as a 'straitjacket' that prevent your models from 'jumping the guns' and fitting the data too well.

4. **Early Stopping**: In this method, training is halted as soon as

the validation error starts increasing (after initially decreasing), i.e., the model's learning plateaus. It's like stopping the practice once the player's performance starts to decline, to prevent injuries due to overtraining.

5. **Ensembling**: Ensembling involves combining predictions from multiple models to give the final prediction. This can reduce error variance and help protect against overfitting. Think of it as seeking advice from multiple experts rather than relying on a single opinion.

6. **Reducing Model Complexity**: Simpler models are less prone to overfitting. Starting with a simpler model prevents the learning algorithm from capturing the noise along with the underlying pattern in the data. In trading, it could mean preferring linear models over high-degree polynomial models.

7. **Data Augmentation**: This involves creating new synthetic data points, which aids in making the model more robust and generalizable to unseen data. A trivial example can be mirror flipping an image in computer vision. In trading, time series augmentation techniques can be used.

Remember, an overfitted model resembles an over-zealous student memorizing the questions instead of understanding concepts. Just like a good teacher uses diverse teaching methods, we use the above strategies to prevent our trading models from overfitting.

7.4   Discuss the importance of data pre-processing and cleaning in ML-based trading.

In the world of machine learning for algorithmic trading, data preprocessing and cleaning is often deemed as a crucial initial step. It is akin to a chef preparing ingredients for a gourmet meal. If you start with poor quality, uncleaned ingredients, the final dish will likely leave a lot to be desired.

The same applies to ML-based trading algorithms. Regardless of how sophisticated or well-designed your models might be, they'll likely perform poorly if the initial dataset is riddled with errors, inconsistencies or irrelevant information.

The primary aim of data preprocessing and cleaning is to create a 'clean' dataset by addressing a myriad of problems which include:

1. **Noise:** In real-world data, noise is common and it may negatively affect the learning process leading to less accurate results. Noise is sort of like 'static' on a phone call which makes it harder for you to understand what the person on the other side is saying. In the same way, noise in your dataset can make your machine learning algorithm less accurate.

2. **Missing Data:** Incomplete datasets are problematic because missing entries can dramatically skew your models. It's equivalent to trying to complete a puzzle with missing pieces – the final picture just won't come together correctly without filling in the gaps.

3. **Outliers:** Outliers are extreme values that can heavily impact the learning process of an algorithm and often result in less accurate, skewed results. Think of outliers as rogue elements that disrupt the harmony and balance of your ML model, akin to the way a disruptive student might throw off the balance of a well-running classroom.

4. **Irrelevant information:** When you've got irrelevant features in your dataset, it can throw off your model and reduce your model's performance. It's like having irrelevant ingredients when you're cooking a dish. Even if it's a really great ingredient, if it doesn't go with the dish you're making, it's just going to spoil the flavor.

With data preprocessing, we address these issues through a variety of techniques like noise filtering, data imputation for addressing missing values, outlier detection and removal, and feature selection for weeding out irrelevant information.

In trading, failure to address these issues could lead to inaccurate predictions about market trends leading to unnecessary financial risks. Thus, data preprocessing is a vital prerequisite phase to building effective ML-based trading systems.

Remember, your algorithm – be it a Deep Neural Network, Support Vector Machine, or a simple Linear Regression model – is only as good as the data you feed it with. Just like you can't prepare a gourmet dish with spoiled ingredients, you can't expect high-quality results from messy and incorrect data.

7.5   How do you evaluate the performance of a machine learning trading model?

Evaluating the performance of a machine learning trading model is similar to checking the health of a competitive athlete. Just as a coach would monitor different aspects of an athlete's performance, we need to check different metrics for our trading model.

Some common methods and metrics used to evaluate machine learning models in trading (our "athletes") include:

1. Sharpe Ratio: Like a coach checking an athlete's speed-to-strength ratio, the Sharpe Ratio measures the performance of an investment compared to a risk-free asset, after adjusting for its risk. It's the average return earned in addition to the risk-free rate per unit of volatility or total risk. The formula is:

$$SR = \frac{R_p - R_f}{\sigma_p}$$

where R_p is the asset return, R_f is the risk-free return, and σ_p is the standard deviation of the asset excess return. Higher Sharpe ratios are better, as they indicate a better risk-adjusted return.

2. Sortino Ratio: Think of this like examining an athlete's performance on uneven terrain. The Sortino Ratio is like the Sharpe ratio, but it only considers harmful volatility. This is important in trading contexts where downside volatility is considered more harmful.

3. Maximum Drawdown (MDD): MDD is like checking how long an athlete takes to recover after a fall. It measures the largest fall in asset value over a specified period. Traders wish to minimize this value as much as possible.

4. Area Under the Curve (AUC): An excellent machine learning model has AUC near the 1 which means it has good measure of separability. A horrible model has AUC near the 0 which means it has worst measure of separability and it means it is reciprocating the result. It is predicting 0s as 1s and 1s as 0s. And when AUC is 0.5, it means model has no class separation capacity whatsoever.

5. Precision, Recall & F1 Score: These three metrics are commonly used to evaluate the correctness of a classification model, which is common in predicting market movements (up or down). Precision measures the accuracy of positive predictions. Recall measures the ratio of correctly predicted positive observations to all the observations in the actual class. F1 Score is the weighted average of Precision and Recall.

Remember, just as with athletes, no single measurement can encapsulate all the strengths and weaknesses of a trading model. Each provides a different perspective, and they should be used in conjunction to get a comprehensive understanding of model performance. Also, it might be more beneficial to focus on the metrics that are the most relevant to the specific trading strategy and risk tolerance.

7.6   Why is feature engineering crucial in machine learning for trading?

Feature engineering is an integral part of machine learning in trading for several reasons, which can best be understood using a grocery shopping analogy.

Let's say you are going to a grocery store to buy the most delicious ingredients for a meal. In machine learning, these ingredients are your features, and the meal represents the outcome or the prediction.

You may find that certain kinds of ingredients make your meal taste better. Similarly, in machine learning for algorithmic trading, certain features can provide more valuable information to the algorithm, and identifying these important features is what we call feature engineering.

The process of feature engineering can involve creating new features from existing ones, selecting the most relevant features, and preparing (e.g., scaling, normalizing) data for the algorithm.

Perhaps you realize that the freshness of the ingredients matter, so every time you are at the grocery store, you check every ingredient for its freshness (creating new features). Perhaps you realize that the dessert you used to buy is not as important as the main meal, so you only focus on the ingredients for the main meal (selecting important features). Or maybe, you have a better idea of how much of each ingredient you need, no matter the size of the meal, so you normalize the quantities (scaling and normalization).

Here are a few reasons why feature engineering is crucial:

1. **Improvement of Algorithm Performance**: As in our analogy, the choice of the right ingredients can drastically enhance the taste of your meal. Similarly, the right set of features can substantially improve your algorithm's performance in predicting stock prices or trading signals.

2. **Algorithm Efficiency**: If you clutter your shopping list with unnecessary items, it will take you longer to buy everything and cost more. Similarly, irrelevant features will slow down the learning process of the algorithm and consume more computational resources. By keeping only the most relevant features, feature engineering improves the efficiency of your algorithm.

3. **Generalization and Overfitting**: If you only learn to cook specific meals with specific ingredients (say, dessert with lots of sugar), that doesn't mean your cooking overall is great. You might struggle with healthier recipes. Similarly, an algorithm trained with redundant features may not generalize well and may perform poorly with new, unseen data (this is known as overfitting). Feature engineering aids in creating robust models that generalize well by screening out noise and irrelevant details.

Thus, feature engineering plays a vital role in machine learning for algorithmic trading by improving the predictive power, efficiency, and robustness of the trading algorithms.

7.7 How would you create features that capture market momentum or volatility?

Creating features that capture market momentum and volatility is a critical task in applying machine learning to algorithmic trading. Let's talk about these two concepts: "momentum" and "volatility", and then dive into the process of creating features capturing them.

"Momentum" in markets is similar to the momentum in physics. Imagine you're rolling a ball down a hill - once it starts going, it keeps going in the direction down the hill until it's interrupted by an external force. Market momentum operates in a similar manner, it tends to persist in its current direction. Capturing this information could help predictive models to determine if prices will swing upwards or downwards in the future.

"Volatility", on the other hand, is a measure of how much the price of an asset moves in a given set of returns. Think of it as turbulence in an airplane; the erratic shaking can't tell you in which direction the plane will move, but it does indicate the intensity of the movement. Volatility is crucial in risk management and is often used in algorithmic trading to identify periods of fiscal stress.

Now, how to generate features to capture these?

1. To capture **momentum**, we might consider **moving averages**, **price rate of change**, or more complex indicators like the **Relative Strength Index (RSI)**. Moving averages can be calculated by taking the average of the asset price over a specific number of days (e.g., the 10-day moving average). Price Rate of Change is a straightforward indicator calculated as $\frac{P(t)-P(t-n)}{P(t-n)}$ where 'P(t)' is the price at time 't' and 'P(t-n)' is the price 'n' periods ago. RSI is a bit more complex, leveraging previous gains and losses to identify if an asset is 'overbought' or 'oversold'.

2. Capturing **volatility** often involves generating features like **standard deviation of returns**, **Average True Range (ATR)**, or **Bollinger Bands**.

- The standard deviation of returns is a simple and effective measure of volatility. The larger this value, the more the returns tend to differ from their average, which indicates higher volatility.

- ATR is an indicator that measures market volatility by decomposing the entire range of an asset price for a period.

- Bollinger Bands are made up of three lines, with the middle line being the simple moving average and the outer lines being a certain number of standard deviations away from this moving average. The width of these bands can provide a measure of market volatility.

These are just examples of many potential features to capture momentum and volatility. In general, feature engineering in algorithmic trading involves a lot of creativity, domain knowledge, and experi-

mentation. Remember that different algorithms might respond optimally to different features, so it's a good idea to have a diverse set of
features at hand.

Remember, also, machine learning in trading like a journey: sometimes it will feel like you're cruising down freeways, and sometimes
it will feel like you're stuck in traffic. But with each step and new
feature you create, you will get closer to your destination. Happy
travelling!

7.8 Discuss the importance of normaliza-
tion and scaling in feature engineering.

Feature engineering in Machine Learning (ML) is as much an art as
it is a science, especially in the context of algorithmic trading. One
vital aspect of feature engineering is the practice of normalization and
scaling. Now, you might wonder why that is so crucial. Let's dissect
these two aspects further.

Normalization

Normalization is like teaching a multilingual crowd, where each individual speaks a different language (consider each language as a different scale), a common language (common scale) for effective communication.

In an ML model, each feature could be interpreted as an individual
speaking a different language - they could represent different ranges
of quantitative values such as price, volume, etc. To comprehend
these data points effectively, we normalize them, bringing them all to
a common scale range.

In mathematical terms, normalization typically means adjusting values measured on different scales to a common scale, often in the range

-1 to 1 or 0 to 1.

Normalization ensures that each feature contributes approximately proportionately to the final prediction, and one feature does not dominate the others just because of its scale.

For example, if you are trying to predict the price movement of a stock by looking at the average price and volume of the trades, the average price might be in hundreds or thousands, but the volume of the trades will be much larger. Normalization ensures these features contribute proportionately to the final prediction.

Scaling

Analogously, scaling is like converting temperature readings from Fahrenheit to Celsius. Even though the two different scales measure the same underlying principle (temperature), they do so with different starting points and increments.

Scaling modifies the range of data but not the distribution. Typical scaling includes min-max normalization (bringing data to range between 0 and 1), Z-score standardization (mean of 0 and standard deviation of 1), and Yeo-Johnson transformation (handling both positive and negative values while stabilizing variance and normalizing the distribution).

In the case of algorithmic trading, scaling is vital to create meaningful features for ML models that can handle the variations in the market data and can interpret these features sensibly.

For instance, if your model takes as input the price of the asset, the price could range from a few dollars to several thousand dollars. But, a price change from 50 to 51 might be much more significant for a $50 stock than for a $1,000 stock. Scaling addresses this issue by converting these different scales into something more digestible and comparable for ML models.

So, normalization and scaling play a crucial role in crafting meaningful and interpretable input to our ML models in algorithmic trading.

They are the organizers at our multilingual event and the translators in our conversation - ensuring that every piece of necessary information gets its due consideration.

7.9 How do you handle multicollinearity in your features?

Multicollinearity refers to the predicament in which two or more features in your machine learning data are highly correlated with each other. It can introduce redundancy into the model, impairing the precision of the estimation and interpreting the individual predictive importance of the features.

In the context of algorithmic trading, let's say you have included both the indices S&P 500 and NASDAQ composite in your model. Since these two market indices are highly correlated, it might be a case of multicollinearity.

Handling multicollinearity often requires careful feature selection. Here are some common ways used to mitigate multicollinearity:

1. **Variance Inflation Factor (VIF):** VIF quantifies how much the variance is inflated due to multicollinearity. A VIF higher than a certain threshold (often 5 or 10) implies severe multicollinearity. You can remove the feature with the highest VIF and re-evaluate until all features have a VIF under the threshold.

2. **Correlation Matrix:** Visualizing a correlation matrix can help you spot highly correlated features. From this, one can manually select features to keep or discard.

3. **Principal Component Analysis (PCA):** You could use PCA to reduce the dimensionality of your feature set. This technique creates principal components which are linear combinations of your features that capture the most variance in your data, effectively reducing multicollinearity. However, these components can be harder to interpret

compared to the original features.

4. **Regularization Techniques:** Techniques like Ridge and Lasso regression add a penalty term to the loss function, shrinking the coefficients towards zero which can reduce the impact of correlated variables.

In the analogy of baking a cake, multicollinearity is like adding two cups of sugar when the recipe calls for one. While sugar makes the cake sweet, adding too much can ruin the taste. Similarly, while each feature in a model can offer valuable insights, including highly correlated features can reduce the model's performance. Thus, like carefully selecting ingredients for a cake, one must carefully select the features for the model.

7.10   Can you give examples of derived features that might be useful for predicting stock prices?

In the context of algorithmic trading, we'd leverage Machine Learning not to directly predict the price (as stock price prediction is largely an inefficient endeavour due to market efficiency), but rather to predict the probability of a future event - such as an increase or decrease in the price.

When it comes to using Machine Learning in algorithmic trading, we are dealing with a time series problem. Therefore, feature derivation becomes a crucial task because the machine learning model's performance highly depends on the predictive power of the features.

Here are some examples of derived features that could be used:

1. **Lagged Values:** These are historical data values that can be used as inputs to predict future events. For example, if we're trying to predict tomorrow's price, we might include the price and volume

data for the last N-days as features.

2. **Moving Averages:** This includes indicators like SMA (Simple Moving Average), EMA (Exponential Moving Average) or Weighted Moving averages. Moving averages can be used to capture the underlying trend in a time series. For instance, if the current price is above its moving averages, it might indicate an uptrend.

For example, consider moving averages are like a road leading you to a mountain (the mountain being an increase or decrease in price). The moving averages would be like your map, showing you the general direction to go.

3. **Price Rate of Change** (ROC): It measures the percent change in price from one period to another. The ROC grows more positive as the price continues to grow and vice versa.

4. **Volatility Measures:** Indicators such as Bollinger bandwidth, Average True Range (ATR) or historical standard deviation measure the amount of uncertainty or risk about the size of changes in a security's value. A higher volatility means that a security's value can potentially be spread out over a large range of values.

Volatility is similar to the weather forecast, you'd have thresholds to indicate calm or stormy weather, and it can affect your decision to go outside or not. Similarly, higher volatility means the stock price can potentially have a large range of values, influencing your decision to trade or not.

5. **Relative Strength Index (RSI):** It is a measure of momentum that identifies overbought or oversold conditions in a market. Values of 70 or above indicate that a security is becoming overbought or overvalued and may be primed for a trend reversal or corrective price pullback. An RSI reading of 30 or below indicates an oversold or undervalued condition.

Remember, we might not build predictive models on these features directly. Instead, these might be useful inputs to machine learning models that also consider many other types of features, like macroeconomic indicators, sentiment data from news and social media, or even fundamental and sector-specific indicators for individual stocks.

Remember, machine learning models can be black box and might be hard to interpolate. Therefore, each of these features should be chosen carefully and added to the model logically and intentionally.

7.11 How do decision trees and random forests differ in their application to trading?

Decision trees and random forests are both machine learning methodologies that can be employed in algorithmic trading. However, they differ in several ways. First, let's briefly define what each one is:

- A decision tree is a flowchart-like structure in which each internal node represents a feature (or attribute), each branch represents a decision rule, and each leaf node represents an outcome. It's a bit like playing a game of "20 Questions" to predict the outcomes.

- A random forest, on the other hand, is a ensemble learning method that operates by constructing multiple decision trees during training and outputting the class that is the mode of the classes (classification) or mean prediction (regression) of the individual trees. It is as if you assemble a diverse panel of experts (each tree being one "expert") and each one votes to decide the outcome.

Now, let's talk about how these two methods diverge in trading:

Accuracy & Overfitting: Random forests tend to hold an edge when it comes to prediction accuracy. Simple decision trees are highly susceptible to overfitting the data, especially if the tree is allowed to grow to an unregulated depth. To use an analogy, a decision tree might be akin to a trader who uses a very specific and rigid set of rules to decide when to buy or sell, which might work exceptionally well with historical data but fail in the real market due to overfitting. A random forest, with its multitude of decision trees, works like a team of traders who add a layer of statistical robustness to the decision-making process, thereby reducing the risk of overfitting.

Interpretability & Complexity: On the flip side, decision trees are generally easier to interpret. You can visually inspect the tree (especially if it's small) to understand the decision process, much like a flow chart. This is akin to a trader being able to explain the rationale behind every single one of his trades. Random forests, however, are much harder to decipher because of the multitude of decision trees it contains. This makes it harder to explain the reasoning behind each trade, as the final decision is derived from numerous smaller decisions made by individual trees.

Noise tolerance: Random forests typically perform better with noisy data because they take into account the voting from multiple trees. This is like having a panel of experts where even if a few make a poor decision due to a noisy signal, the overall consensus may still be accurate.

Feature importance: Both methods can determine the importance of features (or factors influencing trades). However, random forests provide a more robust measure as they account for interactions between features across numerous trees. It's like having multiple traders assess the importance of various signals, thereby providing a more comprehensive view.

In conclusion, both decision trees and random forests have their role in algorithmic trading. The choice often comes down to the specific scenario: the resources available (data, compute), the complexity of the problem, the level of interpretability desired, and the trade-off between bias and variance one is willing to tolerate.

7.12   What are the potential advantages of using neural networks in trading strategies?

Neural Networks, a key foundation for modern machine learning, have recently found profound applications in algorithmic trading. Here's why they can be particularly beneficial:

1. **Predictive Capability**: Neural networks are like the weather forecasting systems of algorithmic trading. Once they "learn" from historical data, they excel at predicting future outcomes, such as predicting potential market movements based on patterns observed in past and present data. This is akin to predicting a rainfall based on the current humidity and patterns seen in the past.

2. **Non-Linear Complex Models**: Financial markets are complex and often don't follow a linear pattern. The beauty of neural networks is that they can deal with non-linearity and model complex functions effectively. Imagine trying to manually assemble a 10,000-piece 3D puzzle. This is similar to a human trying to construct a profitable trading algorithm by incorporating all possible market factors, which is practically overwhelming. A neural network, on the other hand, can deal with such a large number of dimensions efficiently.

3. **Adaptability**: Neural networks can improve their performance through continual learning and adapting to new data trends. In essence, they are like a kind of 'trading chameleon', able to evolve its color (model parameters) to match the changing landscape (market conditions).

4. **Noise Filtering**: They excel at ignoring "noise" and focusing on key patterns. This might be comparable to a detective hunting for clues, able to discard irrelevant information and highlight the critical evidence leading to the "crime" (price action).

However, it's important to note the caveats. Neural networks require extensive computational resources and data for training. They are also susceptible to overfitting and can mistake noise for signals if not properly optimized. Understanding the statistical and mathematical basis, as well as the structure and nuances of the financial markets are vital to using neural networks successfully in algorithmic trading.

7.13   How do you handle the interpretability challenges with complex models like neural networks?

Interpretability is indeed an important aspect when it comes to using machine learning models in Algorithmic Trading. While complex models like neural networks can help in building more accurate and powerful prediction systems, they are famously known as 'black boxes' due to their lack of interpretability.

Handling the interpretability challenge with such models involves a balance between performance and transparency. It's similar to trying to pick your favourite dessert at a buffet where you can only have one. The delicious and exotic unknown dessert (complex ML models like neural networks) might be enticing, but the familiar taste of chocolate cake (simple models) is something reliable and you know what to expect from it. Well, one solution to this buffet dilemma would be - why can't you understand what's in the exotic dessert and possibly enhance your cake with it?

One method for achieving this balance is called Model-Agnostic Interpretation. Here, regardless of the complexity of the machine learning model, we use sophisticated analysis tools to figure out how the inputs relate to the outputs. It's like listing all the ingredients of the complex exotic dessert along with the recipe and then using that information to enhance your familiar dessert - the information isn't perfect, you might not be aware of how to process certain unique ingredients or the effects of them on human taste buds, but the information gives you a credible starting point.

There are numerous techniques in this category, such as Partial Dependence Plots (PDPs), Accumulated Local Effects (ALE), and Individual Conditional Expectation (ICE) plots, that can help us understand the model behavior over its inputs.

Another popular method is the use of SHapley Additive exPlanationS (SHAP). SHAP connects game theory with local explanations and unifies several previous methods and represents the only possible consistent and locally accurate additive feature attribution method based on expectations (the SHAP value). It is equivalent to having a game where each feature value of your model is a "player", they cooperate to predict the output, and the "payout" (the prediction) is distributed among these players depending on their contribution to the victory of the game (the prediction).

Model-specific interpretation methods are also available if you are working with Neural Networks. Techniques like saliency maps, activation maximization, and class activation maps can help in attaining insights about the model behavior.

Remember, the goal of interpretability is not always to fully understand every aspect of the complex model, but rather to gain enough insights to trust the model's decision, measure the model's uncertainty, or have an idea of the model's limitations - to know if the exotic dessert is worth tasting. When we can't get a simple explanation for the model, the validation of its performance and robustness becomes even more crucial. This is done by analyzing the model's generalization error and performance over out-of-sample data.

In conclusion, just like understanding recipes, achieving model interpretability, especially in complex models, never comes in a one-size-fits-all manner. Depending on the specific application, practitioners may find one or the combination of methods mentioned above helpful in their quest for interpretability.

7.14 How can ensemble methods be beneficial in trading predictions?

Ensemble methods in machine learning can provide significant benefit in algorithmic trading predictions. One way you can think of ensemble methods is that they are like the advice you might get from a committee, instead of relying on only one expert for making decisions, we collect different perspectives and make more enlightened decisions.

Let's discuss it with a bit of mathematical formalism. Given a trading model, let's denote y as the true trading signal and $f(x)$ as the prediction from a single model trained on features, x. We aim to minimize the expected prediction error $E[(y - f(x))^2]$. In ideal case, when we have infinite access to data and compute power, a single model trained on all possible features can be perfect. However, in reality, our model is often biased or variance due to insufficient data or biased sampling.

This is where ensemble methods come into play. The basic idea is to build several different models, $f_1(x), f_2(x), ..., f_n(x)$, and aggregate their predictions. The final prediction will be the average (in the case of regression) or majority voting (in the case of classification) of individual predictions:

$$f_{ensemble}(x) = \frac{1}{n} \sum_{i=1}^{n} f_i(x).$$

The aggregation of models can increase the robustness and stability of the predictions, decrease the generalization error, and tackle the overfitting problem that a single model might face.

There are various ways to generate an ensemble of models, including:

- Bagging: such as Random Forests, it helps in reducing the variance error.

- Boosting: such as <i>AdaBoost</i> or <i>Gradient Boosting</i>, it helps in reducing bias error and building strong predictive models.

- Stacking: where predictions of several models are used as features for a 'meta-learner', improving overall performance.

In the context of trading, an ensemble of models can imbibe different features, such as technical indicators, fundamental analysis data, sentiment analysis, macroeconomic factors etc., allow the model to capture the complex and nonlinear relationship in the market and make more accurate trading predictions.

One key note: while ensemble methods are powerful, they have the potential to be much more computationally expensive, and they can also be prone to overfitting if not used with appropriate caution. The key to applying them successfully is a robust method for validating and tuning these models which often involves careful cross-validation and regularized training procedures.

7.15   What are the challenges in using deep learning models for trading?

Using deep learning models for trading comes with several unique challenges:

1. **Data Availability and Quality**: Theoretical finance assumes stock markets are efficient, and this means that all useful information is already reflected in the prices. This makes it hard to find reliable, clean data that holds exploitable patterns. Another issue is data granularity; a fresh stream of minute-by-minute price for many years is much harder to handle than end-of-day prices.

2. **Overfitting**: Overfitting is a major problem in machine learning, and it's especially critical in financial applications where the cost of a false prediction can be very high. It's like building a robot to pick a perfect apple from a tree, based on thousands of previous examples. If the robot is overly-optimized in the training field and has only ex-

perienced perfectly ripe apples, if a less ripe apple appears, the robot might discard it because it doesn't match the overly-specific pattern in its training data.

3. **Noise vs. Signal Ratio**: Financial markets have a high level of randomness (noise), and the actual signal we're trying to extract is often very tiny. Imagine yourself in a rock concert trying to hear a whisper from across the room. This is the amount of noise one needs to filter out to get the desired signals in financial markets.

4. **Non-Stationarity**: Financial markets evolve and change. This is similar to predicting the weather. You could be using last year's data the predict the weather tomorrow, and it works sometimes, but it's surely not a reliable method since weather patterns change and evolve. The algorithms must be able to adapt to new, unseen market conditions and this is a significant inherent challenge when using deep learning.

5. **Interpretability**: Complex models like deep learning offer valuable predictions but offer little understanding on why the prediction was made. This is like having a cook who can make an exquisite dish but can't share the recipe. Financial institutions like to understand the decision making process to further improve trading models and answer to regulatory demands.

6. **Delayed Rewards**: In trading, an action now might result in a reward or punishment much later. This is akin to planting a seed and waiting for it to fruit. Most deep learning models work on immediate reward/punishment feedback.

In conclusion, while deep learning offers a promising avenue for algorithmic trading, navigating the challenges necessitates careful and thorough application of data science and machine learning principles. It's like crossing a river full of crocodiles, one must carefully plan each step, but the rewards on the other side could be well worth the perilous journey.

7.16 Describe the basic premise of reinforcement learning in the context of trading.

Reinforcement Learning (RL) is a type of machine learning that's quite fascinating - it's a bit like training a dog. You want your dog (the trading model, in this case) to learn specific behaviors (trades); when the dog does something good (makes a profitable trade), it gets a treat (positive reward). If the dog does something not so good (e.g., makes a losing trade), it might get a mild reprimand (negative reward). Over time, guided by this system of rewards and punishments, the dog (the model) learns to do more of the stuff that earns treats (profitable trades) and less of what earns reprimands (losing trades).

To translate this into more technical language, RL models have an agent (the "dog"), a set of states (the market conditions), actions (trading decisions) it can take, and rewards (profits or losses based on its trading decisions). The model's goal is to learn a policy – a guide for choosing actions based on states – that maximizes the sum of rewards over time.

The secret sauce in RL is exploration-vs-exploitation. Sometimes, the agent needs to explore by taking random actions, to learn about the consequences of different actions in different states (this is like letting your dog sniff around a new park). But other times, the agent needs to exploit what it already knows in order to "cash in" on its knowledge and get rewards (like a trained dog performing tricks it knows well).

In trading, RL can be used for tasks like optimizing the execution of large trading orders over time (to minimize market impact), deciding when to buy/sell/hold financial instruments, or allocating assets in a portfolio.

One challenge with RL in trading is that rewards are sparse and time-delayed (profits or losses may not be immediate after action is taken), market conditions are non-stationary (the market's statistical properties can change), and feedback is noisy (price movements have a lot of random 'noise'). Despite these challenges, RL has a lot of potential for algorithmic trading if used carefully and in combination with other tools.

7.17 How do reward structures get defined in reinforcement learning for trading?

In reinforcement learning (RL), reward structures effectively define the end goal of an agent's actions. They provide the "carrot-and-stick" for the agent, motivating it to optimize its actions and strategies.

Let's imagine reinforcement learning as a game of soccer. The player (or our trading algorithm) has an objective: to score a goal (or, in our case, maximize profit). Now, how we define a "goal" is essentially the reward function.

In trading, the simplest reward function might just be the profit or loss made by an algorithm, calculated as the difference in portfolio value between the current and previous steps. This is akin to simply rewarding a soccer player for scoring a goal, and ignoring everything else.

However, a more sophisticated reward system might take into account many different factors. For example, instead of just looking at raw profit and loss, we can adjust these values for risk, mimicking a risk-adjusted performance metric like the Sharpe Ratio. In this case, taking on a larger amount of risk gets you less reward, like a soccer player who only gets full points when hitting the goal from the middle of the field, and fewer points when scoring from close range.

We could also include trading costs in our reward function, which would penalize the agent for making too many trades, similar to a soccer player losing points for more foul plays.

The key feature of defining the reward structure in reinforcement learning, is that it should be defined based on the objectives of the trading strategy and should promote the behavior that gets us closer to that goal.

In essence, coming up with a reward function in reinforcement learning for trading is all about aligning the algorithm's goals with our own. It's the rulebook that our player (the algorithm) follows in the game of soccer (the trading world) to achieve its goal (maximizing returns or any other objective) while playing the game smartly (keeping risk, trading costs and other factors in check).

7.18   What are the challenges in applying reinforcement learning to trading?

Applying Reinforcement Learning (RL) to trading certainly holds immense potential through exploiting its capacity for adaptive decision-making. However, its application poses several substantial challenges that one needs to consider carefully.

1) **Imperfect Information and Noisy Data**: Unlike a game of chess, where all of the pieces and their positions are visible, financial markets are more akin to a game of poker, where there's incomplete information and bluffing. RL models function best in environments with clear and immediate feedback mechanisms. However, in finance, your losses today might not mean your strategy is wrong; it might just be a bad day. This scenario is akin to an RL model being punished for taking a step in the right direction but stepping on a proverbial banana peel. There's too much noise in financial data.

2) **Non-Stationarity**: Markets are ever-evolving due to a myriad of factors such as policy changes, economic events, and shifting investor sentiments. This characteristic makes them non-stationary, which challenges the fundamental assumption of RL that the environ-

ment is stationary and the probability for each state is independent of time. If you've ever tried to walk on a moving walkway (like those found in airports), you know how disconcerting it can be when the ground beneath keeps shifting. Now, imagine an RL agent trying to learn in a constantly changing environment.

3) **Exploration-Exploitation Dilemma**: This is an age-old problem in reinforcement learning. It's like the question of whether you should eat at your favorite restaurant (exploitation) or try a new place (exploration). In trading, this dilemma translates to whether to keep using a working strategy or to experiment with a novel - and potentially better - strategy. The wrong choice can prove costly.

4) **Feature Selection**: Financial markets are affected by numerous factors, both quantitative (such as interest rates) and qualitative (such as investor sentiment). Selecting appropriate features for model's states and capturing all necessary information is a daunting task. It's like trying to cook a complex dish, but you're unsure which spices to use and in what quantity.

5) **Delay in Rewards**: In reinforcement learning, rewards serve as a learning signal. In trading, often a considerable period may elapse between an action (or set of actions) and the resulting payoff. This delay can confuse the RL agent while it's still learning. Think of it as planting a seed (action) and waiting for it to bear fruit (rewards).

Thus, while reinforcement learning offers exciting possibilities for algorithmic trading, substantial hurdles need to be overcome.

7.19   How does Q-learning apply to trading scenarios?

Q-learning is a model-free reinforcement learning algorithm, which seeks to learn the optimal policy to get an agent from one state to another while maximizing a reward. In terms of the stock market, you can think of the agent as a trader and using a Q-learning algorithm can be a way to automatically determine the most profitable trading strategy.

To spot out the parallelism between trading and Q-learning, we must first define a few contrasting parts. Firstly, the state in a trading environment can be represented by technical indicators like moving averages of certain time periods, MACD, RSI etc. Secondly, the actions here refer to Buy, Sell or Hold (Hold as in not perform any trade). Lastly, the immediate reward function can be the net profit of the performed action, which is simply the difference between the selling price and the buying price.

In trading scenario, Q-Learning starts initializing every action pair (state-action) to 0 and then, as it navigates through the trading data, it begins updating these values (using a formula known as the Bellman Equation) whenever some profit or loss (reward) is encountered for a specific action carried out in the given state. The ultimate objective is to maximize the overall reward. Formally, here is how the update rule looks like in a mathematical form:

$$Q(state, action) \leftarrow (1 - \alpha) \cdot Q(state, action) + \alpha \cdot (reward + \gamma \cdot max_a Q(nextstate, a))$$

Where,

- α is the learning rate,

- γ is the discount factor,

- $Q(state, action)$ is the current estimate of the quality of the trade,

- $reward$ is the profit of the trade,

- $max_a Q(nextstate, a)$ is the estimate of optimal future profit.

Think about it like a cartoon character in a maze full of rewards and penalties. The goal for him is to learn by trying different paths and observing the resulting rewards and penalties, and over time, he forms a map of the most fruitful path. Same way Q-Learning observes the prices and teaches itself what actions to take under which conditions in order to yield maximum long-term profits.

It's important to understand that Q-learning in trading has its restrictions and is no golden ticket to guaranteed profits. Main constraint here is that the trading problem, in reality, can be considered as partially observable which implies that important features such as future dividends, foreign exchange rates and central bank decisions can greatly affect prices, yet they cannot be directly observed. Nevertheless, the goal here is to gain a statistical advantage over random strategies in the long run.

7.20 Discuss the concept of exploration vs. exploitation in reinforcement learning for trading.

In Machine Learning, specifically in the realm of Reinforcement Learning (RL), an important dynamic to consider is that of exploration versus exploitation. Let's imagine you're visiting a new city with a vast variety of restaurants. How do you decide where to eat?

- You could opt to try a different place every time (Exploration), which allows you to gain knowledge about the various options available, but there's a risk involved - you might end up at a less-than-great restaurant.

- You could also find a place you like on your first day and decide to eat there every single time (Exploitation), ensuring a pleasing experience but possibly missing out on potentially even better places.

Reinforcement Learning algorithms face a similar dilemma when learning to trade in the capital markets.

With the restaurant example in mind, let's dive deeper into these two key concept and their interplay in algorithmic trading using RL:

1. **Exploration:** This is the act of trying new strategies or actions to see how they perform. In the context of algorithmic trading, the RL agent may choose to buy, sell, or hold a particular asset to understand the consequences of such an operation. This approach enables the

agent to learn about new potential profitable strategies that might not have been apparent from the beginning. However, it carries the risk of poor performance, similar to ending up at a bad restaurant.

2. **Exploitation:** Here, the RL agent leverages the knowledge it already has to make trades that it believes will yield the highest reward, based on its current understanding. This is equivalent to continually eating at the restaurant you already know and like. The exploitation approach aims at maximizing immediate performance, but it may miss out on long-term possible gains from yet undiscovered, potentially more profitable strategies.

Striking a balance between exploration and exploitation - often referred to as the exploration-exploitation tradeoff - is at the heart of reinforcement learning. Early on in the learning process, more weight is often given to exploration to discover as much about the environment as possible. As time goes by and the agent gradually gains understanding of its environment - in our case, the market and its dynamics - the focus shifts towards exploitation.

In algorithmic trading, this balance is crucial. If an RL agent spends too much time exploring, it could make numerous bad trades, resulting in substantial financial loss. Conversely, if it only exploits known strategies, it may miss out on discovering innovative trading strategies that could yield higher profits.

Sophisticated algorithms and strategies have been developed to manage this exploration-exploitation dilemma, including -greedy, Softmax Exploration, Upper Confidence Bound (UCB), and Thompson Sampling, among others.

In essence, creating an efficient trading bot using RL is somewhat akin to being a savvy tourist - you need to explore different choices to learn more about the environment (i.e., trading strategies), and then exploit your learnt knowledge effectively to enjoy the best outcome, be it good food or high profit.

Chapter 8

Risk Management

8.1 Why is risk management paramount in any trading strategy?

Risk management is absolutely crucial in any trading strategy for the same reason that airbags and seat belts are crucial in cars: they might not make the ride any more enjoyable, but they're absolutely vital in the event of a crash.

In the context of algorithmic trading, "crashes" are losses that can be incurred due to unexpected market events, errors in the algorithm, or even simple bad luck. If a trading strategy doesn't have any risk management practices in place, a single bad event could wipe out all of its profits, or even lead to bankruptcy.

There are three main principles in risk management:

1. **Diversification**: This principle is all about not putting all your eggs in one basket. Imagine you're a farmer with a hundred eggs. If you put all your eggs in one basket and accidentally drop it, you're

out of luck. But if you put your eggs in ten baskets, a single accident won't be as disastrous. In trading, instead of eggs and baskets, we have assets and investment portfolios.

2. **Position Sizing**: This principle is about not betting too much on a single trade. Let's play a game where you have a 51% chance of doubling your money and a 49% chance of losing all of it. If you bet all your money on every game, you're likely to go broke regardless of having an edge. This is because you might lose everything before your edge has time to materialize. In a similar vein, it's key to keep the size of any one trade small enough that it won't substantially hurt your portfolio if it fails.

3. **Stop-Losses**: Imagine you're on a ship and it starts to leak. A prudent sailor would have a plan to stop the water flooding in before it sinks the ship. In a similar way, a stop-loss order is designed to cap your losses at a pre-determined level should a trade doesn't go as planned.

In sum, proper risk management lets you live to fight another day in the market and play the game in the long term. Trading without risk management in place is like trying to drive a car without a seatbelt - not a good idea.

8.2   How can algorithms be designed to adapt to changing market volatilities?

Indeed, changing market volatilities are one of the biggest challenges to algorithmic trading. In essence, volatility refers to the degree of variation of a financial instrument's trading price. To understand it, imagine you are on a roller coaster and the weather keeps changing - sometimes it's calm and sunny, other times it's stormy with lots of winds. The goal for your trading algorithms, in this case, is to keep the ride as smooth as possible no matter the weather.

One commonly adopted approach to adapt to changing market volatilities is to incorporate dynamic risk management features into the algorithms.

1. **Volatility Forecasting:** Algorithms can be designed to use statistical models like GARCH (Generalized Autoregressive Conditional Heteroskedasticity), EWMA (Exponentially Weighted Moving Average) etc., to forecast volatility. If you could predict the weather, would receiving a storm alert not make the roller coaster ride much smoother?

2. **Volatility Trading Strategies:** Based on the volatility forecast, the algorithms can then adjust their trading strategies accordingly. For instance, if high volatility is predicted, the algorithm may reduce position sizes, widen stop-loss orders, or hedge against the market risk, similar to slowing down the roller coaster during stormy weather.

3. **Volatility Triggers & Measures:** Sometimes, the algorithms may incorporate 'volatility triggers' that when market volatility exceeds a certain threshold, the algorithm either exits its position or reduces its trading. Moreover, various measures of volatility can be incorporated into the decision-making process, like historical volatility and implied volatility.

4. **Machine Learning & AI**: Incorporating AI and machine learning capabilities into the algorithms can help the system to learn from previous market movements, enhancing its ability to adapt to market volatilities. This is like the roller coaster ride being more adapted each time the weather changes.

5. **Portfolio Diversification**: Lastly, algorithms can also control portfolio diversification that helps mitigate risk by spreading out investments. This scenario is like not putting all your eggs in one basket, which is a risk mitigation strategy that can help in uncertain conditions.

However, one must note that despite the best algorithmic strategies, there is always a certain degree of risk associated with trading in volatile markets. Hence, taking additional measures like stress testing, scenario analysis and diligent monitoring of the algorithms' performance is crucial to ensure effective risk management.

8.3   Discuss the trade-offs between risk and reward in trading strategy design.

In developing an algorithmic trading strategy, one of the key considerations to keep in mind is the balance between risk and reward. This is akin to sailing a boat in the vast ocean - you want to reach your destination as fast as possible, but pushing too hard might damage your vessel or even capsize it.

The same quandary applies in algorithmic trading. Pushing for higher rewards often means taking on more risk; conversely, overly wary strategies may reduce risk but also limit the potential rewards. So, let's delve into the concepts of risk and reward.

The "reward" in trading refers to the profit potential of a particular trading strategy. It is the hopeful consequence of well-grounded market predictions. This could be viewed as the speed at which you can sail your boat - the better your predictions, the faster you arrive at your destination.

Meanwhile, the "risk" in trading refers to the potential for losses that result from market fluctuations. In the context of our metaphor, this can be seen as poor weather conditions or underwater hazards that could damage your boat or slow you down.

A profitable trading strategy needs to strike a balance between these two - akin to a sailor navigating swiftly but cautiously to reach the destination safe and fast.

Mathematically, this trade-off is often expressed using the Sharpe Ratio, which is defined as:

$$SharpeRatio = \frac{E[R_p - R_f]}{\sigma_p}$$

where $E[R_p - R_f]$ is the expected return of the trading strategy above a risk-free rate, and σ_p is the standard deviation of the trading strategy's returns (a common measure of risk). The Sharpe Ratio thus quantifies the return per unit of risk taken, and a higher value is desirable - it signifies that the strategy earns more return per unit of risk.

One common way to manage the risk-reward trade-off in algorithmic trading is by using stop-loss orders and take-profit orders. Stop-loss orders help limit the downside risk by selling assets when they reach a certain price level, while take-profit orders help lock-in profits when assets reach a certain price level. This could be seen as using safety equipment or advanced navigation technology in our sailing analogy.

Another approach is the diversification of the portfolio, spreading investments across different assets to mitigate the risk of substantial loss from a single asset. This is like investing in multiple boats with different destinations - if one fails to reach, others might make it.

However, it's important to note that risk management strategies themselves may have trade-offs. For instance, setting tight stop-loss orders can protect against large losses, but could also result in selling assets prematurely during normal market volatility. This is akin to too cautiously sailing - you reduce the chance of accidents but might end up much slower than you could have been.

In conclusion, an effective algorithmic trading strategy requires a carefully considered balance between risk and reward- much like a skilled, calculated sailor steering his boat through the ever-changing seas.

8.4 How do you measure and monitor the risk of a portfolio in real-time?

Risk management is one of the most critical aspects of algorithmic trading, and effectively it's not unlike being a traffic controller at a busy intersection – constantly monitoring all the incoming and out-going cars (trades), ensuring the smooth and safe flow of traffic (volumes), while being on the lookout for potential risks and undertaking damage control.

So how do we do it in a trading context? We have various risk measures and monitoring systems in place:

1. **Value at Risk (VaR)**: This is a statistical model to measure the maximum potential loss under normal market conditions over a certain period of time. Basically, it's like checking the speed limit and the typical average speed of vehicles passing through a junction. If a car is moving way faster than the limit, it poses a risk.

VaR relies on historical data and statistical techniques; for instance, a VaR of 5% over a week means that we are 95% confident that the worst loss will not exceed this value over a week under regular market circumstances.

2. **Conditional Value at Risk (CVaR)**: Also known as Expected Shortfall (ES), it calculates the expected return of a portfolio in the worst-case scenario. It's more of a pessimistic approach; think of it as preparing for the worst traffic condition, like an unexpected rally or a marathon cutting through your town.

3. **Stress Testing**: Stress tests measure the performance of a portfolio under radical changes or severe market conditions. This technique is like training and preparing your traffic control for the worst, like an extreme weather event.

These measurements should ideally be checked at regular intervals. Larger firms even calculate VaR and CVaR in real-time, aided by the capabilities of algorithmic trading platforms and efficient infrastructure.

Beyond these measures, positions are also monitored against defined limits set by the firm. Think of it as lanes and traffic signs at the junction, regulating traffic based on capacities and road-rules.

Risk management also involves monitoring the leverage and liquidity of the portfolio, as well as evaluating counterparty risks and sector or group exposure.

All in all, risk management in portfolio and algorithmic trading is akin to a highly coordinated traffic system, constantly balancing between smooth operation and swift responses to emergencies, ensuring the safe navigation of vehicles in this vast financial highway.

8.5   What are some common risk metrics used in the industry?

Risk management is an essential part of algorithmic trading and is used to quantify and manage the risk associated with trading strategies. Commonly used risk metrics in the trading and finance industry include:

1. **Value at Risk (VaR):** VaR is one of the most popular measures of risk. It describes the maximum potential loss on an investment portfolio over a specific time period at a given confidence level. For example, if the 1-day 99% VaR is $1 million, it means that there is a 1% chance that the portfolio will decline in value by more than $1 million over a 1 day period. VaR is often criticized for not capturing tail risk effectively.

2. **Conditional Value at Risk (CVaR) or Expected Shortfall (ES):** CVaR is an extension of VaR which is used to estimate losses that occur in the tail of the distribution of possible returns. In other words, it's the expected value or average of all losses which are worse than

the VaR. It's a measure of extreme or tail risk, taking into account not just the probability of a large loss, but also the magnitude of the loss.

3. **Standard Deviation / Volatility:** These are common measures of dispersion or risk in finance, often used to represent the market risk. It measures the amount by which the returns on an investment can vary, which can be interpreted as the risk associated with the investment. Volatility can be used to calculate VaR.

4. **Beta:** Beta measures a portfolio's sensitivity to market movements (like a stock market index). A beta greater than 1 indicates that the portfolio is more volatile than the market, while a beta less than 1 indicates that the portfolio is less volatile. Beta is a key input in the Capital Asset Pricing Model (CAPM), a model used to calculate expected returns.

5. **Maximum Drawdown:** This is the largest cumulative percentage decline in portfolio value. It serves to quantify the peak-to-trough decline in portfolio value, emphasizing the worst possible scenario.

6. **Sharpe Ratio**: While not being a pure risk metric, Sharpe ratio is a measure for calculating risk-adjusted return. It is the average return earned in excess of the risk-free rate per unit of volatility or total risk, thus, capturing both risk (volatility) and return components.

Imagine risk management in algorithmic trading as being the captain of a ship in stormy seas. You want to navigate the sea (market conditions) in such a way that you reach your destination (profit targets) without capsizing your ship (exposing the portfolio to undue risk). The risk metrics are like different navigational tools, each giving you different but crucial information about the sea conditions. Using them together allows you to map out the optimal route for your journey.

8.6 Explain the concept of Value at Risk (VaR) and its importance.

"Value at Risk" or VaR is a statistical measure used in financial risk management that quantifies the maximum loss that a portfolio or investment can incur over a specific time period at a certain level of confidence. That might sound a bit abstract, so let's break it down with a simple example.

Consider a friend inviting you to go out on a gambling night. However, you want to restrict your potential loss to no more than $100. Then that $100 limit could be considered your "Value at Risk" for your gambling activity.

In the world of finance, let's say you have a portfolio of stocks that has a one-day 1% VaR of $1 million. This means that there is a 1% chance that the portfolio will drop in value by more than $1 million over a one-day period. Note that VaR measures the potential loss in value of a risky investment or portfolio over a defined period for a given confidence interval.

Why is VaR so important? It's one of the key metrics that decision makers in the financial world use to assess levels of financial risk within their procedures or portfolios. For an investment bank, it's crucial to estimate how much they could lose from extreme market movements. VaR is essentially a yardstick that measures the worst expected loss under normal market conditions over a specific time interval.

It's like being able to gauge how much you'll likely get wet before deciding to step out into the rain, depending on how heavy the rain is or how long you'll be out there. Having this measurement allows a certain amount of control and preparedness, enabling better decision making under uncertainty.

It's important to note however, that while VaR is a commonly used risk measure due to its simplicity, it doesn't account for the severity of losses beyond the VaR threshold. Hence, it should be used in conjunction with other risk measures such as Expected Shortfall (ES) for comprehensive risk management.

In terms of formulation in finance and statistics, VaR is frequently calculated via three methods: the variance-covariance method, the historical simulation, and the Monte Carlo simulation. But delving into the details of these methods is another topic that we can discuss separately.

This measure has been widely implemented across financial service firms and has become an international standard for reporting financial risk. Despite its limitations and criticisms, it continues to play an important role as a robust initialism in financial risk management.

8.7   How does Conditional VaR (or CVaR) provide a different perspective than VaR?

Conditional VaR (CVaR) indeed provides a different perspective and often, a more comprehensive insight into the riskiness of a portfolio compared to VaR (Value at Risk).

To understand the distinction, let's start by defining what VaR and CVaR are:

- VaR specifies the maximum expected loss over a given time horizon at a certain confidence level.

- CVaR, on the other hand, measures the expected loss in the event of a tail risk scenario (i.e., when losses exceed the VaR level).

To illustrate the difference, suppose you're planning a road trip. **VaR** would represent the maximum distance you plan to travel with a certain level of confidence, say, 95%. It implies you're confident that your road trip mileage will be less than that maximum point 95% of the time. However, it doesn't say anything about what could happen in that remaining 5% of instances.

But what if you got lost and significantly exceeded your planned maximum distance? That's what **CVaR** tries to answer. It projects upon the worst-case scenarios — the included 'tail' in the distribution. It gives an idea of how bad things could become if you indeed get lost. Thus, it provides a fuller picture by accounting for the severity of losses when things go really bad.

In mathematical expressions,

If the loss random variable is X, and the VaR at the confidence level $1 - \alpha$ is $VaR_\alpha(X)$, then the CVaR at the confidence level $1 - \alpha$ is denoted and calculated as:

$$CVaR_\alpha(X) = E[X|X > VaR_\alpha(X)]$$

This accounts for expected losses beyond the VaR point, providing an average of tail losses. This is especially useful in handling so-called 'black swan' events in financial markets, which are rare but have extreme impacts.

While VaR's simplicity has made it popular in industry applications, CVaR is considered a more robust and informative measure, with a focus on the impact of extreme market scenarios.

8.8   Why is drawdown considered a critical metric for trading strategies?

Drawdown plays a very significant role in risk management for trading strategies. Drawdown refers to the degree of loss from the peak to the trough of a portfolio, before a new peak is attained. It's akin to sliding down a hill from the peak to the bottom before you start climbing again.

The importance of drawdown comes from its potential impact on a trader's capital and emotional well-being. If I can borrow an analogy from everyday life, it's like going on a diet. Let's say you're trying to lose weight and you put a plan into action. You're doing great initially, losing a few pounds every week. Suddenly, you hit a plateau or even worse, you start gaining weight. That's your drawdown period. It's an interval where despite your best efforts and discipline, you're not seeing the results you want. It's demotivating, often leading to self-doubt and, in worst cases, you going off your diet plan.

Similarly, experiencing a drawdown in trading can dampen the spirits of a trader. Considerable drawdown can damage a trader's confidence, often leading them to abandon their strategy at the worst possible time or take larger than necessary risks to recover losses.

Furthermore, drawdown is important for practical mathematical reasons. Say a portfolio lost 50%, theoretically, it should only need 50% to bounce back. But in reality, it needs 100% gain to come back to break-even point. This is because it's now working with a lower base capital, stemming from the loss. To continue with the diet analogy, if you gain back the weight you lost, you'll have to put in considerable effort to lose it again, often even more than what you put in the first time. So, keeping drawdowns small helps the portfolio to recover faster.

It's crucial for a trading strategy to take into account both the frequency and the depth of potential drawdowns. Both algorithmic and discretionary traders strive to design strategies that minimize drawdown for these reasons. It provides a real-world assessment of the worst-case scenario that a trader has undergone or might go through, providing critical insights for decision-making in risk management.

8.9 How do you estimate VaR for non-linear portfolios or portfolios with options?

Estimating Value at Risk (VaR) for non-linear portfolios or portfolios containing options is a bit more complex than for linear portfolios due to the non-linear payoffs of options. There are several ways to estimate VaR for such portfolios, but three popular methods are: Delta-Normal VaR, Historical Simulation VaR, and Monte Carlo Simulation VaR.

1. **Delta-Normal VaR:** In this method, we first linearize the portfolio using a Taylor series expansion around the current asset price, which leads us to the concept of Greeks (the partial derivatives of the portfolio) such as Delta, Gamma, Vega, Theta, and Rho. For example, the Delta approximates the change in the portfolio value for a small change in the underlying asset price.

The Delta-Normal method is simple and computationally efficient but makes the key assumption that returns are normally distributed and the market factors move linearly, which is not always realized in financial markets.

2. **Historical Simulation VaR:** In this method, we re-price the entire portfolio for each point in our historical dataset. This method is very simple and doesn't require any assumptions regarding return distributions. However, it is computationally intensive and assumes that the future will be like the past.

3. **Monte Carlo Simulation VaR:** In this approach, random numbers are generated to simulate returns on market factors. These simulated returns are then used to reprice the portfolio and calculate the potential losses. The VaR is then calculated from the distribution of these simulated losses. While it's one of the most accurate methods, it is computationally intensive, making it less suitable for larger portfolios.

For non-linear portfolios, the use of one method over another depends on various factors including the portfolio's complexity, computational resources, and the risk manager's level of comfort with the assumptions underlying each model. For complex portfolios, a mixture of these approaches might be utilized.

Think of these techniques as different types of navigation tools. Delta-Normal VaR is like using a straightforward road map (simple and easy to read, but lacking in detail), Historical Simulation VaR is like using a compass and a topographical map (more detailed and accurate but requires more effort), and Monte Carlo Simulation VaR is like using a GPS system (most accurate and detailed, but reliant on the availability of power and signal).

8.10   Discuss the limitations and potential pitfalls of relying solely on VaR as a risk metric.

Value at Risk (VaR) is a widely used risk metric in financial modeling, specifically in the field of algorithmic trading. Its appeal lies in its simplicity. VaR gives us a straightforward number - a maximum possible loss - over a given horizon and at a certain confidence level.

However, relying solely on VaR for risk metrics faces several limitations and potential pitfalls:

1. **Underestimation of Tail Risk**: VaR, by design, only looks at risk up to a certain confidence level. For instance, if you're calculating 99% VaR, you're ignoring those 1% of most extreme events (in the tail of the distribution). These ignored events could potentially incur huge losses far beyond the VaR estimates.

Think of it like this: if you're planning an outdoor birthday party and you check the weather forecast, seeing there is only a 1% chance of rain, you might not plan for a backup indoor venue. This '1% event' i.e., the rain, is the tail risk event that VaR ignores - and if it does rain, it could ruin your party.

2. **Lack of Subadditivity**: VaR does not always satisfy the property of subadditivity, i.e., the total risk of a combined portfolio can sometimes be more than the sum of the individual risks. This property is fundamental to diversification, which is a key risk management strategy.

Similar to packing for a trip in a single suitcase versus multiple ones; consider each suitcase to be an asset - the total weight you could carry could theoretically be more in individual suitcases (each filling up to their individual 'risk' capacity) than in a single one (where the combined 'risk' is less flexible and could exceed total capacity).

3. **Not Discriminating Between Loss Distributions**: VaR doesn't differentiate between loss distributions beyond its confidence cut-off point. Two portfolios with the same VaR might have vastly different loss potentials in the tail end of their loss distributions that isn't captured within the VaR confidence level.

For example, you might have two routes to reach a destination with the same expected arrival time (VaR), but one might have far more traffic jams and accidents (tail risks). VaR doesn't account for these.

To mitigate these limitations, financial experts often use other risk measures in conjunction - like Conditional Value at Risk (CVaR), which measures expected losses beyond the VaR cut-off point, some stress testing against extreme events, or even non-parametric methods for full losses distribution evaluation. It's like carrying an umbrella even with a 1% chance of rain, considering the amount of items to pack both individually and in combination, and planning not just for estimated arrival time but possible road disruptions as well.

8.11   Why is position sizing crucial in risk management?

Position sizing is an integral part of effective risk management in algorithmic trading. At its core, it is about determining the right amount of stocks, futures contracts, or forex lots you should trade, in order to align your trades with your risk appetite.

Let's take an example to illustrate this. Imagine you are at a carnival playing a game of ring toss. Your goal is to win a big, cuddly teddy bear for your beloved. The operator tells you that you can throw the rings ten times. But here's the twist: you only have $20 in your pocket and each ring toss costs $2. If you miss all your tosses, you leave the carnival empty-handed.

In this scenario, your available cash ($20) is your "investment capital," and the cost of each throw ($2) symbolizes your "position size." If you throw all the rings without any strategy, you're risking your entire investment capital. You might be forced to leave without the teddy bear, with your beloved disappointed, and with empty pockets.

This simple game is very similar to the concept of position sizing in trading. If you invest your entire capital in a single trade (or throw all your rings at once) without considering the probability of success or capital at risk, you stand a high chance of being wiped out by the market.

Reverting back to Finance, for example, if you risk too much on one trade, you are more likely to lose a significant part of your capital if the trade goes south. Therefore, keeping the position size at an appropriate level is crucial to ensure that your trading system can survive over long periods.

In conclusion, position sizing is your bet size in the trading game. If you bet too much, you might end up losing your entire capital. If you bet too small, your profits could be insignificant. Therefore, determining the right position size - one that aligns with your risk tolerance and investment objectives - is the key to successful and sustainable trading.

8.12 How can algorithms dynamically adjust position sizes based on market conditions?

Algorithmic trading strategies often include dynamic position sizing based on market conditions, which forms an integral part of risk management in algorithmic trading. The concept is akin to driving a car: you adjust your speed depending on the road conditions, traffic, potential hazards, and rules - essentially risk factors of your trip. Likewise, algorithmic trading adjusts its position sizing based on risk factors like the current market condition or volatility, to mitigate losses and optimize returns.

Here are a couple of ways that we can perform such adjustments:

1. **Volatility Adjustment:** This is a common way to manage risk where algorithms reduce or increase investment sizes based on market volatility. For instance, the algorithm can increase investment sizes when volatility is low and decrease sizes when volatility is high.

This is done using a measure of market volatility, often with the standard deviation or the Average True Range (ATR). The position size is then inversely proportional to the determined market volatility:

$$PositionSize = \frac{Constant}{Volatility}$$

In this equation, PositionSize decreases as Volatility increases and vice versa.

2. **A Portfolio Heat Approach:** In this approach, algorithms manage risk by controlling the total risk of the portfolio, often referred to

as the 'heat' of the portfolio.

Similar to having a thermostat set to a particular 'comfortable' temperature, you adjust the heat output from the system, in this case, investment sizes, according to changes in the environment.

Here, the algorithm computes the total portfolio risk, often a sum of individual bet sizes multiplied by their respective instrument risks:

$$TotalRisk = \sum_{i=1}^{n} BetSize_i * Risk_i$$

If TotalRisk is above a certain threshold, the algorithm proportionately scales down the size of future bets until the total risk is back to a comfortable level.

These are just a few ways algorithms may adjust position sizes dynamically based on market conditions. The key takeaway is that, like a cautious driver or smart thermostat, an efficient algorithm is designed to dynamically adapt to changing conditions by adjusting its 'output' – in this case, position sizes, to manage risk effectively.

8.13   Explain the concept of leverage and its implications for trading risk.

Leverage in trading is a concept that can be compared to using a lever and a fulcrum to lift a heavy weight. In trading, this "heavy weight" is the capital required to make a certain investment, and the "lever" is the borrowed funds a trader can use to gain exposure to large quantities of an asset without having to pay for it entirely upfront. The "fulcrum" would, in this case, be the broker or financial institution providing the leverage.

Conceptually, leverage involves using borrowed money to increase the potential return on an investment. This is represented in a ratio format - for example, a leverage of 2:1 allows a trader to double his trade size, while 10:1 leverage allows him to trade 10 times his original investment.

Mathematically, if you have $10,000 in your trading account and you trade with a leverage of 10:1, you would be able to trade up to $100,000 in value.

Although leverage can magnify profits, it also has the potential to magnify losses. This is the primary risk involved with leverage – just as it can multiply your gains, it can also compound your losses to a great extent.

Think of it like driving a fast car: the faster you go (i.e., the more leverage you use), the higher the risks, but also potentially the bigger the thrills (or profits). Just as you'd need good driving skills and safety measures (risk management) to survive at high speeds, you'd need good trading skills and risk management to survive in high-leverage trading.

If we translate this analogy to equations, given an initial trading capital of C and leverage L, a trader can execute trades up to a value of $C \times L$. However, if a trade goes wrong, a loss is also multiplied by the leverage, i.e., L. So, proper risk management includes not just understanding potential profits but also potential losses in the context of leverage.

Another fundamental point is the risk of a margin call, where the broker requires the trader to deposit more money to cover potential losses. This could lead to the liquidation of positions if the trader can't cover the margin call, and again, this risk is magnified by leverage.

In essence, while leverage can be a powerful tool for traders willing to accept higher risks in order to potentially reap larger rewards, it's a double-edged sword that can also lead to substantial losses. Consequently, it's imperative that traders deeply understand the risks involved and utilize robust risk management strategies when using leverage.

8.14 How do trading algorithms account for margin requirements and leverage constraints?

In trading algorithms, risk management and adhering to margin requirements and leverage constraints is of paramount importance. Just as a responsible driver checks the fuel gauge, speedometer, and other dash indicators before and during a car ride, so should a trading algorithm monitor its risk metrics.

Let's understand margin requirements and leverage constraints in simple terms first.

The margin requirement is like a security deposit on your flat rental – it's an assurance that you eventually have sufficient resources to cover your obligations.

On the other hand, leverage, in the context of trading, is like using a lever to lift a heavy object – it gives you the capacity to trade larger quantities with a fixed capital, similar to how a lever lets you lift more weight with the same effort.

Now, let's delve into how they are managed in trading algorithms.

Firstly, trading algorithms continuously calculate the margin requirement for each transaction that is being planned. This is done by considering the initial and maintenance margin requirements of the broker and the exchange. It involves a set of mathematical formulas which depend on the type of instrument being traded - whether it is equities, futures, or options.

As per the formulas, the margin required increases with position size and also varies with the price volatility of the instrument. For instance, if the trading algorithm is considering opening a long futures position in crude oil, it would keep track of the initial margin requirement for crude oil futures, which is set by the exchange.

Next, on to Leverage Constraints.

Imagine you are playing the game of tug of war. If the other team is substantially stronger, you may not want to put your full strength into pulling the rope, because if your team loses footing, you could be pulled across the line and lose. If the other team is equally strong, you might go all in, pull as hard as you can. This is essentially what leverage is: taking on risks that are proportionate, more, or less than your overall size or capital.

Algorithms account for this by setting a limit on the maximum leverage that they can undertake. This is done via a 'Leverage Limit' parameter, which is set based on the risk tolerance of the trading strategy. The algorithm is coded to always check on its leverage before making a trade. When a new position is being considered, the algorithm will calculate the leverage that would result if the trade was executed. If this is more than the preset 'leverage limit', the algorithm will not execute the trade.

Here, leverage is usually calculated as the ratio of the total market value of open positions to the total trading capital.

In conclusion, a good trading algorithm's risk management strategy is akin to a vigilant night watchman, always on the lookout for any possible sign of danger or undue risk. It exercises caution before making every trade, and ensures that it never goes beyond the boundaries it was set to operate within. Very importantly, it ensures that the system never bites off more than it can chew - in terms of margin or leverage.

8.15   Discuss the dangers of over-leveraging a trading strategy.

Leveraging is akin to driving a race car at top speed around a twisting, hilly circuit. Manage your speed and control well, you might cross the finish line faster. Misjudge a corner or mismanage your control, and you can crash out, often spectacularly.

Over-leveraging in trading amplifies both potential profits and losses. Essentially, leverage is borrowed capital that increases the potential return of an investment, but it also magnifies potential losses. In trading, the leverage ratio represents the margin requirements—the amount a trader has to deposit into their trading account. For example, a 1:100 leverage in forex allows a trader to control a $100,000 trade with $1,000.

In an ideal scenario, leveraging can significantly amplify your gains. But in real markets, prices don't move in a smooth, predictable fashion. Imagine our race car driver again; he risks severe crashes if he only assumes straight paths and clear weather. The reality is curvy roads and unpredictable weather conditions (akin to market volatility).

Over-leveraging creates danger by increasing the exposure of your portfolio to market fluctuations. Consider a simple trading strategy where you go long (buy) if you predict the price will rise and go short (sell) if you predict the price will fall.

Suppose you use leverage of 1:1 and you placed a long order expecting a price gain. If the price falls by, say, 5%, you lose 5% of your investment. Had you used a leverage of 1:50, the same price change would cause a loss of 250%. It becomes worse if the price change is much larger than your prediction, which is common in trading due to the random walk nature of price series.

Additionally, over-leveraging can lead to a margin call, where a broker demands an investor deposits additional money or securities into the account to cover possible losses. If you can't meet the margin call, your broker may liquidate your assets at a loss to meet the obligation.

Lastly, over-leveraging leaves less room for error. Modeling the market accurately is a hard task; even highly sophisticated models with thousands of variables can only explain a small part of price changes. The less accurate market prediction combined with over-leverage, the faster the crash can be.

The bottom line is since we can never accurately predict all price changes in the market, over-leveraging amplifies these prediction errors, which can lead to large losses that can wipe out your trading capital. Taking a conservative and risk-controlled approach of managing leverage is crucial for long-term success in trading.

Chapter 9

Behavioral Finance and Algo Trading

9.1 Name and explain common psychological biases that affect trading decisions.

Algorithmic trading is largely designed to exploit psychological biases that typically impair human decision-making. Traders, like all people, can be subject to a number of biases, even when making informed and data-based decisions. Understanding these biases can aid algorithmic design and improve trading strategies.

Here are some common psychological biases that affect trading decisions:

1. **Overconfidence Bias:** Overconfidence bias, as the name suggests, is when traders believe their ability to pick stocks, predict market trends, or timing the market is better than it actually is. It's like

a amateur darts player believing he could beat a professional just because he had a few good rounds.

2. **Confirmation Bias:** This is a tendency to favor and seek information that confirms one's existing beliefs while ignoring contradictory information. A good analogy would be like listening to a song with lyrics you agree with, and skipping over the parts you don't like. In trading, it could manifest when, for instance, a trader makes a decision to buy a stock because they favor news articles and reports that show a positive trend for the company.

3. **Loss Aversion Bias:** Also known as the disposition effect, this bias stems from the psychological pain of selling a security that has lost value. It's like holding onto a dud firework hoping it will eventually go off, despite evidence to the contrary. Traders prefer to hold onto a losing investment in the hope that it will rebound, rather than recognizing the loss and moving on.

4. **Herd Mentality:** This bias occurs when traders follow what other traders are doing, rather than their analysis. It is as if seeing everyone in a store rushing to buy a certain product, makes you want to buy it too, even though you have no idea about the product's value or utility.

5. **Anchoring Bias:** This occurs when traders anchor their thoughts to a reference point - even though it may not have any logical basis. It's like buying a shirt because it's 50% off without considering whether the original price was inflated to begin with. Your anchor is the original price.

These biases lead traders to make sub-optimal decisions while trading. Algorithmic trading can exploit these biases to deliver superior returns or be programmed to avoid these biases for more rational trading decisions. Recognizing these biases can allow traders and algorithm creators to work around them, delivering a more efficient and effective trading strategy.

9.2   How can algorithms be designed to exploit or mitigate these biases?

Algorithmic trading aims to maximize market efficiency, and designing algorithms which can exploit, or mitigate behavioral finance biases is definitely one potential approach in increasing this efficiency.

Let's conceptualize this through a simple analogy. Imagine you're in a bustling city market. The sellers are humans, who sometimes price their goods not just on the basis of costs and expected profit, but also based on their emotions, personal biases, and the behavior of the crowd around them. Now imagine a smart, unemotional robot (our algorithm) that can keep track of all the prices and can analyze the patterns behind the seller's behaviors to buy cheap and sell at a profit. That's a small glimpse into what algo trading aimed at exploiting human biases might look like.

Algorithmic trading can utilize behavioral finance concepts in a couple of main ways:

1. **Exploiting Behavioral Biases:** Algorithms can be designed to identify patterns that indicate behavioral biases in the market. For instance, the Disposition effect, which states that investors tend to sell assets that have increased in value but hold onto assets that have dropped in value, can be exploited. An algorithm could be programmed to identify the stocks investors are irrationally holding onto (creating an artificial downward pressure on the price), and buy these undervalued assets.

Similarly, algorithms can also exploit trends following market overreaction and underreaction, commonly associated with Prospect Theory. When overreaction occurs, prices are temporarily over-inflated. Conversely, underreaction is when positive or negative news about a stock doesn't immediately affect its price. Identifying such instances can allow algorithms to act on the predictable correction that will follow.

2. **Mitigating Behavioral Biases:** On the other hand, algo trading can also help to reduce the effect of behavioral biases. This is especially applicable for big financial institutions, fund managers, and individual traders who use these algorithms for their own trading. For instance, a fund manager may have a personal bias leading to the overconfidence effect, whereby they trade excessively based on superior information or personal belief. This could result in transaction costs eating into profits. An algorithm here would help execute trades based on pre-set rules and conditions, effectively eliminating these harmful biases.

In the similar fashion, algorithms can also help mitigate 'herd behavior', where traders follow the trend set by the majority, even against their own judgment. If the algorithms determine that such behavior is causing an asset to be overpriced or underpriced, they can execute trades to profit when the market eventually corrects itself.

In conclusion, algorithms have a high potential in exploiting and mitigating behavioral biases for better trading performance. Nonetheless, these algorithms are as good as their underlying design. Therefore, ongoing research in behavioral biases and continuous model improvement are crucial to achieving desired outcomes.

9.3 Discuss the concept of herding in financial markets and its implications.

In financial markets, "herding" refers to a behavioral phenomenon where traders or investors mimic the decisions of a larger body of investors, irrespective of their own private information or analysis. The concept of herding has a root in behavioral finance, which studies the psychology of financial decision-making.

Let's illustrate this with a simple analogy. Imagine a group of sheep. When one sheep decides to move, the rest tend to follow, even if it might not be the best decision for individual sheep. The same pattern can sometimes apply to market participants and this is what we call "Herding Behavior".

This phenomenon comes into play particularly in stressful times, such as during an economic downturn, where investors might ignore their own information and analyses and just follow what everyone else is doing. 'Buy' when others are buying, 'sell' when folks are selling.

From an algorithmic trading perspective, understanding herding behavior and its implications are important for a few reasons:

1. **Pricing Inaccuracy/Market Inefficiency**: Extreme herding behavior can lead to situations where the market price of an asset drifts away from its intrinsic value. If our algorithmic trading model can identify such cases, it can exploit these opportunities, buying undervalued assets and selling overvalued ones.

2. **Risk Management**: Herding can escalate market volatility. Recognizing herding behavior can assist in managing risk in an algorithmic trading strategy by adding some sort of risk control measures when herding is detected.

3. **Algorithm Adaptation**: If herding behavior is detected in certain market conditions, our trading algorithm can be tuned to adapt to such market dynamics. For instance, some algorithms may decide to decrease trading in such volatile conditions.

In mathematics notation, herding behaviour can be illustrated through herding coefficients in a linear regression model.

Given a regression model,

$$r_{i,t} = \alpha + \beta r_{m,t} + \epsilon_{i,t}$$

The "beta" (β) in this context could be seen as a herding coefficient. A larger β implies more herding, as it shows an asset's returns are highly correlated with market-wide returns.

However, studying and detecting herding behavior is challenging due to the inherent complexity and noise in financial markets. Advanced techniques such deep learning and big data analysis are being used to spot herding patterns with better accuracy.

Thus, blending the principles of behavioral finance with the computational prowess of algorithmic trading systems can offer exciting new opportunities in the financial market.

9.4   How might recency bias impact trading decisions and market trends?

Recency bias is a cognitive bias that gives more relevance and importance to most recent information and experiences rather than those from the past. This bias is observed not just in our daily lives, but is also quite evident in the world of finance, specifically, in trading decisions and market trends.

To illustrate the potential impact that recency bias might have, let's consider an analogy with a championship sports team. Suppose you have a favorite football team that has had a stellar track record and has consistently won the championship over the last five years. However, in the current year, the team hasn't performed as well as they have in their past games. As a staunch supporter, if you were to predict the outcome of an upcoming match, would you still continue to back your favorite team, considering their past performance over the years, or whether you'd let their recent performance sway your expectations?

If you let the recent underperformance weigh more than the historical trend, you're exhibiting recency bias. In this context, traders swayed by recency bias could sell off a historically profitable stock following a handful of bad quarterly results, while disregarding the long-term upward trend.

Let's link this example to trading algorithms. If an algorithm takes into account or gives more weight to recent data, it could potentially optimize trades based on short-lived market fluctuations. Depending on the time-frame of trading, focusing on more recent data might not always be a bad strategy. Indeed, high frequency trading algorithms base their strategies around minute-by-minute changes in individual stock prices.

However, if the trading algorithm doesn't balance recent with historical data, it might misinterpret a temporary market downturn as a lasting bear market. This could lead to improper position sizing, poor portfolio selection, and increased trading costs due to frequent trades, each of which could negatively impact investment returns.

In essence, recency bias in financial markets could lead investors or trading algorithms to over-react to recent trends while dismissing longer-term market movements. Therefore, to avoid this bias, it is always essential to validate our strategies across different market periods and to try finding a balance between recent and older data.

9.5   Explain the "disposition effect" and its relevance in trading.

The "disposition effect" is an interesting concept in behavioral finance which highlights our innate human quirks and how they can influence our investment decisions. It was first described by economists Hersh Shefrin and Meir Statman in 1985.

It's akin to the emotional struggle we all might have experienced when we're playing a game and find ourselves winning; we tend to cash our wins too early for fear of losing them. On the other side, we tend to cling onto our losses for too long in the hope that luck will turn and they'll transform into gains. Translated into the world of trading, the disposition effect refers to the tendency of investors to sell assets that have increased in value too early (the winners) while holding onto assets that have dropped in value for too long (the losers).

Now, you might wonder why the disposition effect is relevant to algorithmic trading, given that, by definition, algo trading is designed to strip out the human element and operate purely on logic-based algorithms. However, it's precisely for this reason that understanding the disposition effect is key for those involved in algo trading. Here's why:

1. Improved trading strategies: Knowing that many human traders are susceptible to the disposition effect enables those involved in algo trading to fine-tune their algorithms to exploit this known bias. For instance, an algorithm might be designed to anticipate price increases of assets that are widely held and have recently increased in value, under the assumption that they'll likely be sold off too early.

2. Understanding market behavior: Trading algorithms not only trade against each other but also against human traders. As such, having knowledge about behavioral biases like the disposition effect helps in the design of smarter algorithms that can factor in likely human trading responses to market events.

Basically, viewing the markets through the lens of human psychology (like the disposition effect) adds another dimension to investment strategies. It's like being aware that some people at a fruit market tend to undervalue high-quality apples just because they've had a few bad ones in the past. This knowledge could help you build a business model around buying these undervalued apples and selling them at a proper price elsewhere.

Incorporating behavioral finance insights into algorithmic trading is an emerging area and has the potential to lead to more efficient and sophisticated trading algorithms.

9.6 How might algorithmic trading strategies exploit behavioral biases in retail investors?

Algorithmic trading, an area often described as being where finance meets statistical analysis and predictive modeling, is continuously evolving, and one of its surprising connections is with behavioral finance. Behavioral Finance focuses on the cognitive and psychological aspects of investing. Simply put, it's all about the biases and irrationalities that investors, mostly retail, may demonstrate in their investment decisions. Algorithmic trading strategies, on the other hand, take advantage of these biases to make systematic and data-driven investment decisions. So let's discuss how they interact and how algo-trading can exploit these behavioral biases.

1. **Herd Behavior**: This is an extremely common behavioral trait amongst retail investors. Here, investors tend to follow what everyone else is doing - almost like a herd of sheep. For example, in a rising market, this may lead to a buying frenzy, and in a falling market, a selling frenzy. Some algorithmic trading strategies are developed to track such abnormal volume spikes, significant price movements, and social media sentiments, which may hint towards such herd behavior. Once such behavior is detected, algorithms can quickly act by either buying before the price increases further or selling before the price drops.

Using a football game as an analogy, the algorithmic strategy is like a player who anticipates where the ball (i.e., market movement) is going and positions itself there ahead of everyone else.

2. **Disposition Effect**: This effect refers to the tendency of investors to sell assets that have increased in value while keeping assets that have dropped in value. It's driven by the anticipation that the good performance will continue and the bad will reverse. Algorithmic trading models can be designed to detect such price patterns and exploit these situations to buy low and sell high.

In terms of analogy, you can compare disposition effect to holding onto a losing lottery ticket, hoping it will somehow become a winner later, and selling a small winning ticket, expecting its value won't increase any further. The algo-trading strategy, in contrast, behaves like an astute trader who knows when to cut losses and book profits.

3. **Overconfidence Bias**: Here, retail investors tend to be overconfident about their abilities to predict the stock market. This bias often results in excessive trading and risk-taking. Algorithmic trading strategies can exploit this by taking the opposite side of these unsustainable positions, often resulting in profit when the market corrects itself.

4. **Confirmation Bias**: Retail investors have a tendency to interpret new information in a way that confirms their existing beliefs and theories. Thus, they might disregard vital market information that contradicts their positions. Algorithmic trading, however, doesn't suffer from this bias. It continuously adapts and learns from new information, enabling it to position optimally within the market dynamics and take advantage when retail investors neglect valuable data.

In conclusion, algorithmic trading can be viewed as a sort of antidote to many of the behavioral biases that retail investors suffer from. With its data-driven, emotionless, and systematic approach, it can exploit these existing biases in the market and potentially generate superior returns.

9.7 How can algorithms help professional traders avoid falling victim to their biases?

Behavioral finance is a field that combines psychological theory with conventional economics to explain why and how people make irrational financial decisions. One of the key principles in this field is that individuals are not always rational, and they are, in fact, influenced by certain biases when making decisions, even in financial matters. The same principle applies to finance professionals, including traders. They can fall victim to overconfidence, anchoring (relying too much on the initial piece of information encountered), confirmation bias (favoring information that confirms pre-existing beliefs), loss aversion, and so on.

Algorithmic trading, in contrast, is a method of executing a large order using automated pre-programmed trading instructions accounting for variables like time, price, and volume to send small slices of the order (child orders) out to the market over time. It's comparable with setting an autopilot on an airplane. The airplane still needs a human to code the flight path, but the autopilot ensures that the airplane sticks to the path without letting human factor (like fatigue or emotional stress) affect its operation.

Now, how can algorithmic trading help avoid these biases? Here's how:

1. **Emotionless Trading**: Algorithms do not experience fear, greed, hope, or anxiety. They strictly follow the strategy that has been programmed into them in a highly disciplined manner. When a pilot is in turbulence, he could panic and make a poor decision. But an autopilot would stick to the course, effectively negating the panic factor.

2. **Consistency in Actions**: By predefining trading parameters, algorithms ensure consistent execution of a trading strategy. It is as if you set google maps before starting your journey. No matter how many unfamiliar turns it asks you to take, you follow them to reach your destination.

3. **Risk Management**: Algorithmic trading requires traders to define their risk parameters, which can prevent impulsive trading decisions fuelled by fear or overconfidence. This is similar to a car's automatic brake system; it keeps the speed in check so the car doesn't go too fast and skid off the road.

4. **Backtesting**: Algorithmic trading allows traders to backtest their strategy with historical data before putting it into real operation, minimizing the potential influence of hindsight bias. This can be compared to simulating the airplane flight in a controlled virtual environment before the actual flight.

5. **High-Speed Decisions and Execution**: Algorithms are high-speed, capable of processing vast amounts of information and executing trades within milliseconds. This mitigates the influence of anchoring bias–the tendency to rely too heavily on initial information–as algorithms can swiftly update their decision-making based on the most recent data.

6. **Diversification**: Algorithms can efficiently diversify investments to a degree virtually impossible for human trader, which can mitigate the influence of herding behavior – the tendency for individuals to mimic the actions (rational or irrational) of a larger group.

So, in this way, algorithms can help traders keep their biases in check and make more systematic, rigorous, and objective decisions. However, it's also worth noting that the effectiveness of algorithmic trading is highly dependent on the accuracy, robustness, and efficiency of their underlying models and assumptions.

9.8   Discuss the ethical considerations of algorithms exploiting behavioral biases.

The ethical considerations of algorithmic trading exploiting behavioral biases are analogous to surfers turning a blind eye to a lurking shark while riding a wave. The surfers are the market participants, the wave is the market trend that everyone wants to ride, and the shark is the algorithmic trading systems waiting to take advantage of behavioral biases.

These systems prey on two major biases.

1) Loss Aversion: Participants are usually afraid of booking losses and would rather hold on to losing positions in the hope of a swing around. This is similar to a gambler doubling down after a stretch of losses. Algorithms can intelligently identify such situations and exploit these tendencies, thereby creating ethical concerns.

2) Herding: Another bias is the instinctive tendency of individuals to follow the crowd. Like lemmings, investors often join the bandwagon without questioning if the direction is right or wrong, this can potentially sway markets in one direction. Algorithms can use this to their advantage in trying to push the market in a specific direction, leading to ethical issues.

So what's the ethical problem here?

Its predatory nature raises ethical considerations, as it puts less-informed participants at a disadvantage, distorting the level-playing field that markets should ideally be. This is akin to playing a chess match with a novice where he isn't even aware that the opponent is a grandmaster.

There is also the question of market manipulation. Algorithms, especially high-frequency trading (HFT) ones, can use strategies like quote stuffing or momentum ignition to mislead other market participants or create artificial market conditions. This would be like Lucius Fox controlling Gotham City's entire water supply in Batman Begins, changing the natural course, flow, and availability of water.

Moreover, there is also the fairness and equality of opportunity issue. By taking advantage of faster data feeds and cutting-edge technology, these algorithms are playing a different league of the game against individual investors or traditional investors. It's like running a 100-meter race but giving a headstart of 50 meters to some runners - not exactly the epitome of fair competition.

Behavioral biases exploited by algorithmic trading:

1) *Loss Aversion*: Fear of losses, akin to a gambler doubling down after losses. Trading algorithms can exploit these tendencies, leading

to ethical considerations.

2) *Herding*: A tendency to follow a crowd, similar to lemmings joining a bandwagon without questioning the direction. Algorithms can push markets in that specific direction, creating ethical issues.

Ethical Considerations:

1) **Predatory Nature**: Distorts the level-playing field in the market, disadvantaging less-informed participants.

2) **Market Manipulation**: Creation of artificial market conditions or misleading market participants.

3) **Fairness and Equality of Opportunity**: Advantage of faster data feeds and cutting-edge technology, leading to unequal playing field.

9.9   How might algorithms adjust to a market where most participants are also algorithmic traders?

In a market where most participants are algorithmic traders, there is a high degree of automated decision making. This environment often becomes a game of fast reactions and predictions based on statistical models. It's akin to a digital racetrack where all the cars (algorithms) are trying to be the quickest to respond to changes on the road (the market).

If you think of the market as being a bit like an ecosystem, with different creatures (traders, manually or algorithmically driven) interacting, then in this digital jungle, the algorithmic creatures have to evolve to handle different scenarios, like a lion learning to hunt different types of prey.

To survive and thrive, algorithms need to be adaptive in several ways:

1. **Speed**: In an algorithm-dominated market, being fast is crucial. It's the equivalent of a sprinter trying to outrun his competitors. High-frequency trading (HFT) algorithms, for instance, aim to buy or sell assets within microseconds.

2. **Machine learning**: Machine learning algorithms can process large amounts of data and make predictions based on this data. They adjust over time as they 'learn' from their performance. In our ecosystem analogy, that's like a bird which over time learns to choose the best branches to gather for building its nest.

3. **Noise filtering**: Market data is flooded with noise - random or irrelevant data. Algorithms should be able to filter out this noise to make sound trading decisions. This is akin to a fish which can filter out unnecessary information to find the relevant signals indicating where food is.

4. **Statistical arbitrage**: Some algorithms use statistical arbitrage strategies that capitalize on market inefficiencies, like mispricings. They make a high number of trades, and though the profit from each trade might be small, in aggregate, it can be substantial. This is somewhat like ants carrying tiny bits of food back to their anthill - each piece might be small, but together, it all adds up.

5. **Anomaly detection**: Algorithms can adjust by preempting unusual market behavior, such as drastic price drops, and respond accordingly. Continuing our analogy, this would be similar to animals adapting to and preparing for season changes.

6. **Game theory**: Some advanced algorithms utilize game theory to figure out potential moves from their algorithmic competitors, like a chess player predicting his opponent's moves.

These are some of the ways that algorithms adjust in a market dominated by their own kind. Remember, as the ecosystem gets more complex, the survival and success of these trading algorithms depend on how well they can adapt and evolve.

9.10 How can understanding behavioral finance enhance the effectiveness of a trading algorithm?

Behavioral finance provides us with insights about the cognitive biases and patterns of irrationality that pervade human financial decision-making. These biases may result in price patterns and market inefficiencies that can be exploited by algorithmic trading models. Let's dive a bit into how this works.

1. **Incorporating Psychological Factors:** By understanding certain biases such as herd behavior (where investors follow the market trend) or overconfidence bias (where traders overestimate their knowledge), an algorithm could potentially take a contrarian stance and profit from price corrections when these biases correct themselves. Think of it as a savvy fisherman who knows where the fish (the market players) are likely to be based on their predictable patterns (behavioral biases), and casts his net (algorithmic trading strategy) accordingly.

2. **Identifying Market Inefficiencies:** Behavioral finance suggests that markets are not always efficient, contrary to the theory of Efficient Market Hypothesis (EMH). Behavioral patterns can lead to systematic errors that create market inefficiencies, which are interesting opportunities for algorithmic traders. Imagine it like a treasure hunter who, knows where people tend to lose things (market inefficiencies), could develop a more effective treasure map (trading algorithm).

3. **Market Sentiment Analysis:** Understanding social and emotional factors influencing the market might help algorithmic traders to refine their strategies. For example, negative sentiment might give a sign of upcoming market sell-offs and vice versa. This could be similar to a weather predictor using data on temperature and humidity (market sentiment) to forecast whether it will rain (market movement).

4. **Anchoring:** Traders often anchor, or hold onto specific reference points when making decisions. For instance, they might place too much importance on the initial purchase price of a stock. Algorithms can account for this and devise strategies on this basis.

Adding these facets of behavioral finance into an algorithm makes it more adaptive and representative of the market's reality, in turn standing a better chance against the ever-fluctuating financial markets. Therefore, understanding behavioral finance can add a dimension to quantitative models that may enhance the effectiveness of a trading algorithm.

Chapter 10

Regulatory and Ethical Concerns

10.1 What regulations currently impact algorithmic traders the most?

Algorithmic trading is a rapidly evolving field and numerous regulatory challenges and ethical issues have emerged in this industry. A few major regulations that algorithmic traders need to be cognizant of are:

1. **Market Abuse Regulation (MAR)**: Introduced in the European Union in 2016, MAR significantly places high requirements on market participants to ensure they are not manipulating the market, engaging in insider trading, or committing other forms of market abuse. Traders using algorithmic strategies are responsible for ensuring their trades comply with these regulations.

2. **MiFID II, MiFIR, and Dodd-Frank Act**: These regulations are designed to increase the transparency of the financial markets and

reduce potential systemic risk. They also impose strict controls on algorithmic traders, including a requisite for the firms to maintain an effective system to manage risk associated with algorithmic trading.

3. **Automated Trading Regulations in the U.S by CFTC**: CFTC has published a set of proposed new rules known as Reg AT (regulations on automated trading). They apply to futures trades and would affect algorithmic traders. Firms subject to Reg AT will require to maintain a copy of the algorithmic trading source code and related records in a recordkeeping system subject to inspection by the regulators.

Comparing these regulations with traffic rules can make us understand these effectively. It is like you're driving the car of algorithmic trading on a highway. The MAR are the speed limits ensuring you drive in an ethical speed (trade responsibly). MiFID II, MiFIR, and Dodd-Frank Act are the traffic lights and road signs indicating when to stop, go, merge lanes, etc. (these provide guide on reducing market risks). And the Reg AT is like car insurance, making you have ownership and proper maintenance records so that if an accident is caused, the investigators would trace out the cause.

These above-mentioned regulations are in place to ensure that the marketplace operates fairly and ethically. They also aim to make the participants accountable, protect investors and the public, improve market transparency and integrity, and prevent systemic risk. Violating these can lead to hefty penalties, reputational damage, suspension, disqualification, or even criminal charges.

10.2   How do regulations ensure transparency and fairness in markets dominated by algorithms?

Regulations play a vital role in ensuring transparency and fairness in markets dominated by algorithms.

The primary ones include mandating disclosure, enforcing strict standards for testing and use of algorithms, and real-time surveillance of algorithmic activity.

To visualize this, let's say algorithmic trading is like a car race. Without clear rules and referees, drivers may use underhanded tactics to win, endangering everyone in the process. Regulations serve as the rules and referees, ensuring every driver competes fairly and responsibly.

1. **Disclosure Laws:** Regulations requiring firms to disclose their trading strategies are akin to rules that require racers to disclose any modifications made to their vehicles. This ensures that everyone has the same information and no one is given an unfair advantage.

In the US, for instance, the Securities and Exchange Commission (SEC) requires firms to notify them before they deploy algorithmic trading strategies.

2. **Testing and Use of Algorithms:** Like safety checks in car races, stringent regulations around the testing and use of algorithms are designed to prevent unexpected mishaps. Before going live, algorithms are required to undergo rigorous testing to ensure that they don't cause market disruptions.

This is seen in MiFID II (Markets in Financial Instruments Directive) introduced by the European Union, which requires firms to have effective systems and risk controls in place, like ensuring algorithmic strategies are thoroughly tested.

3. **Real-Time Monitoring and Surveillance:** Just as referees monitor races for any foul play, regulatory bodies continuously monitor market activity, looking out for irregular patterns that could indicate market manipulation or abuse.

In addition, significant market events can trigger 'circuit breakers' or 'volatility interruptions', mechanisms that temporarily halt trading to prevent extreme price swings. This is like pausing the race if weather conditions become extremely unfavorable, to ensure the safety of the participants.

Therefore, by mandating disclosure, enforcing strict use and testing standards, and providing constant surveillance, regulations foster a level playing field in the fast-paced, competitive arena of algorithmic trading. They are designed to mitigate the potentially harmful impacts of unchecked algorithmic activity, thus promoting transparency, fairness, and market integrity.

10.3 Discuss the regulatory response to flash crashes and other market anomalies.

Flash crashes and other market anomalies have raised significant concerns with market regulators globally. These events — spontaneous, sharp declines in stock index values — suggest potential vulnerabilities in the financial system and have propmted regulatory responses.

Regulators have sought to develop initiatives to prevent these anomalies and ensure market integrity. They are like parents setting rules in a playground, trying to ensure that all the children (market participants) play fairly and nobody gets hurt (economic damage).

Here are a few key regulatory initiatives that have been introduced in response to market anomalies:

1. **Circuit Breakers:** One response to flash crashes is the implementation of "circuit breakers". Much like a circuit breaker in your home that cuts off electricity to prevent an overload, market circuit breakers halt trading if prices drop too quickly, giving the market time to digest the information and preventing a panic sell-off.

2. **Regulation National Market System (Reg NMS):** In the US, the SEC implemented the Reg NMS to modernize and strengthen the national market system for equity securities. The rule is like a

traffic guide, steering trades to the exchange that offers the best price and preventing trade-throughs, which are trades executed at subpar prices.

3. **Algorithm Testing and Governance:** After the Knight Capital fiasco in 2012, where a software glitch led to a loss of $440 million in 45 minutes, regulators have put immense stress on proper algorithm testing and governance. It's akin to a car manufacturer being mandated to thoroughly test a car's braking system before selling it to consumers. Likewise, trading algorithms have to be tested in different scenarios before they can go live.

4. **High-Frequency Trading (HFT) Oversight:** The rising prominence of HFT, characterized by executing large numbers of trades in fractions of a second, has drawn regulatory attention. Think of it like a speed limit on a highway to keep the traffic flow smooth and manageable. Regulators are considering measures to control this aspect of the market, preventing unfair advantages or market manipulation.

Ethically, the key concern revolves around a level playing field for all market participants. Some argue that HFT and algorithmic trading privilege a small number of participants with faster access to markets and information. The debate is analogous to a race where some participants have sports shoes while others run barefoot. Increasing transparency, ensuring all participants have access to the same information, and placing some checks and balances on high-speed trading are ways regulators are trying to keep the race fair.

However, these regulatory responses are not without their criticisms and challenges. For example, imposing too many restrictions might stifle innovation and competition. That would be like telling soccer players they could only use one foot, making the game fair but less dynamic. Regulators are hence constantly walking a tightrope, balancing market efficiency, fairness, and innovation.

10.4 How do regulations vary for algorithmic trading across different global markets?

Algorithmic trading and its related field, high-frequency trading, are subject to different legislative and financial regulatory measures across the globe. Though international standards exist, with regulatory bodies such as the European Securities and Markets Authority or the SEC (Securities and Exchange Commission) in the U.S. providing guidelines, the interpretation and implementation of these standards may vary by country or region.

In the United States, for instance, the Dodd-Frank Wall Street Reform and Consumer Protection Act of 2010 introduced several amendments that are pertinent to algorithmic traders. The Act aims to prevent abusive practices and systemic risk. One can liken this to a referee in a basketball game seeking to deter foul play and ensuring fair games. One example is the Volcker Rule, which prohibits banks from speculative trading, much like preventing a basketball player from making reckless moves that could cause injuries.

Meanwhile, Europe's Markets in Financial Instruments Directive II (MiFID II) is another regulatory framework that has significant impact on algorithmic traders. The MiFID II was introduced to improve the functionality of financial markets in light of the 2008 financial crisis and to strengthen investor protection. More concretely, MiFID II requires all algorithmic traders to be licensed and to test their algorithms to minimize systemic risk.

The situation is slightly different in emerging markets, where the regulatory framework firmly in place in the U.S. and Europe may be absent or less comprehensive, and the adoption of algorithmic trading is less advanced. Developing markets may not have enough monitoring measures, which is a bit like playing a competitive game without a referee.

In regions like Asia, the regulatory approach can be varied. Some countries like Japan, with a mature financial market, apply stringent rules akin to the West. But there are others, like India, that have a more conservative approach, imposing strict conditions on high-frequency trading to mitigate excessive speculation and market volatility.

So, the regulatory landscape for algorithmic trading is much like the rules of sports: all enforce obeisance to broad, universally accepted standards to ensure fair play, but specifics can differ based on the country, sport, or in our case, market. Change in circumscribing factors like technology or market conditions may also lead to regulatory evolution over time.

10.5 What are the reporting and audit requirements for algorithmic trading firms?

Algorithmic trading firms operate in a tightly regulated environment due to the potential for significant financial and systemic risk. The specifics may vary by jurisdiction, but the reporting and auditing requirements are generally extensive. They exist to ensure transparency, prevent manipulation, minimize systemic risk, and maintain market integrity.

Firstly, regulatory bodies often require firms to report on their trading activity. For example, in the US, the SEC Rule 606 requires trading entities to disclose order routing practices quarterly, and Rule 605 mandates monthly electronic execution quality reports. Besides, if a firm is considered a "High-frequency trader," it might fall under stricter reporting frameworks, such as the CFTC's proposed 'Regulation Automated Trading'.

Additionally, many jurisdictions have provisions necessitating self-monitoring and auditing. For instance, under MiFID II in the EU, firms are required to store algorithmic trading records for five years, and these records can be requested by competent authorities at any time.

Algorithmic trading firms also need to conduct and submit regular testing and validation reports of their algorithms to attest they aren't contributing to disorderly trading conditions or breaching regulatory conditions.

To put it into simpler terms, this reporting and auditing requirement is a lot like having a driver's dashboard camera in your car. If you drive well and obey all the traffic rules, the footage from the camera is just a routine recording. If, however, there is an accident or violation, the authorities can use the footage to determine what really happened.

Additionally, some jurisdictions also impose requirements related to systems, risk controls, and business conduct. And failure to meet the stipulated terms carries potential consequences, including regulatory penalties and reputational damage. Thus, compliance should be a prerequisite, just like a seatbelt in a car: it might seem inconvenient at times, but not having it on can lead to severe consequences.

Finally, ethical concerns come into play in this highly quant-driven approach where humans are largely absent in the decision-making. Since algos make decisions based on pre-programmed instructions, the responsibility to ensure fairness, morality, and legality in trading amplifies, just like the ongoing debates on AI ethics in other industries.

In summary, the reporting and auditing requirements for algorithmic trading firms intend to ensure fairness, transparency, and orderliness in financial markets, prioritizing investors' protection and market integrity. It's essential that firms understand and observe these guidelines as they build and operate their trading algorithms.

10.6   Explain the mechanics of a flash crash.

A flash crash is a drastic drop in the stock markets, often triggered by high-frequency trading (HFT) and algorithmic trading systems. The mechanics of a flash crash can be explained by considering it as a very unruly version of a sports game, in which all players start running in the same direction without coordination, causing chaos and ultimately resulting in a stampede.

Here is how it occurs on a trading level:

1. **Initial Decline**: This could start due to several reasons: from an unexpected news event, a rapid selling pressure in an individual security or a sector, or even a misplaced or erroneous trade ("fat finger" error). In our sports analogy, imagine if suddenly one player starts rushing in one direction due to a miscalculation or misunderstanding.

2. **High-frequency and Algorithmic Trading Aggravates the Decline**: High-frequency trading systems and algorithms are designed to make trades based on certain predetermined conditions such as market volatility, liquidity, etc. When these conditions meet the algorithm's criteria, it can generate sell orders, thereby exacerbating the initial decline. This is comparable to other players seeing the initial rush and, due to either misunderstanding or a desire to follow the crowd, also start running in the same direction.

3. **Liquidity Disappearance**: As the trades are executed rapidly, a lot of sell orders hit the market, but not enough buy orders are there to match. It results in an acute loss of liquidity, i.e., securities become harder to sell. In the sports game, this is like most players ending up on one side of the field, leaving the other side empty.

4. **Market Calm Down**: Eventually, the market either halts trading of the affected securities (a bit like blowing a whistle and stopping the game) or buyers step in, seeing a good opportunity to buy at lower prices (like some players realizing they can now easily score on the empty side of the field). Liquidity slowly comes back, and the market recovers.

From a regulatory perspective, flash crashes can pose systemic risks to market stability and investor confidence. After experiencing a significant flash crash on May 6, 2010 in which the Dow Jones Industrial Average plunged about 1000 points and then recovered within minutes, regulatory bodies put measures in place to halt trading on significant price moves in order to curtail such events.

From an ethical standpoint, the role of HFTs and algorithmic trading in flash crashes brings into question the fairness and integrity of the market, as these systems can trade on information quicker than human traders and potentially manipulate the market. Regulators are thus faced with the challenge of ensuring fair and orderly markets in an increasingly automated trading environment.

10.7   How have past flash crashes influenced the public's perception and regulation of algorithmic trading?

Flash crashes, severe and rapid price declines followed by a quick rebound, create substantial market instability and have played a significant role in shaping public perception and regulation of algorithmic trading.

To many retail investors, algorithmic trading has come across as a mysterious alchemical operation overseen by Wall Street wizards tinkering with arcane mathematical models. The occurrence of flash crashes has further painted these 'wizards' in a nefarious light and pushed regulatory bodies to impose stricter control.

The 'Flash Crash' of May 6, 2010, for instance, was a pivotal event that shaped the discourse around algorithmic trading. In a span of few minutes, the Dow Jones Industrial Average (DJIA) suffered a precipitous drop of around 600 points, around 9

Many attributed this incident to a phenomenon known as High Frequency Trading (HFT) - a type of algorithmic trading characterized by high speeds, high turnover rates, and high order-to-trade ratios - which leverages sophisticated technological tools and computer algorithms to rapidly trade securities.

In response to the flash crash and the resultant outcry, the regulatory bodies scrambled to introduce changes to enhance the stability of the markets and to prevent future flash crashes.

For instance, tighter regulations regarding circuit breakers were introduced. A circuit breaker is a kind of passive regulation that's designed to prevent free-falling (or skyrocketing) markets by pausing trading after prices move by a certain percentage in any direction. Think of it as the trip switch in your home's electrical system - if the system is overwhelmed, the switch 'flips', momentarily cutting the power to prevent damage.

Further, regulators have actively pursued cases of illicit market manipulation using algorithmic strategies. A famous example is the case of Navinder Singh Sarao, a trader who was implicated in the 2010 flash crash. He used an algorithmic strategy called "spoofing", artificially creating a large sell pressure by placing orders and then quickly cancelling them, leading to market instability.

Regulators have also increased their focus on risk management in algorithmic trading, requiring firms to have stronger systems and controls in place. For instance, firms are required to perform daily backtesting of their trading algorithms using the previous day's data to ensure the algorithm's performance is stable.

Regulatory and ethical issues in algorithmic trading continue to evolve with the advancement in technology and market dynamics. Just as traffic laws and road designs need periodic updates to keep pace with the evolution of automobiles, so too do trading regulations need reshaping to address the challenges posed by algorithmic trading. These regulations, if carefully designed and effectively enforced, can help curb the adverse effects of algorithmic trading while allowing markets to reap its benefits.

10.8   How can trading algorithms be designed to avoid contributing to flash crashes?

To design trading algorithms that can help stem flash crashes, we must first understand what causes these sudden, fleeting dips in market prices. Typically, flash crashes are triggered by a combination of drastic price changes paired with rapid trading, often instigated by algorithmic trading systems that can place thousands of trades in mere seconds. You can think of this like a snowball rolling down a hill. It starts small - a small price change causes an algorithm to trade. But it quickly picks up size and speed as other algorithms react to the change, causing a flash crash.

So, to prevent our trading algorithm from contributing to potential flash crashes, we could deploy several strategies:

1. **Trading braking system**: Imagine you're driving a car, and you suddenly see the traffic lights turn red. Instead of slamming on the gas pedal, you hit the brakes to stop your car and avoid a crash. In a similar manner, we can incorporate a "trading brake" into your algorithm. This feature would pause trading when it detects drastic price swings within a very short timeframe (i.e., the 'red lights'). This concept is also applied in actual stock exchanges in the form of "circuit breakers" which halt trading during extreme market volatility.

if $|CurrentPrice - PreviousPrice| >$ Threshold within Δt time, pause trading

2. **Stability over profitability**: A good trading algorithm should prioritize stability over short-term profit. This means that it should avoid aggressive strategies that exploit small market fluctuations for quick profits, which can potentially destabilize the stock market. Like trying to squeeze in a line, there's a chance we might squeeze too hard and cause disruption. Instead, the algorithm can utilize strategies that slowly accumulate profit over a longer period of time, helping to

maintain overall market stability.

3. **Risk measures**: Incorporate robust risk management by ensuring that risk is adequately spread and not concentrated in certain high-velocity trades - much like not putting all your eggs in one basket that may break at once.

4. **Feedback loops consideration**: The algorithm should be designed to avoid perpetuating feedback loops, especially negative ones. A negative feedback loop in this context might be one where a price drop triggers further selling, inducing further price drops - like a descending spiral staircase. Algorithmic detection and avoidance of such trends in real-time can help break these unfavorable patterns.

5. **Human involvement**: Lastly, despite the allure of 'set it and forget it' algorithmic trading, humans should still be involved in overseeing the algorithms - acting as a safety net. Just like how autonomous vehicles still often have a human overseer, this ensures that, in the event of unforeseen market conditions, a human can intervene to prevent a spiraling disaster.

Remember, these strategies can help reduce your algorithm's contribution to flash crashes, but since the market is a complex system influenced by many players and factors, it is impossible to completely eliminate the risk of flash crashes.

10.9 Discuss the role of circuit breakers in preventing flash crashes.

Circuit breakers are important regulatory mechanisms used to curb dramatic volatility in financial markets and prevent spiraling phenomena like flash crashes. To explain their function in a relatable way, consider an electric circuit at your home. If an unexpected power surge occurs (a sudden, dramatic increase in electricity), then your circuit breaker kicks in, temporarily interrupting the electrical flow. This saves your electrical devices from experiencing a damaging overload. Similarly, in the financial market, circuit breakers interrupt trading during periods of extreme volatility.

Flash crashes are like the electrical power surges. These are sudden, dramatic sell-offs in one or more markets occurring within a very short time period, sometimes just within a few minutes. They can cause significant damage to market integrity if not controlled. The 2010 Flash Crash in the U.S. stock market is a prime example where the Dow Jones Industrial Average dropped about 1,000 points (more than 9%) only to recover those losses within minutes.

Circuit breakers are designed to halt trading temporarily in such scenarios, to offer a 'cooling off' period for the market. These can be at individual security levels or at whole market levels based on predefined thresholds typically set as a percentage change in a particular market index like the S&P 500. Once the market or security hits that threshold in a single day, trading halts for a certain period, allowing traders to reassess their strategies, absorb new information, and make more level-headed decisions.

Even algorithmic trading systems, which operate at high speeds and can sometimes contribute to market volatility, are designed to respect these circuit breakers. By doing this, they help to maintain an orderly market and provide participants a fair opportunity to enter or exit trades, enhancing overall market integrity.

However, while circuit breakers slow down markets during turbulent times and can prevent some immediate harm, they do not entirely eliminate the risk of losses. Much like how a home's circuit breaker doesn't prevent the lightning strike that caused the surge, but merely reacts to prevent further damage. It's vital, especially for algorithmic traders, to have risk management strategies in place beyond relying on regulatory failsafes like circuit breakers.

10.10 What lessons have been learned from notable flash crashes in the past decade?

Algorithmic trading, a primary driver of the financial market's evolution, enables rapid trading decisions based on complex mathematical models. However, flash crashes in the last decade, such as the May 2010 Flash Crash or the October 2016 Sterling Flash Crash, highlight some serious regulatory and ethical concerns that arise due to algorithmic trading.

Let's walk through some of the major lessons learned:

1. **Need for Breakers:** Just like having a circuit breaker in your home to prevent any potential electrical disasters, financial markets need similar safety mechanisms. These "circuit breakers" or safeguard mechanisms can temporarily halt trading when price movements in a market exceed a certain threshold within a short time frame. The 2010 Flash Crash was a wake-up call, following which several exchanges implemented or reinforced various types of circuit breakers.

2. **Transparency Requirement:** A significant part of algorithmic trading occurs in "dark pools", away from public eye. This lack of transparency can contribute to market instability if not properly regulated. Imagine playing a game of poker where you cannot see all the players - the uncertainty and risk skyrocket. Post the notorious flash crashes, there has been growing demand for more transparency in these areas.

3. **Robustness of Algorithms:** The flash crashes have shown us the importance of ensuring the robustness of algorithms against extreme market scenarios. Algorithms are coded rules that should be applicable in all environments. Let's consider them as 'GPS for trading'. Now, if the path suddenly experiences extreme weather, you would want the GPS to still function and guide you safely. This necessitates the development of stress testing scenarios during the design phase to validate the performance of these algorithms in diverse market conditions.

4. **Backup Plans:** The crashes reminded us of the importance of having a manual override or backup plans when algorithms fail or when unexpected events occur. It's like having a fire exit in a building - you hope you'll never need it, but it's crucial for safety.

5. **Ethical Responsibility:** The flash crashes underlined that algorithmic traders and firms need to take greater ethical responsibility for their strategies. In our GPS metaphor, if the GPS guides you to drive in the wrong direction or dangerously fast, the blame shouldn't solely be on the GPS system but also on the developer for setting it up that way. High-speed and high-frequency trades that induce market instability for personal gain pose an ethical problem in finance.

In conclusion, the flash crashes provided a rather harsh lesson on the regulatory and ethical concerns of unchecked algorithmic trading. They showed us the areas where regulatory bodies need to focus on to ensure fair, transparent, and stable financial markets. And, of course, they underlined that while technology can do wonders, it needs to serve the market's health and stability, not endanger it.

10.11   How can algorithmic trading potentially manipulate market prices or volumes?

Algorithmic trading is a powerful tool in modern financial markets, facilitating high-speed execution, risk management, efficiency, and liquidity. However, it's crucial to use this tool responsibly due to its potential for market manipulation. Here are a few ways algorithmic trading can potentially influence market prices or volumes unethically:

1. **Quote Stuffing**: Algorithmic trading can generate a considerable number of buy or sell orders in the market within milliseconds. This technique, called quote stuffing, can overburden certain trading channels and can result in artificial price movements. It's like causing

a traffic jam in a road system, with an ulterior motive of benefiting from the slow movement of some vehicles.

2. **Layering and Spoofing**: Algorithms could place multiple deceptive orders to create the illusion of increased supply or demand, which can artificially drive the stock prices up or down. It's akin to a vendor in a market place spreading out their merchandise on multiple stalls to create an illusion of scarcity, thereby manipulating the price. Once the desired price level is reached, these orders might be cancelled. This strategy, referred to as layering or spoofing, is against trading regulations.

3. **Front running**: If a trading algorithm becomes aware of a pending large trade, it can transact on that information before the large trade is executed, a practice known as front running. Imagine you're in a line for a popular concert ticket, but someone who hears about your intention cuts the line and buys the ticket before you, then sells it to you at a higher price.

4. **Pinging**: Similar to a submarine using sonar to detect objects, "pinging" involves placing small orders to find hidden orders or determine the market's direction. This information can then be used to manipulate prices.

It's worth noting that these practices are deemed illegal and unethical by most regulatory bodies globally, such as the Financial Industry Regulatory Authority (FINRA) in the U.S and the Financial Conduct Authority (FCA) in the U.K. Penalties may include hefty fines, bans, or even criminal proceedings.

Notice that market manipulation isn't unique to algorithmic trading. But it's the speed, efficiency, and anonymity of algorithms that can potentially magnify these issues. Additionally, as algorithms become more advanced and make use of AI and machine learning, the ethical and regulation concerns will likely continue to evolve.

10.12 What ethical responsibilities do algorithmic traders have towards retail investors?

Algorithmic trading involves a great deal of power and responsibility, due to its capability to execute trades at a much faster rate and larger scale than human trading. Despite its vast potential, it carries a set of ethical obligations to ensure fair pitching ground for all types of investors, including retail investors.

1. **Transparency**: Algorithmic traders are ethically bound to provide a clear understanding about the working principles of their bots to regulatory bodies. This can still be done while protecting one's proprietary information. It's like handing over the recipe of a dish (the algorithm) without giving away the secret sauce (the unique data or processes used to refine the algorithm).

2. **Fairness**: Algorithmic traders should not create systemic biases against retail investors. Their algorithms should not deliberately exploit market events to disadvantage retail investors. This would be equivalent to a professional footballer competing against school kids. The significant speed and information processing advantage that algorithmic traders have should not turn into an instrument of manipulation or unfair advantage.

3. **Avoiding Market Manipulation**: 'Quote stuffing', 'spoofing' or outputting misleading signals to move the market in a direction beneficial to the algorithmic trader, is both unethical and illegal. These tactics are akin to a magician using sleight of hand to trick an audience—using speed and confusion to mislead.

4. **Error Management**: Traders have the responsibility to ensure adequate risk controls and safeguards are put in place to prevent erroneous orders or disruptive events ('Flash Crashes'). It's somewhat like a motor vehicle manufacturer—though accidents may not always be due to the vehicle's operation, the manufacturer has a responsibility to ensure robust safety features.

5. **Feedback Loop Prevention**: Algorithms that result in feedback loops can lead to destructive market events. Traders are expected to test their algorithms diligently and have safety measures in place in case of unintended repercussions. It's comparable to the story of the Sorcerer's Apprentice, where the apprentice's lack of understanding leads to a magic broom endlessly repeating its task and causing chaos—a small error in the algorithm, scaled up, could lead to industry-wide issues.

The bottom line is, even in the digital age, the age-old principle of 'do unto others as you would like them to do unto you' holds good. As algorithmic traders, our actions against retail investors should reflect the way we would want to be traded against.

10.13 How do regulations address the ethical concerns in algorithmic trading?

Algorithmic trading has brought speed, efficiency, and quantitative rigor to the financial markets, but it also raises significant ethical concerns such as unfair access to markets, potential market manipulation, and systemic risks due to algorithmic glitches or misbehaviors. These ethical concerns, in turn, trigger several regulatory responses designed to mitigate such risks and maintain fair and transparent markets.

Let's briefly examine the major regulatory strategies related to algorithmic trading:

1. **Pre-Trade Risk Controls:** Similar to requiring a car to have brakes before it can be legally driven, regulators generally require brokers to implement pre-trade risk controls to minimize the potential negative impact of trades, including price, quantity and order duplicate checks. These controls serve as a crucial first-line defense against algorithmic errors or rogue algorithms that could disrupt the

markets.

2. **Market Fair Access Rules:** Some ethical concerns centered around algorithmic trading revolve around fairness. For instance, people may question if it's fair for algorithmic traders with ultra-low-latency connections to exploit small price discrepancies before anyone else can. Regulators address this by mandating fair access for all market participants through rules like Regulation NMS in the U.S. or MAR in EU, which ensure all traders have equal opportunity to trade.

3. **Regulation on High-Frequency Trading (HFT):** In the spirit of ensuring a fair race (like an Olympic 100m race), regulators focus on regulating HFTs which have capacities to execute trades in microseconds. Regulations require HFTs firms to maintain robust risk control measures and to regularly test their algorithms to minimize trading errors and systemic risks. Some jurisdictions even impose 'speed bumps' to prevent excessively fast trading and level the playing field.

4. **Transparency and Disclosure Requirements:** Transparency is an antidote to potential unethical conduct. Hence regulators require firms to disclose details of their trading algorithms if requested, which is a bit like showing the ingredients of your secret sauce or recipe on the menu. This fosters accountability and allows regulators to ensure trades are not being conducted in manipulative manners.

5. **Systemic Risk Management:** From a macro perspective, regulators are primarily concerned about protecting the financial system from systemic risk - a domino effect where the failure of one component can lead to the collapse of the entire system. In algorithmic trading, a poorly designed or malfunctioning algorithm can rapidly trigger cascading failures. Regulations address this by requiring firms to have kill switches to quickly halt trading activities if certain risk conditions are triggered.

To ensure these regulations are complied with, firms engaged in algorithmic trading are expected to maintain comprehensive records of their all activities. Non-compliance can result in fines, sanctions, or in extreme cases, cessation of operations.

Finally, one key takeaway about regulatory and ethical concerns in algorithmic trading is that the intersection between technology and financial markets is a rapidly evolving space. Therefore, ongoing dialogue among regulators, traders, and technologists is essential to balance the benefits of innovation with the need for fairness, integrity, and stability in our financial systems.

10.14 Discuss the balance between innovation in algorithmic trading and ethical considerations.

Algorithmic trading, like a high-speed train, has revolutionized the financial industry by accelerating and enhancing trade execution, optimizing trading strategies, and reducing costs. However, like any fast-moving train, it is necessary to implement adequate controls and considerations to avoid potential crashes, hence the emergence of regulatory and ethical concerns.

Before diving into the balance between innovation in algorithmic trading and ethical considerations, let's first understand algorithmic trading. In a nutshell, algorithmic trading is the process where preprogrammed trading instructions, accounting for variables such as time, price, and volume, are used to automatically carry out trades.

This is akin to an autopilot system in airplanes; once the coordinates (in our case, trading parameters) are set, the system executes the journey (trades) without requiring human interaction. But, such automation can also pose risks regulatory and ethical risks.

From a regulatory perspective, uncontrolled algorithmic trading can lead to abrupt market events like the "Flash Crash" of 2010. In an instant, market indices tumbled due to aggressive sell-off algorithms, which led to widespread panic and financial loss. It was the equivalent of a high-speed train derailing due to a software glitch.

Ethically, algorithmic trading can create inequity in market access. Large institutions with advanced trading algorithms have an upper hand over individual investors, akin to having a faster train running on a parallel track. It's important that these "faster trains" do not hinder or pose risks to others on the rail network.

Striking a balance between innovation and ethical considerations involves regulating algorithmic trading without stifling innovation. Regulators can enforce risk management practices and improve market transparency, much like traffic rules and signals that manage train movement and prevent mishaps.

On the ethical front, providing equitable market access and ensuring fair market practice is the fulcrum. This could be equivalent to providing all trains, irrespective of their make or speed, the same right to use the rail network.

In conclusion, like the delicate equilibrium needed in managing a rail network, a balance between fostering advancement in algorithmic trading and ensuring compliance with regulatory and ethical principles is critical in maintaining the integrity and efficacy of financial markets.

Afterword

As we reach the concluding pages of this exploration into the intricate world of algorithmic trading, it's both a time to reflect and to gaze forward. We've navigated the labyrinthine corridors of financial markets, decoding the sophisticated algorithms that pulse at its heart and grasping the statistical, technological, and ethical quandaries that they present.

"Algorithmic Trading: Questions and Answers" was conceived as a beacon, illuminating the often-murky waters of a field that melds finance with cutting-edge technology. With each chapter, we aimed to unravel complexities, offering clarity on subjects that can often seem impenetrable. The questions posed and the answers provided are not just intellectual exercises; they are a testament to the dynamic nature of markets and the relentless human endeavor to understand and harness them.

In the course of this book, we've traversed from foundational concepts to advanced strategies, but the world of algorithmic trading, like any vibrant field, is ever-evolving. New challenges will arise, and with them, innovative solutions. As you move forward, armed with the knowledge you've gained here, remember that learning is a continuous journey. The questions might change, but the quest for answers — the very essence of inquiry — remains constant.

The future of trading lies at the intersection of human intuition and machine precision. As algorithms become more sophisticated and markets more interconnected, there will always be new frontiers to explore. It's our hope that this book serves not as an endpoint but as a catalyst, inspiring you to delve deeper, question further, and innovate boldly.

Thank you for accompanying us on this journey. May the insights you've gleaned here serve you well, whether you're charting new territories in algorithmic trading or simply sating intellectual curiosity.

Made in the USA
Monee, IL
08 January 2025